The Gemstone File

The
GEMSTONE
FILE

edited by Jim Keith

IllumiNet Press
Atlanta

Library Of Congress Cataloging in Publication Data

The Gemstone File / edited by Jim Keith. — 1st ed.
    p.   cm.
  ISBN: 0-9626534-5-4 : $14.95
  1. United States — Politics and government — 1945-1989.
  2. World politics — 1945-
  3. Political corruption — History — 20th century.
  4. Conspiracies — History — 20th century. I. Keith, Jim, 1949-
E839.5.G38   1992
909.82—dc20   92-18217

Cover art by James Koehnline

This book comprises an investigation of unsubstantiated "underground"
documents, with the purpose of analyzing them and proving or disprov-
ing their allegations. Printing these documents does not constitute a statement by the editor or publisher that the documents in question are believed to be factual, or should be construed as such.

IllumiNet Press
P.O. Box 746
Avondale Estates, GA 30002

First IllumiNet Press Edition, 1992

10 9 8 7 6 5 4 3 2 1

Printed in the United States of America

Dedicated to Mae Brussell

The editor wishes to thank the following people for their contributions to the research: Matt Love and the Cabot Cabal, Vicky Bolin, Ron Bonds, Len Bracken, Stephanie Caruana, Jerry Smith, Tim Cridland, Mae Brussell, John Judge, Walter Alter, Micro Associates, Anarchist Alliance of Aotearos, and Mike Gunderloy.

Contents

Introduction

Jim Keith

> *Park's response was innocence laced with Oriental humility. But, sir, all this surely could not be contained in the Gemstone File?*
>
> *Hoover chuckled. No, my dear friend. Gemstone is a composite of critical data principally exposing the collusion of the American overworld with the American underworld, dating back to 1934.*
>
> *What names would one find in Gemstone?*
>
> *Quite a variety, Mr. President.*
>
> *It would be helpful for me, dear friend, to acquire those names.*
>
> *Yes, Hoover responded softly. I'm certain it would be.*
>
> From *The Circle* by Steve Shagan

The *Gemstone File* is one of the wilder and woolier legends of research into political conspiracy. Penned by Bruce Roberts (of which not a great deal is known other than the bare facts of his life and that he died, either by brain tumor or cancer, on July 30, 1976), this document of reportedly over one thousand handwritten pages was passed in part in 1975 to Mae Brussell, the now-deceased researcher into matters conspiratorial. Brussell talked about the File on the air, devoting two of her weekly radio shows to it, and, after Roberts' death, offered to sell her copy for $100,000 to the first publishing house willing to print it. She reported that she had been offered $30,000 by an unnamed British movie studio, but had turned it down because she didn't feel they would do a good job with their adaptation of the File. Brussell apparently put some stock in Gemstone, or at least she felt that others might, if the price she placed on it is any indication.

The File was synopsized by Stephanie Caruana (a writer sent to interview Brussell by *Playgirl* magazine, who took and still takes Roberts' revelations with utmost seriousness) and the condensed "A Skeleton Key to the Gemstone File" was then distributed at random and far and wide, reprinted, changed, parodied, added to, and variously hijacked by people heeding its call to make copies and spread them around. When people speak of the *Gemstone File*, they are usually referring to the Skeleton Key, although the term is more correctly applied to Roberts' original Gemstone letters.

The Skeleton Key was the basis for Steve Shagan's popular 1982 espionage novel *The Circle* (which fictionally attributed the File to J. Edgar Hoover) and was even reprinted in Larry Flynt's *Hustler* magazine. One story has it that Flynt was shot due to his publication of the Skeleton Key although, considering the magazine it was printed in, the point is moot.

So what kind of information does the Skeleton Key contain? It is a convoluted and feisty chronology purporting to be the inner track on some of the major events of the Twentieth Century: the Kennedy assassination, the tragedy at Chappaquiddick, and the strange and secret histories of Howard Hughes and Aristotle Onassis. The Skeleton Key describes skullduggery and wheeling and dealing for high stakes indeed: the control of America. The events depicted in the Key are nasty enough, in fact, so that one wonders if they might not be true.

"A Skeleton Key to the Gemstone File" has appeared in a number of additional versions of which we are aware. The original appears to exist in a very rough, partly unreadable photocopy dated May 1, 1975, with a name and address affixed: "Stephanie Caruana, 75 Prosper St., San Francisco, Ca 94114." The Caruana version includes an interesting section on heretical religion and a listing of individual Gemstones that is not included in all later versions... no doubt for the sake of discretion. Caruana has mentioned another "expanded" Skeleton Key of sixty-odd pages, including photographs, although this version has so far been unobtainable.

At least ten other anonymous typed or typeset versions of the Skeleton Key are in our possession, including one that intersperses the nearly-as-wild conspiracy/metaphysical chronology from Neal Wilgus's book, *The Illuminoids*.

The curious "Illuminati Research Report" is, in part, a melding of the Skeleton Key, the infamous Protocols of the Elders of Zion and Wilgus's *Illuminoids* timeline. Although there is no byline on this Gemstone version, it was reportedly written by Dennis Brunelle in the mid 1980s. Brunelle claimed to be a Grand Master in the Ordo Templi Orientis lodge, but to have become disillusioned with their "Illuminati"-derived program, at which time he set out to blow the whistle.

"Small press" or underground magazine appearances of the Skeleton Key include *Shavertron, The Continuing Crisis, Conspiracy Digest, The Fanatic* and my own magazine, *Dharma Combat*.

One interesting permutation of the Skeleton Key, hereafter referred to as the Kiwi Gemstone, incorporates lengthy references to international and, especially, Aotearoa (New Zealand) politics, and was printed in the New Zealand anarchist publication *The State Adversary*. It was reportedly the subject of a legal suit prior to this publication, and that is fairly easy to understand. The Kiwi Gemstone is included in this book and, regardless of whether you have any interest in Aotearoan politics, it should be read, if only because of the stunning depiction of a Mafia/big business takeover and details of subliminals used for mass brainwashing. The Kiwi Gemstone is believable and I would even say instructive as to what Gemstone might have been.

Without a doubt the strangest of the Gemstone versions we have is the version photocopied from an original typed on lined notebook paper, replete with the antics of Chevy Chase, Goldie Hawn and Rowan and Martin. X. Sharks DeSpot has taken credit for this Gemstone version and has admitted it to be a hoax. While contributing greatly to the present volume with his research, Mr. DeSpot has asked that I not include his "Jokestone File" out of concern that loonies might harass Goldie Hawn.

In an elegant segue: during the course of editing this book, I received a phone call from W. Scott Walker, the publisher of a book called *Beyond the Gemstone Files*. I had written to him, wondering about the content of the book, whose title I had encountered a few times but had never been able to locate, even having gone so far as to consult the Library of Congress. Walker told me in quiet, grave tones that I would be "violating copyrights held by the CIA," if I was so foolhardy as to go ahead with my proposed book.

His story was that the author of *Beyond the Gemstone Files*, Peter Renzo, was an ex-CIA man authorized by the Company to release the *Gemstone Files*, which (Walker confided) are the G. Gordon Liddy files "he thought he had burned." Walker maintains that Renzo was a member of the "Fighting Tigers Assassination Squad," and that the CIA simply won't allow me to do the book: this book.

After questioning Mr. Walker about the nature of the files he had published (via Vantage Press, a well-known subsidy press, bastion of the terminally unpublishable, and now, we find, Company asset), it became apparent that it was the Caruana Skeleton Key which the "CIA" had so boldly authorized him to go where so many had gone before.

I sensed Walker was a little dismayed when I confided I have the Key in at least eleven different versions and am in correspondence with the original editor, and when I filled him in on a little of the background as I know it, Fighting Tigers Assassination Squad, aside.

Since speaking with Walker I have had a chance to review Renzo's book which is composed of, as I had guessed, the Caruana Skeleton Key coupled to stories about the author's supposed CIA connections and the murder of his friend amid the overwhelming odor of "apple pie," i.e. Roberts' dreaded sodium morphate. Renzo also tells of a sojourn in Laos where he found a secret temple and a giant idol that, after pressing a concealed button, opened to disgorge precious "gemstones." On the way out of the temple Renzo fends off an attack by giant cobras. A tacked-on segment about the Philadelphia Experiment (now you see the Atlantic Fleet, now you don't) and some photos of Renzo posing with tigers and aiming guns and kicking things fills out its formidable 65 pages.

The original Skeleton Key concludes with the kind of note

familiar to aficionados of conspiracy broadsheets and badly-xeroxed rants found affixed to telephone poles: "At present, the only way to spread this information here in America is via hand to hand." Be that as it may, what you have in your own hands is the certified CIA-unauthorized "A Skeleton Key to the Gemstone File," printed seventeen years after its original appearance.

In preparing this edition we have gathered the original text of the Skeleton Key along with related documents and commentaries from a number of researchers. Our most important resource during the book's preparation was correspondence with Stephanie Caruana, the original editor of the Skeleton Key and friend of Bruce Roberts. After several failed attempts to contact Ms. Caruana, she was located by accident in a coincidence I leave to more Illuminated minds to grapple with. Ms. Caruana has increased our understanding of the document and its background, while dissipating at least a portion of our original skepticism.

Notes on the Skeleton Key by sundry hands conclude the volume in an attempt to examine the data and to offer leads and theories to future researchers.

Now all that remains is for you to read and evaluate the book. Then you may decide whether the *Gemstone File* is a true telling of momentous world events or a strange — strange as real life — hoax.

A Skeleton Key to the Gemstone File

May 1, 1975

[The following is the original text of the Skeleton Key, including spelling and punctuation. Numerical references refer to Notes beginning on page 188.]

The Gemstone File was written in many segments over a period of years by an American man named Bruce Roberts. Parts of the file were released to certain Americans beginning in 1969. The number of handwritten pages is well over a thousand, of which I have read about four hundred. I have been able to verify some of the statements made in the file, but do not have the time or the research facilities to verify the entire story. Perhaps others can help.

Since the scope of the work is so large, and the events described so complex and interlocking, it may be more easily understood with this skeleton outline of the Gemstone thesis. Individual papers can then be read with greater comprehension.

1932: Onassis, a Greek drug pusher and ship owner who made his first million selling "Turkish tobacco" (opium) in Argentina, worked out a profitable deal with Joseph Kennedy, Eugene Meyer, and Meyer Lansky. Onassis was to ship booze directly into Boston for Joseph Kennedy. Also involved was a heroin deal with Franklin and Elliot Roosevelt. (1)

1934: Onassis, Rockefeller and the Seven Sisters (major oil companies) signed an agreement, outlined in an oil cartel memo: Fuck the Arabs out of their oil, ship it on Onassis's ships; Rockefeller and the Seven Sisters to get rich. All this was done. (2),(3),(4),(5)

Roberts, studying journalism and physics at the University of Wisconsin, learned these things via personal contacts. His special interest was in crystallography—and the creation of synthetic rubies, the original Gemstone experiment.

1936-1940: Eugene Meyer buys the *Washington Post*, to get control of news media. Other Mafia buy other papers, broadcasting, T.V., etc. News censorship of all major news goes into effect.

1941-1945: World War II; very profitable for Onassis, Rockefeller, Kennedys, Roosevelts, I.G. Farben, etc., etc. Onassis selling oil, arms and dope to both sides went through the war without losing a single ship or man.

1949: Onassis buys U.S. war surplus "Liberty Ships" in questionable (illegal) puchase. Lawyer Burke Marshall helps him.

1956: Howard Hughes, Texas millionaire, is meanwhile buying his way toward control of the U.S. electoral process with a view toward his own personal gain. He buys senators, governors, etc. He finally buys his last politician: newly elected V.P. Nixon, via a quarter-million-dollar non-repayable loan to Nixon's brother, Donald. (6)

Early 1957: V.P. Nixon repays the favor by having IRS-Treasury grant tax-free status (refused twice before) to "Hughes Medical Foundation" (7), sole owner of Hughes Aircraft, creating a tax-free, non-accountable money funnel or laundry, for whatever Hughes wanted to do. U.S. government also shelved anti-trust suits against Hughes's TWA, etc.

March 1957: Onassis carried out a carefully planned event: he has Hughes kidnapped from his bungalow at the Beverly Hills Hotel, using Hughes's own men (Chester Davis, born Cesare in Sicily, et al). (8) Hughes's men either quit, get fired, or stay on in the new Onassis organization. A few days later, Mayor Cannon of Nevada (now Senator Cannon) arranges a fake "marriage" to Jean Peters to explain Hughes's sudden loss of interest in chasing movie stars. Hughes, battered and brain-damaged in the scuffle, is taken to the Emerald Isle Hotel in the Bahamas, where the entire top floor has been rented for the "Hughes party;" there he is shot full of heroin for thirty days, and later dragged off to a cell on Onassis's island, Skorpios. (9), (10) Onassis now has a much larger power base in the U.S. (the Hughes empire), as well as control over V.P. Nixon and other Hughes purchased politicians. L. Wayne Rector "Hughes" double since 1955, becomes "Hughes".

September 1957: Onassis calls the Appalachin meeting to announce to U.S. Mafia heads his grab of Hughes and his adoption of Hughes's game plan for acquiring power: buying U.S. senators, congressmen, governors, judges, en masse, to take control "legally" of the U.S. government. Onassis's radio message to Appalachin from a remote Pennsylvania farmhouse is intercepted (reluctantly) by FBI's J. Edgar Hoover, on the basis of a tip-off from some Army intelligence guys who weren't in on the plan.

Also in 1957: Joseph Kennedy takes John F. and Jackie to see Onassis on his yacht, introduce John, and remind Onassis of an old Mafia promise: the presidency for a Kennedy. Onassis agrees.

1958: Hordes of Mafia-selected, purchased and supported "grass roots" candidates sweep into office.

1959: Castro takes over Cuba from dictator Battista, thereby destroying the cozy and lucrative Mafia gambling empire run for Onassis by Meyer Lansky. Castro scoops up $8 million in Mafia casino receipts. Onassis is furious, V.P. Nixon becomes operations chief for CIA-planned Bay of Pigs invasion, using CIA Hunt, McCord, etc., and Cuban ex-Battista strong-arm cops ("Cuban freedom fighters") Martinez, Gonzalez, etc., as well as winners like Frank Sturgis (Fiorini).

1959: Stirring election battle between Kennedy and Nixon. Either way Onassis wins, since he has control over both candidates.

1960: JFK elected. American people happy. Rose Kennedy happy. Onassis happy. Mafia ecstatic.

Roberts brings his synthetic rubies—the original "Gemstones" to Hughes Aircraft in Los Angeles. They steal his rubies—the basis for laser beam research, laser bombs, etc., because of the optical quality of the rubies. One of the eleven possible sources for one of the ingredients involved in the Gemstone experiment was the Golden Triangle area. Roberts was married to the daughter of the former French consul in Indochina. In that area Onassis's involvements in the Golden Triangle dope trade was no secret. Roberts's investigation revealed the Onassis-Hughes connection, kidnap, and switch.

"Gemstones"—synthetic rubies, and sapphires with accompanying "histories"—gemstone papers—were sold or given away to consular officials—in return for information. A worldwide information network was gradually developed—a trade of the intelligence activities of many countries. This intelligence network is the source for much of the information in the Gemstone File.

January 1961: Joseph Kennedy had a stroke, ending his control over John and Bobby. The boys decide to rebel against Onassis's control. Why? Inter-Mafia struggle? Perhaps a dim hope of restoring this country to its mythical integrity?

They began committing Mafia no-no's. Arrested Wally Bird, owner of Air Thailand, who had been shipping Onassis's heroin out of the Golden Triangle (Laos, Cambodia, Vietnam), under contract with the CIA (Air Opium); arrested Teamster Mafia Jimmy Hoffa, and put him in jail. Declared the $73 million in forged "Hughes" land liens, deposited with S.F.'s Bank of America, as "security" for the TWA judgement against Hughes, to be what they are: forgeries.

April 1961: CIA Bay of Pigs fiasco. Hunt, McCord, CIA, Battista's Cubans and Mafia angry about JFK's lack of enthusiasm. Mafia Onassis has his U.S. right-hand man,

"Hughes's top aide", former FBI and CIA Robert Maheu (nick-named "IBM," for Iron Bob Maheu), hire and train a Mafia assassination team to get Castro. The team of a dozen or so includes John Roselli and Jimmy (The Weasel) Frattiano (11), expert Mafia hitmen, assisted by CIA Hunt and McCord and others. This was reported recently by Jack Anderson, who gets a lot of his "tips" from his friend, Frank (Fiorini) Sturgis—also on the Castro assassination team. The team tries five times to kill Castro, with everything from long-range rifles to apple pie with sodium morphate in it. Castro survives.

1963: Members of the Castro assassination team arrested at Lake Pontchartrain, La., by Bobby Kennedy's Justice boys (12). Angered, Onassis stops trying to kill Castro. He changes targets, and goes for the head: JFK, who, according to Onassis, "welched" on a Mafia deal.

JFK sets up "Group of 40" to fight Onassis.

August 1963: Two murders had to occur before the murder of JFK, or people would understand the situation and might squawk:

Senator Estes Kefauver, whose Crime Commission investigations had uncovered the 1932 deal between Onassis, Kennedy, Eugene Meyer, Lansky, Roosevelt, et al. Kefauver planned a speech on the Senate floor denouncing Mafia operations; instead, he ate a piece of apple pie laced with sodium morphate (used in rat poison), and had a sodium-morphate-induced "heart attack" on the Senate floor. (13)

Phillip Graham, editor of the *Washington Post*. Phillip had married Katherine Meyer, Eugene Meyer's daughter, who had inherited the *Washington Post* and allied media empire. Graham put together the Kennedy-Johnson ticket and was Kennedy's friend in the struggle with Onassis. According to Gemstone, Katherine Meyer Graham bribed some psychiatrists to certify that Phil was insane. He was allowed out of the nuthouse for the weekend and died of a shotgun wound in the head, in the Graham home in Washington; death ruled "suicide."

November 1, 1963: The hit on JFK was supposed to take place in true Mafia style: a triple execution, together with

Diem and Nhu in Vietnam. Diem and Nhu got theirs, as scheduled. Onassis had invited Jackie for a cruise on the *Cristina*, where she was when JFK got tipped off that big O planned to wipe him out. (14) JFK called Jackie on the yacht, from the White House, hysterical: "Get off that yacht if you have to swim," and cancelled appearance at a football stadium in Chicago, where the CIA-Mafia assassination team was poised for the kill. (15) Jackie stayed on board, descended the gangplank a few days later on Onassis's arm, in Turkey, to impress the Turkish Bey, Mustapha. Madame Nhu, in the United States bitterly remarked "Whatever has happened in Vietnam?"

One of the assassination team (Tom Mallee, a double for Oswald) was picked up in Chicago, with a rifle, and quickly released by the police.

Three weeks later the Mafia's alternate and carefully arranged execution plan went into effect: JFK was assassinated at Dallas. A witness who recognized pictures of *some of the people arrested at Dealey Plaza* as having been in Chicago three weeks earlier, told Black Panthers Hampton and Clark.

The JFK murder: Onassis-"Hughes's" man Robert Maheu, reassigned the Mafia-CIA Castro assassination team to the murder of JFK, adding Eugene Brading, a third Mafia hitman from the Denver Mafia Smaldones "family". Two months earlier, Brading, on parole after a series of crimes, applied for a new driver's license, explaining to the California DMV that he had decided to change his name—to "Jim Braden." Brading got his California parole officer's permission for two trips to Dallas, in November on "oil business"—the first time to look things over; and the second time when JFK was scheduled for his Dallas trip.

Lee Harvey Oswald, CIA, with carefully planted links to both the ultra-right and to the Communists, was designated as the patsy. He was supposed to shoot Gov. Connally, and he did.

Each of the four shooters—Oswald, Brading, Frattiano, and Roselli—had a timer and a back-up man. Back-up men were supposed to pick up the spent shells, and get rid of the guns. Timers would give the signal to shoot. Hunt and McCord were there to help. (16) Sturgis was in Miami. (17), (18)

Frattiano shot from a second story window in the Dal-Tex building, across the street from the Texas Book Depository. He apparently used a handgun; he is an excellent shot with a pistol. Frattiano hit Kennedy twice, in the back and in the head. Frattiano and his back-up man were "arrested," driven away from the Dal-Tex building in a police car, and released (without being booked). (The Dallas police office is in the Dal-Tex building).

Roselli shot Kennedy once, hitting the right side of his head and blowing his brains out, with a rifle, from behind a fence in the grassy knoll area. Roselli and his timer went down a manhole behind the fence and followed the sewer line away from Dealey Plaza.

The third point of the triangulated ambush was supplied by Eugene Brading, shooting from Kennedy's left, from a small pagoda at Dealey Plaza, across the street from the grassy knoll. (Brading missed, because Roselli's and Frattiano's shot had just hit Kennedy in the head from the right and the rear, nearly simultaneously). Brading's shot hit the curb and ricocheted off. Brading was photographed on the scene, stuffing his gun under his coat. He wore a big leather hat, its hatband marked with large conspicuous X's. (Police had been instructed to let anyone with an X-marked hatband through the police lines; some may have been told they were Secret Service). After his shot, Brading ditched his gun with his back-up man and walked up the street toward the Dal-Tex building. Roger Craig, a deputy sheriff, rushed up to Brading, assuming he was "Secret Service," and told him he had just seen a man come out of the Book Depository and jump into a station wagon. Brading was uninterested. Brading walked into the Dal-Tex building to "make a phone call." There he was arrested by another deputy sheriff, showed his "Jim Braden" driver's license, and was released— without being booked.

Oswald shot Connally twice from the Texas Book Depository. He split from the front door. His back-up man was supposed to take the rifle out of the building (or so Oswald thought); instead he "hid" it behind some boxes, where it would be found later.

Three men dressed as "tramps" picked up the spent shells from Dealey Plaza. One was Howard Hunt. Then they drifted over to an empty boxcar sitting on a railway spur behind the grassy knoll area, and waited. A Dallas police officer ordered two Dallas cops to "go over to the boxcar and pick up the tramps." The three "tramps" paraded around Dealey Plaza to the Police Department, in the Dal-Tex building. They were held there until the alarm went out to pick up Oswald; then they were released, without being booked. In all, ten men were arrested immediately after the shooting; all were released soon after; none were booked; not a word about their existence is mentioned in the *Warren Report.*

Regarding Lee Harvey Oswald: Officer Tippitt was dispatched in his police radio car to the Oak Cliff Section, where Oswald had rented a room. Tippitt may have met Oswald on the street. He may have been supposed to kill Oswald, but something went wrong. Tippitt was shot by two men, using two revolvers. The "witness", Domingo Benavides, who used Tippitt's police car radio to report "we've had a shooting here," may have been one of the men who shot him. (A "Domingo Benavides" appears in connection with the Martin Luther King shooting, also).

Oswald went to the movies. A "shoe store manager" told the theatre cashier that a suspicious-looking man had sneaked in without paying. Fifteen assorted cops and FBI charged out to the movie theatre to look for the guy who had sneaked in.

Oswald had a pistol that wouldn't fire. It may have been anticipated that the police would shoot the "cop-killer" for "resisting arrest". But since that didn't happen, the Dallas police brought Oswald out for small-time Mafia Jack Ruby to kill two days later. (19)

Brading stayed at the Teamster-Mafia-Hoffa financed "Cabana Hotel" in Dallas. Ruby had gone to the Cabana the night before the murder, says the *Warren Report.*

The rest, as they say, is history. Onassis was so confident of his control over the police, media, FBI, CIA, Secret Service, and the U.S. judicial system that he had JFK murdered before the eyes of the entire nation; then systematically bought off, killed off, or frightened off all witnesses, and had the evidence destroyed; then put a 75-year seal of secrecy over the entire matter. Cover-up participants included (among many): Gerald Ford on the Warren Commission (a Nixon recommendation); CIA attorney Leon Jaworski, of the CIA-front Anderson Foundation, representing Texas before the Commission to see that the fair name of Texas was not besmirched by the investigation; CIA-Dallas Chief John McCone; his assistant, Richard Helms; and a passle of police, FBI, news media, etc.

WHERE ARE THEY NOW?

Johnny Poselli received part of his pay-off for the head shot on JFK in the form of a $250,000 "finders's fee" for bringing "Hughes" (Onassis) to Las Vegas in 1967.

Jimmy Frattiano's pay-off included $109,000 in "non-repayable loans" from the S.F. National Bank. (President: Joe Alioto). Credit authorization for the series of loans from 1961-1965 came from Joe Alioto and a high Teamster official. Dun and Bradstreet noted this transaction in amazement, listing the loans in their 1964-1965 monthly reports, and wondering how Frattiano could obtain so much "credit" as his only known title (listed in D&B) was "Mafia Executioner". Frattiano went around for years bragging about it: "Hi, there, I'm Jimmy Frattiano, Mafia Executioner..." A bank VP told the whole story to the California Crime Commission, where Al Harris heard it, and it was hidden in a file folder there. Al Harris, who later shot his mouth off a little too much, "heart attacked".

When last seen (March, 1975), Frattiano was testifying before an SF Grand Jury in regard to his participation, with East Coast Mafia Tony Romano, in the Sunol Golf Course swindle (which cost SF somewhere between $100,000 and $500,000), with the active help of Mayor Joe Alioto.

In between, Frattiano used his $109,000 in "non-repayable loans" to start a trucking company in the Imperial Valley, where he engaged in a lot more swindling—involving U.S. Government construction contracts. As one California Crime Commission member explained, "The Mafia is doing business directly with the U.S. Government now."

Brading was questioned by the FBI two months after his arrest—and release—at Dallas—as part of the Warren Commission's determination to "leave no stone unturned" in its quest for the truth about the JFK assassination. In spite of the fact that Brading was a known criminal with an arrest record dating back about twenty years, the FBI reported that Brading knew nothing whatsoever about the assassination.

Brading became a charter member of the La Costa Country Club, Mafia heaven down near San Clemente. He also became a runner for the skim money from the Onassis-"Hughes" Las Vegas casinos to Onassis's Swiss banks.

Gerald Ford, of the Warren Commission, went on to become President—by appointment of Nixon, then in danger of even further and more serious exposure—from which position the trust Ford pardoned Nixon one month later, for "any and all crimes he may have committed." That covers quite a lot—but Ford is good at covering things up. (20)

McCone, the head of CIA-Dallas, went on to become a member of the ITT Board of Directors—sitting right next to Francis L. Dale, the head of CREEP.

Richard Helms, McCone's assistant at Dallas, ultimately was rewarded with the post of CIA Director. Leon Jaworski, CIA attorney, became the Watergate Prosecutor, replacing Cox, who was getting too warm. Jaworski turned in a sterling performance in our "government-as-theatre"—the honest, conscientious investigator who "uncovered" not a bit more than he had to—and managed to steer everybody away from the underlying truth.

Dr. "Red" Duke, the man who dug two bullets out of Connally and saved his life, was shipped off to a hospital in Afghanistan by a grateful CIA.

Jim Garrison, New Orleans DA who tried to get Eugene Brading out of L.A. (but used one of Brading's other aliases, Eugene Bradley, by mistake), had his witnesses shot out from under him, and was framed on charges of bribery and · extortion. FBI officers "confiscated" photos of Brading taken on the scene, etc.

FBI officers "confiscated" photos of Brading taken on the scene.

Et cetera.

After JFK's death, Onassis quickly established control over Lyndon Johnson through fear. On the trip back to Washington, Johnson was warned by radio, relayed from an air force base: "There was *no conspiracy.* Oswald was *a lone nut assassin.* Get it, Lyndon? Otherwise, Air Force 1 might have an unfortunate accident on flight back to Washington."

Onassis filled all important government posts with his own men. All government agencies became means to accomplish an end: rifle the American treasury, steal as much as possible, keep the people confused and disorganized and leaderless; persue world domination. JFK's original "Group of 40" was turned over to Rockefeller and his man, Kissinger, so that they could more effectively fuck over South America. (Onassis was one of the first to console Jackie when she got back from Dallas with JFK's body). Silva, a S.F. private detective hired by Angelina Alioto to get the goods on philandering Joe, followed Joe Alioto to Vacaville, to the Nut Tree Restaurant, where Joe held a private meeting with other Mafioso to arrange the details of the JFK-assassination pay-off to Frattiano.

1967: Onassis has always enjoyed the fast piles of money to be made through gambling (in Monaco, and in Cuba under Battista.) (21) Onassis took over Las Vegas in 1967, via the "Hughes" cover. U.S. Government officials explained that it was alright because "at least Hughes isn't the Mafia." (ha ha.) (22) Note: L. Wayne Rector was hired around 1955 by Carl Byoir PR Agency (Hughes's L.A. PR firm), to act as Hughes's double. (23) In 1957, when Onassis grabbed Hughes, Rector continued to act as his stand-in. Rector was the Hughes surrogate in Las Vegas; Robert Maheu actually ran the show; Maheu got his orders from Onassis; (24) the six "nurse-maids," called "The Mormon Mafia", kept Rector sealed off from prying eyes.

June 17, 1968: (25) Bobby Kennedy knew who killed his brother; he wrote about it in his unpublished book, *The Enemy Within.* (26), (27) When he foolishly tried to run for President, Onassis had him offed, using a sophisticated new technique: hypnotized Sirhan Sirhan shooting from the front, "security guard" (from Lockheed Aircraft) Thane Cesar shooting from two or three inches away from Bobby's head—from the rear. Sirhan's shots all missed; Cesar's couldn't possibly miss. Evelle Younger, then the L.A. D.A., covered it all up, including the squawks of L.A. Coroner Thomas Noguchi. Younger was rewarded with the post of California Attorney General later. His son, Eric Younger, got a second generation

Mafia reward: a judge-ship at age 30. (See Ted Charach, L.A., author and director, *The Second Gun,* a documentary film on the RFK murder, bought and suppressed by Warner Brothers, for more details.) (28)

After Bobby's death, Teddy knew who did it. He ran to Onassis, afraid for his life, and swore eternal obedience. In return, Onassis granted him his life and said he could be President, too, just like his big brother, if he would just behave himself and follow orders.

September 16, 1968: Hit and run accident on Robert's car, parked in front of the Russian consulate in S.F.—who routinely take pictures of everything that goes on in front of the consulate. Their photos showed the license plate of the hit-and-run car: UKT-264, on a blue Cadillac belonging to Mia Angela Alioto, Joe's daughter, being driven by Tom Alioto, Joe's son—whose driving license had been revoked. His license, and the car's license, were both fraudulent. To cover up the hit-and-run circumstances, S.F. MP's from the Presidio quickly staged a few more hit-and-runs on the same corner—all duly filmed by the Russians. Kathryn Hollister, the Alioto family nurse, was "persuaded" to take the rap for the hit-and-run. Roberts threatened to spill the whole story—in court—with photos.

Next evening Brading and Frattiano showed up in the Black Magic Bar—Brading wearing his X-marked hat from Dallas—to see whether Roberts recognized it, how much he knew, etc. A S.F. MP from the Presidio piped up from the end of the bar: "I heard they let everyone with an X-marked hat through the police lines in Dallas."

Cover-up support for Alioto in the hit-and-run was complete.

Mafia Joe Alioto had Presidential ambitions, shored up by his participation in the Dallas payoff. Everyone who helped kill JFK got a piece of the U.S. pie. But J. Edgar Hoover, FBI head, blew his cover by releasing some of the raw FBI files on Alioto at the Democratic National Convention. Joe was out of the running for V.P., and Humphrey had to settle for Muskie. Humphrey planned to come to S.F. for a final pre-election rally, sparked by Joe Alioto; Roberts threatened to blow the hit-run story, plus its Mafia ramifications open if Humphrey came to S.F. Humphrey didn't come; Humphrey lost San Francisco, California, and the election.

October 1968: Jackie Kennedy was now "free" to marry Onassis. An old Mafia rule: if someone welches on a deal, kill him, and take his gun and his girl: in this case, Jackie and the Pentagon.

July 1969: Mary Jo Kopechne, devoted JFK girl, and later one of Bobby's trusted aides, was in charge of packing up his files after his assassination in L.A. She read too much—learned about the Kennedy Mafia involvement, and other things. She said to friends: This isn't Camelot, this is murder. She was an idealistic American Catholic. She didn't like murdering hypocrites. She died trying to get off Chappaquiddick Island, where she had overheard (along with everyone else in the cottage) Teddy Kennedy's end of the D.H. Lawrence cottage telephone calls from John Tunney and to Joe Alioto, and Democratic bigwigs Swig, Shorenstein, Schumann, and Bechtel. Teddy's good friend John Tunney called to complain that Alioto's friend Cyril Magnin (29) and others had tried to bribe Jess Unruh to switch from the Governor's race to run for the Senate—for the seat John Tunney wanted—so that Alioto would have an easier run for Governor. Teddy called Alioto, who told him to go to hell; then Teddy called the rest to arrange for yet another Mafia murder. Mary Jo, up to there with Mafia shit, ran screaming out of the cottage on her way to Nader. Drunken Teddy offered to drive her to the ferry. Trying to get away from curious Sheriff Lock, Teddy sped off toward the Bridge, busted Mary Jo's nose when she tried to grab his arm from the back seat, and bailed out of the car as it went off the bridge. (30) Mary Jo, with a busted nose, breathed in an air bubble in the car for more than two hours, waiting for help, while Teddy, assuming she was dead, ran to set up an alibi. Mary Jo finally suffocated in the air bubble, diluted with carbon dioxide from her exhalations. It took her 2 hours and 37 minutes to suffocate, while Teddy had Joseph Kennedy, III, steal a boat and ferry him across to Edgartown. Mary Jo was still pounding on the upturned floorboards of Teddy's car while Teddy called Jackie and Onassis on the Christina. Teddy also called Katherine Meyer Graham, lawyers, etc. Jackie called the Pope on Teddy's behalf, who assigned Cardinal Cushing to help. The next morning, the first person Teddy tried to call after deciding he'd have to take the rap himself was: Lawyer Burke Marshall, Onassis's friend in the U.S. Liberty ships deal back in the forties; and also, the designated custodian for JFK's brains after Dallas (the brains have since disappeared.) (31), (32)

Cover-up of the Chappaquiddick murder required the help of: Massachusetts Highway Patrol, which "confiscated" the plates from Teddy's car after it was fished out of the pond; the Massachusetts Legislature, which changed a 150-year-old law *requiring an autopsy* (which would have revealed the suffocation and broken nose); Coroner Mills, who let Kennedy's aide, K. Dun Gifford, supply him with a death certificate, already prepared, for Hill's signature, listing cause of death as drowning; Police Chief Arenas; Cardinal Cushing's priests, who appeared before the Kopechne's "direct from God," with personal instructions from Him that Mary Jo was not to be disturbed; a Pennsylvania mortuary where Mary Jo's broken nose was patched up; East and West Coast phone companies, which clamped maximum security on the records of calls to and from the cottage (S.F. Police Chief Cahill was reassigned to a new job; Security Chief for Pacific Telephone); The U.S. Senate, who never said a word about Teddy's (required equipment) plug-in phone; the judge who presided over the mock hearing; James Reston, editor of Martha's Vineyard's only newspaper, who never heard a word about Teddy's phone at the cottage, though residents called in to tell the newspaper; the *New York Times, Washington Post*, etc., etc., etc.

John Tunney's sister, Joan, heard her brother's end of the phone call, made from her house in Tiburon, to the Chappaquiddick cottage. The next day, after Mary Jo died, Joan ran away to Norway, where she was kidnapped by Mafia hoods Mari and Adamo. They locked her up in a Marseilles heroin factory for 60 days, where the heroin fumes turned her into a junkie (no needle marks); then they turned her loose outside the factory. Joan's husband complained, so she chopped his head off with an ax, and was subsequently locked up in a nuthouse belonging to the Marquess of Blandford, then Tina Livanos Onassis's husband.

Mari and Adamo got pressed into scrap metal in a New Jersey auto junkyard.

In the panic of trying to cover up Teddy's guilt at Chappaquiddick, many things came unglued. The JFK murder threatened to creep out of the woodwork again; Black Panthers Hampton and Clark were murdered (the Chicago cops fired over Attorney Charles Garry's [illegible] because of what they knew about the JFK murder squad's presence at Chicago on Nov. 1, 1963).

September 1969: "Gemstones," with histories, had been released around the globe for several years. In 1969, Roberts gave a Gemstone, with history, to Mack, head of California CREEP, for Nixon, with the proposition: the Presidency, in return for wiping out the Mafia. The "history" included Teddy's phone calls to, and from, the Lawrence Cottage on Chappaquiddick—billed to Teddy's home phone in Hyannisport. Nixon, being Mafia himself, wasn't interested, but kept the information to use later.

May 4, 1970: Charlotte Ford Niarchos called her ex-husband, Stavros, worried about the Ford Foundations's involvement in the Chappaquiddick cover-up. Eugenie Livanos Niarchos, in bed with her husband, overheard the conversation. Stavros was forced to beat her to death; he ruptured her spleen and broke the cartilage in her throat. Cause of her death was listed as "overdose of barbiturates," though autopsy showed these injuries. (33)

End of 1970: Howard Hughes's presence on Earth was no longer required. His handwriting could be duplicated by a computer. (34) His biography—all the known facts about his life—had been compiled and a computerized biography issued to top Hughes execs. His double—Rector—had been doing "Hughes" for years. And Hughes was ill.

Clifford Irving, author of Hoax, about an art forger, became interested in "Hughes". Living on Ibizza, he heard the Mediterranean gossip that "Hughes" was a hoax, too. He went to "Hughes's" so-called "Mormon Mafia," the six "nurse-maids"—for information. One of them—Merryman—perhaps tired of the game—gave Irving the computerized Hughes biography and from it, Irving wrote his "autobiography".

Hughes's death was expected shortly. Preparations were being made so that it would not interfere with the orderly continuation of his empire.

Irving wrote his book—and the publishers announced it. Onassis knew someone had given Irving the information. He thought it was Maheu, and fired him in November, 1970. On Thanksgiving Eve, 1970, in the middle of the night, "Hughes" (Rector) made a well-publicized "secret departure" from Las Vegas to the Bahamas.

December 1970: Onassis discovered his mistake—and had Merryman killed.

Robert Maheu, accidentally deprived of his half-million dollars annual salary, sued "Hughes" for millions—mentioning "Hughes's" game plan for the purchase of Presidents, senators, judges, etc. Onassis paid off—cheap at the price—to maintain his custodianship of "American democracy" and the "free world"—and keep from hanging for multiple murders.

The "Hughes" Mormon Mafia party, plus Rector, fled around the world—from the Bahamas, where they murdered an uncooperative Governor and Police Chief, to Nicaragua, where they shot the U.S. Ambassador between the eyes for noticing that there wasn't really any Hughes; and thence to Canada, where Mormon Mafia nursemaid Eckersley looted a goodly sum in a swindle of the Canadian Stock Exchange; and on to London to Rothschild's Inn of the Park.

April 18, 1971: Howard Hughes, a human vegetable as a result of serious brain damage during his 1957 hustle, plus fourteen years of heroin, grew sicker and sicker. A final overdose of heroin did him in. His coffin was lowered into the sea from a rocky headland off the coast of Skorpios. Present at the funeral were: Jackie Kennedy Onassis; Teddy Kennedy; Francis L. Dale, Director of CREEP, and an ITT Board of Directors; Tom Pappas, also CREEP; and a South Vietnamese cardinal named Thue. Onassis allowed some pictures to be taken from a distance; he himself did not appear. The pictures were published in Midnight, a Canadian tabloid. (35), (36), (37)

Albanian frogmen, tipped off, were waiting under the water. They seized the coffin and took the corpse off to Yugoslavia, thence to China and Russia, and then, perhaps to Boston, in a foot locker. The corpse's dental work was compared to Hughes's very own dental records, and they matched (38). News of Hughes's death, the U.S. take-over by Onassis, and the facts surrounding the murders of JFK, RFK, Martin Luther King, Mary Jo Kopechne, and many more, and the subsequent cover-ups (involving still more murders) has been circulating around the globe for several years. Any country with this information can blackmail the U.S. Mafia government, which has no choice but to pay up. The alternative: be exposed as a bunch of treasonous murderers. This is why China-hating red-baiting Nixon was forced to "recognize" China (which he now claims as his greatest accomplishment); and why the U.S.S.R. walks off with such good deals in U.S. loans, grains, and whatever else it wants. All they have to do is mention those magic words: "Hughes", JFK, RFK, MLK, Mary Jo—words to conjure by— and the U.S. Mafia government crawls into a hole. Information once leaked can't be unleaked. The only way to end the dilemma is through a nuclear war and that wouldn't be one-sided. The other way would be to throw the Mafia out of the United States. Starting at the top—with Ford, Rockefeller and Kissinger. Super-patriots, please note: No one—not all the radicals and subversives hounded by the U.S. domestic intelligence—put together—has done one fraction of the damage done to the U.S. economy, morality, power and prestige, by the thieves at the top.

On the day Hughes was buried, Clifford Irving's wife presented a publisher's check made out to "H. Hughes" to Onassis' Swiss Bank, for payment. Onassis paid off—cheap at the price.

"Gemstone" papers rolling around the world, here and abroad, kept the situation hot. Everyone was nervous. Rockefeller gave Kissinger $50,000 for Carlson and Brisson to write their "expose", "The Alioto Mafia Web" for *Look*. Their mission: find out everything that was public record about Alioto's connection with the JFK murder (His pay-offs to Frattiano, listed in D&B)—and explain it away—in any way that didn't lead back to Dallas. The idea was to get Alioto to quietly go away but still keep the lid on everything.

May 1971: Tina Livanos Onassis married Stavros Niarchos, her former brother-in-law—until he killed her sister, Eugenie.

May 1971: "Folk hero" Daniel Ellsberg, a well-known hawk from the Rand Corp., who had designed the missile ring around the Iron Curtain countries (how many missiles to aim at which cities), was told to release the faked-up "Pentagon Papers," to help distract people from Hughes, JFK, RFK, MLK, etc. The papers were carefully designed by Ellsberg and his boss, Rand Chief and new World Bank Chief Bob ("Body Count") McNamara, to make the Vietnamese War look like "just one of those incredibly dumb mistakes". This helped to cover up the real purposes of the war: Continued control, for Onassis and his friends, of the Golden Triangle dope trade (Vietnam, Laos, and Cambodia); (39) and for Onassis and the oil people, of Eastern oil sources. To say nothing of control over huge Federal sums, which could be siphoned off in profitable arms contracts, or conveniently "disappear" in the war effort.

McNamara's "World Bank"—handing out American money to "starving nations"—actually set up huge private bank accounts for various dictators in the Onassis-controlled Swiss banks. The money could be used as needed to support and extend Mafia operations. Example: $8 billion in World Bank funds for "starving Ethiopians" wound up in Emperor Haile Selassie's personal Swiss bank accounts. This would make him the richest individual in the world—but other dictators have Swiss accounts, too. Maybe even larger. The money drained from America and other captive Mafia nations to feed a greed that can never be satisfied.

(Rand Corp., one of our major "think tanks" has another goody in store for the public: "Project Star," Rand's cover-up fall-back version of the JFK murder—held in reserve should public restlessness over the *Warren Commission Report* cover-up ever threaten to get out of hand. That ought to confuse the people for at least another twelve years, and by that time most of us will be dead, anyway....)

Note in Passing: The dope trade routes are: Golden Triangle to Taiwan to San Francisco. Heroin from the Golden Triangle was sometimes smuggled into S.F. in the bodies of American G.I.'s who died in battle in Vietnam. One body can hold up to 40 pounds of heroin, crammed in where the guts would be.

Some dope gets pressed into dinner plates, and painted with pretty patterns. One dope bust in S.F. alone yielded $6 billion in heroin "china plates"—the largest dope bust in history—quickly and completely hushed up by the S.F. press Mafia. The dope sat in the S.F.P.D. for a while, then was removed by FBI men and probably sent on its way—to American veins. All of this dope processing and shipping is controlled and supervised by the Mafia, for the Mafia. Dope arrests and murders are aimed at independent pushers and maverick peddlers and smugglers who are competing with, or holding out on, the Mafia. While Nixon was conducting his noisy campaign against dope smuggling across the Mexican border, his dope officer *in charge of protecting the Mafia dope trade* was E. Howard Hunt.

Lots of heroin gets processed in a Pepsi Cola factory in Laos. So far, it hasn't produced a single bottle of Pepsi Cola.

Some dope gets processed in heroin factories in Marseilles (see *The French Connection*).

Still more dope comes from South America—cocaine, and now heroin. U.S. Aid went to build a highway across Paraguay (Uraguay?). Useless for the natives, who have no cars; they use it for sunbathing in the day. All night, airplanes loaded with cocaine take off from the longest landing strip in the world—financed by U.S. tax money for the benefit of international Mafia dope pushers.

And then there is opium from Turkey—morphine. This was the starting point of Onassis' fortune.

In case one is still wondering whether the Mafia can actually get away with such things, consider the benefits derived from controlling the stock market, the courts, the police, etc., in one swindle alone: the 1970 acquisition by "Hughes" of "Air West", which involved swindling Air West stockholders of $45 million. Recently indicted for that swindle by the S.E.C.

(in a *civil suit*) were "Howard Hughes" and Jimmy (the Greek) Snyder, "not usually associated with the Hughes crowd," and others.

June, 1971: *New York Times* began publishing the Pentagon Papers, Rand Corp.'s prepared cover-up of the real reasons for the Vietnamese War.

Nixon had gotten a copy of the first Gemstone Papers, circulated in the U.S. back in 1969. He was now wondering how much information Democratic chairman Larry O'Brian had about Hughes, Onassis, JFK, RFK, et al., and more specifically, how much of the dirt the Democrats planned to use.

Nixon set up the "plumber's unit" to "stop security leaks, investigate other security matters." Ehrlichman, Krogh, Liddy, Hunt, Young, etc. Hunt as "White House consultant" supposedly worked for the Mullen Corp.—a CIA cover. Mullen's chief client was "Howard Hughes". Robert Bennett was the head of the Mullen Corp.

June 28, 1971: Ellsberg indicted for leaking the Pentagon Papers.

September 3, 1971: The Watergate team broke into Ellsberg's doctor's (Fielding's) office to get Ellsberg's psychiatric records. Team members: CIA Hunt and Liddy; Cuban "Freedom Fighters" De Diego, Martinez, Bernard Barker. All except Liddy had worked together back at the Bay of Pigs.

Question: Why the intense battle between Mafia forces? Answer: While Onassis was the recognized crowned head of the Mafia, intense, no holds barred scuffling for the lucrative second spot (control of U.S. presidency, government, and so on) was permissable and encouraged under the Mafia code of rules. The only stipulation: outsiders mustn't know about it. "Hughes" contributed liberally—and equally—to both Democratic and Republican parties for the 1972 election. The winner would get even more money from "Hughes".

September 23, 1971: E. Howard Hunt spliced up the phony cables implicating JFK's administration in the Diem assassination.

October 1971: *Look* magazine apologized to Alioto for their "Alioto Mafia Web" article—and folded. The sticking point: they couldn't *prove* Alioto's Mafia Nut Tree meeting back in '63-re: the JFK murder.

November 1971: Alioto re-elected S.F. mayor.

December 1971: Roberts applied for a "Gemstone" visa from the Russian Consulate—on a tapped phone. Phone was tapped by Hal Lipset, S.F. private investigator, who worked for Katherine Meyer Graham, and others, and routinely monitored Consulate phone calls.

January, 1972: The Watergate team showed up at the S.F. Drift Inn, a CIA-FBI safe-house hangout bar, where Roberts conducted a nightly Gemstone rap, for the benefit of any CIA or FBI or anyone who wandered in for a beer. James McCord, Martinez, Bernard Baker, Garcia, and Frank Sturgis showed up—along with a San Francisco dentist named Fuller. James McCord remarked: "Sand and oil with hydrogen heat makes glass brick"—threat of war to Arab nations. The event, like the other nightly raps, was taped by the Drift Inn bartender, Al Strom, who was paid to do so by his old friend, Katherine Meyer Graham—but told his other friend, Roberts, about it. The bar was also wired for sound by Arabs, Russians and Chinese.

January 27, 1972: Liddy and Dean met in Mitchell's office, with Liddy's charts for his $1 million "plan" of spying, kidnapping, etc. The plans included breaking into Hank Greenspun's Las Vegas office safe, in hopes of recovering Greenspun's file on the Hughes kidnapping and Onassis' Vegas operations, which Greenspun had successfully used to blackmail Onassis out of $4 million or so. (40) A "Hughes" get-away plane would stand by to take the White House burglars to Mexico.

February, 1972: Liddy and Hunt travelled around a lot, using "Hughes Tool Co." calling cards, and aliases from Hunt's spy novels.

Liddy, Hunt and other Watergaters dropped by for a beer at the Drift Inn, where they were photographed on bar stools for Katherine Graham. These photos were later used in the *Washington Post*, when Liddy, Hunt, and the others were arrested at Watergate—because CIA men like Liddy and Hunt aren't usually photographed.

Roberts quoted to Liddy the "Chinese stock market in ears"—the price on Onassis' head—by the ear—in retaliation for a few things Onassis had done; on Wayne Rector, the Hughes double; Eugene Wyman, California Democratic Party Chairman and Mafia JFK pay-off bagman; and on Lyndon Johnson: "four bodies twisting in the breeze".

Roberts: "Quoting the prices to Liddy at the Drift Inn made their deaths a mortal cinch. Liddy's like that—and that's why the murdering slob was picked by the Mafia."

"Gemstones rolling around the Drift Inn in February inspired Liddy's 'Gemstone plan' that became Watergate." (41)

February, 1972: Francis L. Dale, head of CREEP and ITT Board of Directors member, pushed Magruder to push Liddy into Watergate.

In a Mafia-style effort to shut Roberts up, his father was murdered by "plumbers" team members Liz Dale (Francis L. Dale's ex-wife), Martinez, Gonzalez, Barker; in Hahnemann's hospital, S.F.— where Mr. Roberts had been taken after swallowing a sodium morphate "pill" slipped into his medicine bottle at home by Watergate locksmith (Miama's "Missing Link" locksmith shop) Gonzalez. The pill didn't kill him; he had a weak digestion, and vomited enough of the sodium morphate up (it burned his lips and tongue on the way out)—but he had emphysema, and went to the hospital. In the hospital, "nurse" Liz Dale and "doctor" Martinez assisted him to sniff a quadruple-strength can of aerosol medicine— enough to kill him the next day.

The day before, Tisseront, head of the College of Cardinals at the Vatican, was pushed out of a Vatican window. Tisseront had followed the career of the present Pope, Montini (whose mother was Jewish). Montini sodium-morphate-murdered Pope Pius XI; was banished from Rome for it by Pius XII; became Pope in 1963. (42), (43) Tisseront wrote it all down; called the Pope "The Deputy of Christ at Auschwitz," and the fulfillment of the Fatima 3 prophecy: that "The anti-Christ shall rise to become the head of the Church." Tisseront also wrote about all the suppressed secrets of the Roman Catholic Church: ie, that Jesus Christ was an Arab (44), born April 16, 6 BC, at the rare conjunction of Saturn and Jupiter. (45) Arab (Persian) astronomers (the Magi) came to Bethlehem to look for *their* king—an Arab baby—and found him in a stable, because the Jews wouldn't let Arabs Mary and Joseph into their nice clean inns, even then. (46) When Jesus overturned the tables of the money-lenders at the Temple, the Jews had the Romans nail him to a cross. (47) He died on the cross, when the Roman soldiers stuck a spear in his side, pulled out his liver, and ate it. (48), (49) Tacitus, the Roman historian, described it all—in a chunk of history deleted by the Church. (50), (51),(52) Nero burned Rome—but that didn't stop the spreading of Jesus's teachings by the early Christians (Arabs). (53) So the Romans decided to adopt the religion, clean it up, make Christ a Jew and Mary a virgin, and work out a church-state deal to fuck the people in the name of God and country that has been operating ever since. Around 300 AD—at the Council of Nicasa—the Christian Orthodoxy was established; a dissenting bishop had his hands chopped off, another bishop was assigned to round up all the old copies of the Bible and destroy them, in favor of the "revised", de-Arabized version. Cleaned up Matthew, Mark, Luke and John were declared "it"; the other Gospels were declared Apocryphal and heretical. (54), (55) Roman Emperor Constantine became the first "Christian" emperor. (56), (57)

Later—during the "Holy crusades"—the Bible was again rewritten—to include Jesus's warning against the "yellow race." (58)

"27 Gemstones, with histories, to 27 countries, brought Red China into the U.N. and threw Taiwan out."

April 1972: Money pours into CREEP: "Gulf Resources and Chemicals Corp., Houston, Texas" contributes $100,000; illegal, laundered through Mexico, comes back through Liedtke of Pennzoil Corp., Houston. (59) Robert Vesco gives Maurice Stans $200,000 "campaign contribution," etc., etc.

Liddy gives McCord $76,000; McCord buys $58,000 worth of bugging equipment, cameras, etc.

May 1972: J. Edgar Hoover had the Gemstone File; threatened to expose Dallas-JFK in an "anonymous" book, The Texas Mafia. Instead, someone put sodium morphate in his apple pie. The corpse was carted away from his home in the back seat of a VW—and his files were "burned"—but some of them got away.

May 28, 1972: First break-in at Watergate: McCord, Barker, Martinez, Garcia, Gonzalez, Sturgis. De Diego and Pico stood guard outside. Hunt and Liddy directed the operation from a (safe?) distance—across the street. The object was to check on Onassis's two men at Democratic Party HQ: Larry O'Brien and Spencer Oliver. (O'Brien's chief PR; client had been "Hughes"; Oliver's father worked for Onassis). McCord wiretapped their phones.

But!!! Little did McCord know that the Plumbers were being observed by Hal Lipset, Katherine Graham's S.F. detective who had followed two of the Plumbers from Liz Dale's side in S.F. to Watergate. Lipset "watched in amazement" as the Plumbers broke in and bugged the phones; then reported back to his boss, Katherine Graham. Lipset and Graham set the trap for the Watergaters when they returned to remove their bugs and equipment.

June 17, 1972: Bernard Barker was wearing his Sears, Roebuck deliveryman costume—the same one he wore at the Dr. Fielding break-in and at the Hahnemann's Hospital murder of Mr. Roberts.

Hal Lipset, Graham's spy, was dressed as a mailman. He left his mailsack behind when he taped the door at Watergate, watched security guard Frank Wills remove it and walk on; *retaped* the door, and as a result, Frank Wills went across the street and called the police, and McCord, Martinez, Sturgis, Barker and Gonzalez were caught in the act. (Graham had them on tape and film, too, every minute of the time.) Liddy and Hunt, across the street, supervising via walkie-talkie, were not. Liddy called Magruder in California re: the Watergate arrests. Magruder told Mitchell, LaRue and Mardian. (60)

Time to burn files. Liddy shredded the Gemstone files at CREEP.

Dean cleaned out Hunt's safe at the White House, and gave Hunt's copy of the Gemstone file to L. Patrick Gray, acting FBI head: "Deepsix this—in the interest of national security. This should never see the light of day." Gray burned the file.

June 20, 1972: DMC Chairman Larry O'Brien filed a $1 million suit against CREEP—naming Francis L. Dale, the head of CREEP. This was a big Mafia mistake—for Dale led directly back to Onassis.

June 21, 1972: *The 18-1/2 minutes of accidentally erased White House tape:* Nixon, furious over the Watergate Plumbers' arrests, couldn't figure out who had done it to him: *who had taped the door at Watergate that led to the arrests?* Hal Lipset, whose primary employer at the time was Katherine Graham, couldn't tell him. Nixon figured that it had to do somehow with Roberts's running around in Vancouver tracing the "Hughes" Mormon Mafia nursemaid's (Eckersley) Mafia swindle of the Canadian stock exchange; and Trudeau. The 18 1/2 minutes was of Nixon, raving about Canada, "asshole Trudeau", "asshole Roberts", Onassis, "Hughes" and Francis L. Dale. It simply couldn't be released.

Stephen Bull's secretary, Beverly Kaye, later heard the "erased" tape, stored in a locked room in the White House. She was horrified. She sent out some depressed Christmas cards and notes to friends, and sodium morphate "heart attacked" at age 40 in a White House elevator outside the locked safe room where the tapes were stored.

January 1973: Tisseront was dead—but as the Church rushed to destroy every copy of his papers, Roberts received one—and wrote a few of his own, released over New Years':

1. "The Cover-up of the Murder of Christ";

2. "The Yellow Race is not in China—The Yellow Race Dead-Fucks Mary Jo Kopechne"; (61), (62)

3. "Mrs. Giannini's Bank of America financed the murder of JFK at Dallas via Alioto's Frattiano, Brading and Roselli";

4. "Vietnam—Fatima 3—Holy Crusade."

"Four documents; four bodies twisting slowly in the breeze."

Lyndon Johnson: Sodium Morphate "heart attack" at his ranch on the Perdernales River. Among his last words: "You know, fellows, it really was a conspiracy..."

Alexander Onassis's plane crash at the "1000 foot Walter Reuther Level," via a fixed altimeter, at Athens airport.

Eugene Wyman, California Democratic Party Chairman, and JFK assassination pay-off bagman: heart attack.

L. Wayne Rector, Hughes double: killed at Rothschild's Inn on the Park, in London.

"Started the shattering of the Mafia economy."

March 18, 1973: Roberts called Hal Lipset, discussing all these matters publicly—over a tapped phone. Lipset reported to Dean, who had hired him away from Graham after they figured out who had taped the door at Watergate. (Mitchell: "Katie Graham's liable to get her tit caught in a wringer.")

March 19, 1973: Dean to Nixon, nervously: "There is a cancer growing on the Presidency."

March 21, 1973: Nixon said that on this date he "received new evidence on Watergate." Lipset later bragged on TV that he had been the one to bring the "new evidence" to Nixon. Meanwhile, back at the *Washington Post*, Katherine Meyer ("Deep Throat") Graham had been feeding Woodward and Bernstein information for their articles. (63)

May 10, 1973: (64) The first witness at the Watergate hearing, running down the names on the CREEP organizational chart, mentioned the name at the top: Francis L. Dale, Chairman. Dale was never mentioned again during the rest of the trial.

July 9, 1973: Roberts had used Al Strom's Drift Inn Bar as an "open lecture forum" for any and all—and Al Strom taped it, for his boss Katherine Graham. But "Al was fair"—

and told Roberts he was doing it—for which he was murdered on this date.

August 1973: Murder of Chile, by Group of 40: (Rockefeller and his man, Kissinger), working with the CIA and $8 million. Allende's Chile had nationalized ITT. Admiral Noel Gaylor (65), Naval Intelligence, told Roberts 1 1/2 years earlier that Chile would get it; Roberts warned the Chilean consul in advance: Allegria, now "teaching" at Stanford.

ITT has now exacted $125 million payment for its Chilean plants—a good return for their $8 million. Mafia-controlled Chile's annual inflation rate has set a world's record. In the style of the old Holy Roman Empire: a slave nation paying tribute to the conqueror.

October 1973: Another "Holy War"—Israelis vs. Arabs.

January 1974: Joe Alioto grants Sunol Golf Course lease to Mafioso Romano, Frattiano, Muniz, Madeiros, Abe Chapman, and Neil Neilson. Alioto sets up the Dallas murder squad in S.F. for more murders.

January 26, 1974: "Hughes" extradition trial cancelled in Reno, "Alioto Mafia Web" Mafia Judge Thomson, after Moses Lasky, from Mafia Alioto's California Crime Commission, waves the forged "Howard Hughes" signature under his nose. (66)

Maheu "wins" his damage suit against "Hughes"—his blackmail pay-off—after discussing Hughes's "game plan" for buying control of the U.S. by buying politicians: Governors, judges, senators, and presidents.

February 1974: Mafia Hearst's daughter Patty "kidnapped" by Lipset's SLA—in a fake terrorist action. (67)

Martin Luther King's mother was murdered by a black student, a self-declared "Israelite"—"acting alone," who was escorted to the church by somebody—and who had a list of other mothers as targets. (68) Next day, the target, Shirley Chisholm, got the message, and rushed to sign off on the DNC suit against CREEP, naming Francis L. Dale; she had been the last hold-out.

April 4, 1974: Mary McCarthy, a writer who had been given a copy of the Gemstone File, said in an article in the *New York Review of Books* that the key to the formation of Liddy's Gemstone plan lay in the where-abouts and activities of the Plumbers between December, 1971 and February, 1972. Answer: They were in the Drift Inn, watching Gemstones rolling around on the bar top.

August 6, 1974: Nixon and Ford signed a paper at the White House. It was an agreement: Ford could be President; Nixon got to burn his tapes and files, and murder anyone he needed to, to cover it all up.

August 7, 1974: Roberts passed information to Pavlov at the S.F. Russian consulate which led directly to Nixon's resignation: the "More" journalism story review's story about Denny Walsh's "Reopening of the Alioto Mafia Web" for the *New York Times,* killed in a panic; plus a long taped discussion of who and what the Mafia is. Hal Lipset, listening to the conversation in the bugged consulate room, had phone lines open to Rockefeller and Kissinger, who listened, too. Rockefeller sent Kissinger running to the White House with Nixon's marching orders. *"Resign right now."* Nixon and Julie cried. But there was still some hope, if Nixon resigned immediately, of drawing the line somewhere—before it got to the King of the Mountain himself—Onassis. Nixon, on trial, would blurt out those names to save himself: Onassis, Dale, "Hughes". Even "JFK".

August 8, 1974: Nixon stepped down, and Ford stepped up to keep the cover-up going.

August 23, 1974: Frattiano in San Francisco, staying at the Sunol Golf Course. More murders scheduled re: Gemstone cover-up.

August 30, 1974: Ford hires Mafia lawyer Becker to work out a pardon deal for Nixon, who might otherwise name Onassis, Graham, and Pope Montini to save himself.

San Francisco Zebra Murders: A series of "random" kill-ings, dubbed "Zebra Murders" by the police because, suppos-edly, blacks were killing whites. The real target was Silva, the witness to Alioto's Mafia Nut Tree meeting. Silva was shot to death in an alley. Careful Mafia planning went into this se-ries, to kill several birds with one stone: 1. Get witness Silva out of the way, without being too "obvious" about it; 2. Spread fear of "black terrorists," and convince people that the Police Department needed more money, and more repressive power. 3. Blame— and frame—Black Muslims—knock off leaders of the opposition.

September 7, 1974: Roberts had made an agreement with a friend, Harp, of Kish Realty, over a bugged phone. Harp was to buy a Gemstone—with history—for $500, the price of a trip to Canada for Roberts to check into the "Hughes" Mormon Mafia Canadian stock market swindle, and other matters. But Harp was sodium-morphate poisoned be-fore the deal could go through—on this date. (69)

Note: Sodium-morphate: a favorite Mafia poison for centu-ries. Smells like apple pie, and is sometimes served up in one, as to J. Edgar Hoover. Sometimes in a pill or capsule. Symptoms: Lethargy, sleep, sometimes vomiting. Once in-gested, there is a heart attack—and no trace is left in the body. Proof is in the vomit, which is usually not analyzed. Not mentioned in your standard medicine books on poisons, etc. It is a common ingredient in rat poison. (70)

September 8, 1974: Ford pardons Nixon for "all crimes committed from June 20, 1969 (oops, make that January) through August, 1974."

Gemstone papers still floating around the world. Gandhi talks about the "U.S.'s bloody deeds."

October 1974: Ford drops "extradition" of Hughes from the Bahamas. Explanation: "We dropped it because we knew he wouldn't come." That's for sure!

October 3, 1974: The Watergate Trial—the cover-up of the cover-up— got under way, starring Montini's, Ben Veniste, Onassis's Neal, Graham's Jill Volner. In the White

HOuse, Mafia Mayors Alioto, Daley, and Beame met with the "truth squad"—Ford, Scott, and Griffin—and Mike Mansfield, in secret.

October 10, 1974: Tina Livanos Onassis Blandford Niarchos, sodium- morphate poisoned by hubby Stavros; puked, slept, and died of "heart attack."

Losing his son, Alexander, took all the fun out of killing for Onassis. Who was there to inherit the world empire he had dreamed of handing to his son?

December 1974: Brezhnev had scheduled a meeting with Sadat, of Egypt. The outcome wouldn't help the U.S.—no matter how many trips Henry made to the Mid-east with clean socks and blank checks. A new U.S. "secret weapon" was apparently used: a tiny speck of metal, introduced some-how into Brezhnev's lymph system. It lodged in the cluster of lymph nodes over his heart, and there it was coated with layers of phlegm—much as an oyster creates a pearl around an irritating grain of sand. Brezhnev's lymph system clogged up; he got the flu and the meeting with Sadat was cancelled. (71)

Russian doctors x-rayed him and found a huge lump in his chest. Then they put him before a Kirlian camera and checked his aura for cancer. No cancer. Note: Kirlian photography is the latest Russian diagnostic tool. It reveals the presence of disease—physical or moral (it also detects lies). (72)

Brezhnev's "lump" had to be treated with radiation therapy—hence the rumors he had cancer. It took six weeks to clear up.

March 1975: Onassis died. The Mafia organization re-grouped itself. Prince Faisal watched his uncle, King Faisal, silently watch the shift of Mafia power—and couldn't stand it. He shot his uncle, the spiritual leader of 600,000,000 Moslems, who had played ball with Onassis all along.

South Vietnam's Thieu, dubious about which way the Mafia cooky would crumble now that Onassis was dead, decided the time was right for him to split. He abandoned the War Effort, cursed the U.S., and split for Taiwan, his plane so overloaded with gold bullion that he had to dump some of it overboard.

March 15, 1975: Roberts got the "Brezhnev Flu," and spent 2 weeks at U.C. hospital. Doctors there, without the Kirlian photography diagnostic technique, assumed the softball-sized lump over his heart was cancer. It wasn't.

April 1975: The Cambodian domino was no fun at all — it fell right over. Premier Lon Nol fled to exile in a Hawaiian suburb.

CIA Chief Colby, in a fit of spite, "leaked" the "stolen" story of CIA-Hughes Glomar Explorer's raising of the *bodies of drowned Russian sailors* from their sunken nuclear submarine. Purpose: To bug the Russians, and also to halt criticism of the CIA by pointing out how noble, brave, and self-sacrificing they are in their efforts to save us. (73)

The Russians are funny about their dead. They bitterly resented Colby's game. They quietly went through a massive naval "war game" — the reheasal of a nuclear attack of the U.S.

Which brings us almost to the present time. Ford, Kissinger and Rockefeller squat like toads on the corpse of America. By the time of the Bicentennial, the stink may be unbearable.

Ford now plans a propaganda movie version of his book, "Portrait of an Assassin," which will reiterate the exploded cock and bullshit notion that Oswald was JFK's "lone assassin." With singularly inept misunderstanding of the times, he seems to think Americans will take his word for it, and be "reassured" in the face of those "crackpot conspiracy theories." He doesn't seem to realize that he will be reminding, or informing, Americans, of his role on the infamous Warren Commission.

I hope this outline will make individual Gemstone papers easier to understand.

IF YOU FOUND THIS OUTLINE INTERESTING:
You won't be reading it in the papers for quite some time. At present, the only way to spread this information here in America is *via hand-to-hand*. Your help is needed. Please

make 1, 5, 10, 100, copies, or whatever you can, and give them to friends or politicians, groups, media. The game is nearly up. Either the Mafia goes—or America goes. (74)

An Interview with Stephanie Caruana

conducted through the mail by Jim Keith

Q: Please tell me about your association with Bruce Roberts' *Gemstone Files*.

A: I had the very great privilege, about 18 years ago, of knowing and working with the author of the original *Gemstone File* letters, Bruce Roberts, in San Francisco. In order to clarify, in my own mind, the facts he laid out in such profusion in his letters, I wrote a chronological outline, to the extent that I understood what he was saying, which I called "A Skeleton Key to the Gemstone File." At a time when Bruce Roberts was hospitalized with a strange ailment which he claimed was CIA-induced, I made a bunch of copies of the Gemstone "Key" and mailed them out at random. It was a very scary time and ultimately tragic. I also remember, quite vividly, giving a copy of the Key to Paul Krassner [editor of *The Realist*], who said, "Bruce Roberts is a pain in the ass." I had a different view. I thought, and still think, that Bruce Roberts was probably the bravest and most brilliant man I ever met.

This [commenting on various copies of the Skeleton Key in current circulation] was pretty close to what I sent out when Bruce Roberts was in the hospital in California—although there were several "editions" with more or less info added from time to time... I also, at about the same time, "collaborated" with Mae Brussell (oddly enough, the daughter of Cyril Magnin) on an article about Patty Hearst and the fake SLA "army" which had taken Berkeley hostage with its ludicrous "food distribution." The article, was entitled "Is Cinque the First Black Lee Harvey Oswald?", meaning that he was a patsy set up by the authorities — a "yo-yo" they controlled with a string, letting him "escape" from prison after carefully indoctrinating him, in prison, with the idea of a black "army" etc. — all under the supervision of government-paid handlers.

The California prison system had at that time (and still does, for all I know) a system of "black pride" classes, taught by outsiders, the real purpose of which would not stand scrutiny. The "drama of controlling the black savages" is very much on the mind of some very powerful Californians, dictating their tactics of police training, etc., which is why Los Angeles is currently going up in smoke!

The article came out in the *Berkeley Barb*, and I must say we had a pretty good grasp on the phoniness of what was really going on. I see how at least one of your Gemstoners has picked up on this a bit, in terms of how the powers-that-be were trying to use this created and manipulated "army" for fear and terrorist propaganda. I had the — I can't say pleasure, for it was a terrible horror — the week the *Barb* came out with our article, of seeing these people covering their tracks by wiping out the "army." Frying its leader, "Cinque" alive — (after pulling Patty Hearst out of harm's way, of course) with a murderous SWAT team raid, televised live, which I watched, live, on a TV set in the window of a Berkeley shop. This, and a few personal death threats, as well as Bruce Roberts' difficulties and all the other murders he kept talking about, persuaded me that the best thing I could do, if I wanted to get this information out, was to do just what I did: throw it to the wind, and run for my life. Which I did.

At the time, most people who read it were somewhat dazed. Much of the information, or at least the way it was put together, was new and shocking. Since then, a great deal has emerged, and enough has been corroborated from various sources that people don't find it so hard to believe any more. I don't feel paranoid, either, since it's too late to shut me up, by many years! (That was the whole idea.) I've seen

TV shows based on one or another aspect from time to time.

I guess what amazes (and saddens) me the most is that this "Key" seems to be all that has trickled down to the (underground) public of Bruce Roberts' original letters, which were a thousand times more powerful in their writing and effect. I gather that you have never actually seen any of them. I assure that he really did exist, and that he was brilliant, and a great discourser. When he talked about holding forth in one bar or another, that's exactly what he did. Anyone with a tape recorder would have a feast of information.

I think that the Gemstone information is important for people to have. Not that I really think that it will "save" us, because frankly I think we're too far gone for salvation! But at least it may help a bit to understand what is happening. It can give people a broader perspective. For this reason, I think it may be important for people to know this is, or was, real. Somebody, a man named Bruce Roberts, actually wrote those letters; and somebody else (me) actually wrote the Skeleton Key. (How do they think it came into existence??? Spontaneous combustion????)

...About 10 years ago, I got a phone call from—*Penthouse?? Playboy??* They said someone had sent them a copy, and they wanted to use some of the information, but I would have to "document" it first! I said, hey, I ain't going to "document" it. If it feels right, do it! Otherwise, you commit suicide, not me. I ain't getting paid for this, nohow, right? Right, they said. I said, it seems to me, that if this information is true, it will prove itself by being believed when it is read. Ten years from now, your article will be forgotten, but the Gemstone Skeleton Key will still be around. They snickered, and hung up.

What I had in mind was that the Old Testament originally was copied by hand, one letter at a time, and that didn't stop it from getting around. People hunger for the truth. And I believe that what I was passing on was true.

Q: What are your feelings about the continuing interest shown in the *Gemstone File?*

A: I am aware, and I am very pleased, that the information that I released eighteen years ago has been spread around to so many people that it is now "public property," and that, consequently, the danger of getting wiped out for spreading it, which was quite real back then, is probably over for now. However, the shady process of milking people and governments of money which was the "Mafia's" favorite game then, is still going on now, and in many cases, by the same people, or their successors. If I were to appear too publicly to advise and instruct people how to spot and track these ongoing scams, "somebody" might still get mad. I hope you'll understand that I like living, and that a number of my friends (including Bruce Roberts) died because of their involvement in tracing and recording these political and financial manipulations.

Please understand that I have very mixed feelings about all this. One wonders whether, if a real person emerges, "claiming responsibility" for the Skeleton Key to the Gemstone File, whether some of these surviving characters who are accused in the file of murder, blackmail, etc. etc., might want to sue me for millions, or simply wipe me out for the crime of "character assassination," etc. I hope you understand a little simple fear! What "protects" me, if anything, is that the people involved wouldn't want to draw attention to the material by publicly objecting to it. An automobile "accident" on a quiet country road is, however, easy enough to arrange.

Q: What was your first contact with the *Gemstone Files*?

A: The circumstances were, that I was living in Mae Brussell's house in Carmel. I had "offered myself to her as a slave," because I wanted to write articles based on her fat file folders. This started with Patty Hearst and the SLA "Army" where I found myself going nuts trying to figure out what was really going on. While I was working with Mae Brussell, my editor at *Playgirl* asked me if Mae knew anything about Howard Hughes. Mae laughed and said Howard Hughes was dead. We set out to "co-author" an article about Howard Hughes, and she gave me her file folders on Hughes (and Onassis) to read. I had a nasty deadline to meet, and was reading and writing from morning until night.

Then she pulled out her *Gemstone File* letters, and told me I could read them, but only after I had finished working on the article, on my own time at night, locked in my little cell. She also "ordered" me to not actually read the letters, but only to skim over them, and only to read what related to

Howard Hughes! At midnight, exhausted after a long hard day, I started to read. The first page was chocked full of murders, poison, and dirty words. My reaction was: Hey, this guy is a paranoid schizophrenic. I've been told all my life about them. They think everybody's getting killed. In a sense, I had been brainwashed to automatically reject anyone who talked about the things he did, in the ways he did it. I had to pull back and take a look at my own reactions, and to decide that I would read the material with an open mind. It all held together — from first to last page.

Of course, I was reading the Gemstone letters themselves, instead of my own sadly watered-down and abbreviated outline of what they had to say.

The article I wrote "with" Mae was published in *Playgirl* — but their attorney had cut so many holes in it that it came out more like paper dolls than an article. Even so — the editor got fired, and I was banned forever. The editor told me that the day that issue of *Playgirl* appeared on the newsstands, she was in New York and "I never saw so many men in black overcoats running up to buy *Playgirl* in my life!" I personally doubt that they were buying it to see whose cock was in the centerfold, don't you think?

My "working relationship" with Mae came to an end at about that time. I guess she decided that having a slave wasn't all it was cracked up to be, and I got a little tired of it, too. I headed for San Francisco, met Bruce Roberts, and became friends with him.

I guess I thought, or hoped, that what was being kept such a secret from the American people, but was being used abroad by various governments to blackmail the U.S., and in various kinds of global power politics, should belong to the people — if only to see what would happen if people found out what was really going on. You know yourself, that nothing really did happen. The guys playing the crazy games maybe held their breath for a few minutes, to see if anyone could do anything with the truth. Then they continued playing the games. Now we have a situation where although many people understand the game, or at least large parts of it, the Mafia and its associates are well established here. America is like a huge animal with a giant parasite hanging from its throat. Enough blood is being drained that everyone is hurting, and yet no one seems to know how to get rid of the parasite. The parasite itself is wondering what, if anything, we will ever do. It won't however, commit suicide. That is not the nature of the beast.

Q: Could you tell me more about editing the Skeleton Key?

A: Please remember that you are working from a very abbreviated and concise outline, written by another person (me) who was, at the time, struggling to understand a whole pile of complicated and shocking information. My outline consisted of 23 pages, based on a hasty and imperfect selection from an original body of letters of several hundred pages. Some of it was based on my hasty notes made from reading letters which I did not own, and only had the chance to see once. My original impulse was to understand the letters myself, and it helped me to try and make some sort of chronological sense out of them. Roberts was not only a mental giant and a powerful writer, but also a sort of poet. Reading his letters was like reading a history written by James Joyce in his *Finnegans Wake* period. All of historic time (that is, the threads Roberts was interested in) tended to be jumbled together in paragraph-long sentences. Some of my "chronologizing" consisted of picking bits and phrases out of these sentences, and putting them under appropriate dates — sometimes years apart. I stuck to Roberts' own words as much as I could, since I felt that any interpretation I might make of what might be a "poetic" expression on his part, might well be wrong.

My intention at the time was to outline events, not to describe Bruce Roberts. When I decided to release the Gemstone outline, which was done in a hurry under the pressure of fright for his safety, I attempted to include a few explanations, and at least some details about him, so that readers would understand that I was not claiming to be the creator of this body of work, merely an outliner of someone else's writing. If my intention had been to describe Bruce Roberts, I would have said that he, as far as I knew, was brave, tough, real, a player and not a sideline sitter; sometimes scared, very angry, and not in the least way the silly wimp you describe! [in the original draft for my article "Is It True?"]. He wasn't "trying to enter the world of James Bond"—he was

James Bond, or his own version of it. Only, he wasn't "On Her Majesty's Service." He was a freelancer. A street fighter, a Scotsman, a heavy drinker. I know it's difficult for most people who are not embroiled in the center of a universe such as his, to imagine what it's like to be there, but your picture is just wrong.

As far as I know, he never intended or directed his writing for the general public. Therefore your idea that he was attempting to paint himself in one light or another, for self-aggrandizement or whatever other uncomplimentary terms you can think of, is incorrect.

Q: Why did you conclude that the Gemstone letters were not meant for public distribution?

A: They were almost invariably addressed and sent to a specific person. Xerox copies went into the File, and were only given or sold to people like myself or Mae Brussell, who had a special interest in them. As far as I know, they were never publicly distributed, and this seems likely because it appears neither you nor anyone else you know personally have ever seen a copy of a single one, even though I suppose you and everyone else interested in the subject of Gemstone have been asking to see them for years! On the other hand, my "Skeleton Key" was intended for public distribution, and that, my good Watson, is why you have a copy!

Q: Could you describe your personal mindset when you met Roberts?

A: I had completed the article for *Playgirl*, and escaped from solitary confinement with Mae Brussell. After reading the portion of the file that Mae had (possibly 200 pages, dating from around 1970 to 1972), I had been very curious about the author. I asked Mae what he was like, and she said he was "Caspar Milquetoast!" She told me that after her daughter had been killed in an "automobile accident" on a lonely road in Carmel, where her other daughter had been seriously injured, another girlfriend killed, and a fourth girl injured. She had mentioned this on her radio show (Radio Conspiracy). And apparently she mentioned the name of a man who had sympathetically come to visit her after the "accident." After this broadcast, which Bruce Roberts had apparently heard, he came to visit her in Carmel, and gave her a copy of the *Gemstone File* (his letters). He told her that the man who came to see her was the man who had arranged for the "accident," which had been done to persuade Mae to drop her investigations (she was apparently getting too close to some things) — and he, Bruce Roberts, recognized the man's name, and he knew that the reason this man had visited her was to get the warning across to her that she should stop. However, Mae didn't get the message (she believed her first visitor to be sincerely offering condolences), and didn't believe Roberts; she thought he was probably some nut. She read the file, not especially believing it, but later events made her put more credence in it. She told me that she went to visit Roberts in S.F., and that he lived with his mother, a nice little old Scotch/Irish lady who served tea and wore white gloves. All this made Mae think Bruce Roberts was "Caspar Milquetoast."

I was a bit surprised, because the impression I got from his writing had been that of a much more fierce personality, but I adjusted my thinking to "Caspar Milquetoast." I was still very curious to meet him. And I decided that since we had used some of the Gemstone information in the *Playgirl* article, I felt obligated to tell him about it, before it appeared as a journalistic courtesy, at least — though Mae seemed to feel that he had given her permission to use the information as she saw fit. And I also wanted to read the rest of the file — whatever he had written after Mae's portion of the file ended — it was: "And what happened after that???" At the time, I didn't know the file had a name; it was just "letters."

Roberts had mentioned in the letters that his phone was tapped, and I didn't want to call him, so I just drove to the address that he had put on the file, an apartment house in S.F., and rang the bell. I fully expected him to invite me in for tea with his mother. When I finally did meet him, it was clear to me that he wasn't Caspar Milquetoast at all. More like Clint Eastwood/John Wayne, if you want to go Holly-wood for images.

Between Mae Brussell and Bruce Roberts, it was Mae who was the amateur. She was a "filer," as anyone who knew her would tell you. I don't think she ever had any direct con-nection with the events she described. (Except for her contact with Roberts, which she misunderstood at the time). She got most of her information from the press, since she subscribed to about 8 different daily papers, and lots of magazines. Every day she would clip the articles relevant to the stories and people she was following, and since she had a copy machine, she would underline things, make copies, and pop the articles into the right file folders. After a time, she had files on nearly everybody, and that was the (only) basis for her articles on Watergate for Paul Krassner's *Realist*. In terms of brains, she was smart, for a squirrel. I never had the impression that she had any deep understanding of what she had squirrelled away, though as a writer, I found her file folders chocked full of juicy information!

Bruce Roberts, on the other hand, got a lot of his information direct from the source, and from his own experiences. He also "traded" his Gemstone letters to sources around the world, who in turn supplied him with information that was unobtainable elsewhere. It was a worldwide information network on the highest level. For example, I believe this is where he got the information on "Pope Montini" and the original "Christ" — from Cardinal Tisseront at the Vatican before Tisseront's untimely "accidental suicide" through a plate glass window.

Q: Do you believe that Larry Flynt got shot because of the publication of the Skeleton Key?

A: Yes, I do believe Larry Flynt got shot because he believed that stupid jerk, Paul Krassner, who thought that the *Gemstone File* info was "a big joke." I'm glad somebody else said it, not me. Paul thinks everything is a big joke! It's a measure of what a trivial person he is. After Flynt got shot, I heard Paul just didn't want to talk about Gemstone at all, and no wonder. He's a regular stand-up comic! More than one can say for Larry Flynt.

Q: Did you ever see any of Roberts' actual gemstones?

A: Yes, I did see a few. He invited me to meet him one day in front of "Mrs. Giannini's Bank of America" in downtown S.F. He had a safe deposit box there, and he went in and got a few artificial diamonds, and I think a ruby, and showed them to me. They were to be sent out in connection with a letter or letters that he was sending to someone. I have never been big on gemstones, and even though diamonds are supposed to be a girl's best friend, none of them have ever actually befriended me. At the time, I believe he was no longer making gemstones. He told me that he had done so in the past in a garage, which blew up one day due to some mistake, and singed off his eyebrows, etc. I think he may have run out of gemstones at some time, and of course could use anything he wanted as a symbolic "gemstone." Sometimes a coin. Or even a pebble from a certain place. In this case, it was the "history" that accompanied the object that would give it its value. I can't give you much more information than that. He told me some of these things anecdotally, and I never heard the whole story of his life.

Q: Do you know why the G. Gordon Liddy files were also called "Gemstone"?

A: The relationship between Gordon Liddy and Gemstone, as I understand it, is that Roberts was writing his Gemstone letters (letters that he sold, with a gemstone); Gordon Liddy was given a few of these letters, possibly even with a gemstone; he named his White House operation "Gemstone," after Roberts' letters in his "Gemstone file"; that's where the name came from. Liddy's purpose as I understand it was to find out how much of the Gemstone information had leaked out, and damage control. Gordon Liddy isn't "Gemstone"; he was "anti-Gemstone." I see him on TV every now and then. He plays "himself" on *Miami Vice;* a murdering CIA/Mafia slob, and he doesn't need to act. He recently appeared on Jack Anderson's show. Jack Anderson serves as a conduit to release CIA cover stories to J.Q. Public. The CIA is very imaginative and productive, when it comes to creating cover stories. They had Gordon Liddy "explaining" to Jack Anderson how he had been "hired" by the CIA to murder Anderson, and how, in his endearingly clumsy CIA way, he had failed repeatedly. How could anyone be afraid of such a bunch of inept nerds?? (That was the point of the show.) Can't even pull off a good assassination! Did J.Q. Schmoe really believe this bullshit? Who knows? I didn't bother to watch. The difference between media and life gets a little fuzzy, doesn't it? Do you know the difference? In a nutshell: in life, if they decide to bump you off, they actually do it.

Q: What would you venture to say was Roberts' purpose in writing the Gemstone letters?

A: Much of this has to be guesswork, really, since you can't always be sure of another person's motivation, especially when that person isn't around to explain. As I think I may have told you, Bruce Roberts' serious involvement with Hughes began when he tried to sell the Hughes Tool Company his invention, I believe it would be the use of artificial diamonds as cutting tips for oil well drill bits. Last night, half asleep, I was watching a program on lasers. Suddenly this guy from "Hughes" appeared; I forgot his name. He is supposed to have "invented" the use of laser enhancement for shooting a beam of light through an artificial ruby (in 1960, after Hughes stole Roberts' invention). In retrospect, I think Roberts half-explained all this in his letters and conversations with me, though as a scientific ignoramus, I didn't grasp it at all. He was also talking about the potential for power inherent in laser beam technology, still in the process of development. "Hughes" stole a lot more from Roberts than just diamond tips for drill bits, although that may have been the original potential use with which he took his idea to them. Instead of paying him, Hughes Tool stole his invention. The motivating force was rage, and while he was fighting Hughes Tool, he somehow discovered "there wasn't any Hughes," i.e., Onassis had snapped him up and was running the Hughes empire through the "Mormon Mafia" baby-sitters, Robert Maheu, etc. A paperback book on "Hughes" which I used to have had some utterly damning photos of Hughes appearing before a Senate committee or whatever, clearly showing the facial scars he sustained when he escaped the assassination attempt on him in one of his planes; and a "later" photo of "him"; younger and without the scars, handsomer, and clearly not the same human being at all! Just a look-alike, actually one of the doubles who appeared during "Hughes's" increasingly rare public appearances after the real Hughes was snatched by Onassis. This book, I believe written by Noah Dietrich, who had worked for Hughes for years, until the takeover convinced Onassis to pay Dietrich a significant amount of $$$ to shut up and go away, which he did.

Along the way Roberts lost considerable income (not being paid for his scientific discovery, etc.). So a man who might have been a perfectly happy inventor-physicist became a very unhappy man-whose-invention-was-stolen-by-a-big-company. Being an exceptionally brilliant and courageous man, he kept going deeper and deeper, and I suppose formed the habit of keeping journals, since he was also a very gifted writer. The more he learned about Onassis and Onassis's associates, and their strangle-hold on the media, etc., the more became the need to communicate some of what he knew. We all take different paths. Roberts wrote "letters." He was also, I believe, a very humane person; a father (divorced); not a killer. He didn't like Mafia killers. I don't think he appreciated the world being run by these killers, especially when they moved in and took over the U.S. government with the assassination of Kennedy. It really was a secret coup. I guess you can divide people into two groups: the ones who think it's okay to feed people drugs, murder to stay in power and make money, etc., etc., manipulate whole populations, and those who think, when they know about it, that it isn't okay, no matter how much money they can make by being part of it. Or how much they will lose by not being part of it. I suppose you have made a similar choice, or that you believe you would make that choice if it were presented to you as such. I suppose that, while perhaps something of a dilettante, you wouldn't have chosen to explore "conspiracy theory" only provided that it couldn't possibly be true. I suppose you feel you have some decent human instincts that keep you from being a professional killer. Don't you think it might be possible that Bruce Roberts shared these feelings? I always thought he did.

Since Roberts wasn't making money from his scientific work, he had to make it somehow. He once told me that he did construction work (contractor) for a while, putting roofs on buildings, etc. "You have to make a living somehow." At a certain point, he put nine and nine together, and started sending letters, with Gemstones, "cold," and asked the recipients to send him what they thought the letter was worth to them. I guess some of them sent substantial sums, and others sent people to kill him. I know he didn't have very much money; this could have been due in part to various divorces, children, etc., and various disasters that frequently seemed to happen to his cars, etc.

Q: What do you think of the recent *Kiwi Gemstone?*

A: It's the first "Gemstone" result that seems positive. That is, someone has actually used the Gemstone information accurately and courageously as a basis for following current events which are now shaping our world (species) history, and I say, more power to them! It is really a tragic story of how our world has been "united" under the rule of these vicious criminals, monsters in business suits. You can see exactly what dear old George Bush means when he keeps talking about "One World," or whatever the phrase he uses.

Of course, the Kiwi Gemstone phrasing is a bit misleading, in that the wording seems to imply that "Bruce Roberts" wrote all of it. I don't believe anyone writes anything after they are dead, and I think that needs clarifying. If the person or persons responsible for continuing "Gemstone" through the takeover of Australia wish to be anonymous, that's something I do understand. And if they are smart enough to follow the current international financial, political and social manipulations, hopefully they will be smart enough to stay alive.

Q: What about Roberts' reference to sodium morphate? The chemists that I've consulted don't seem to be aware of any such thing.

A: The "sodium morphate" question is one which I also had trouble with. "Sodium morphate" is the phrase Roberts used and I stuck to his words and phrases as closely as possible. I tried to look it up myself, and ran into the same brick wall. I even asked him about it once, and he looked at me blankly and repeated that it was a common ingredient in rat poison. I do know that I have read many references, and have seen the device of such heart-attack inducing poison referred to in many murders, real and fictitious, since then, and I know that such a poison, whatever its technical name, is fairly easily obtainable.

Q: Do you happen to know what Roberts was getting at when he referred to "The Yellow Race"?

A: What comes to mind is the phrase: "The Yellow Race is not in China: the Yellow Race dead-fucks Mary Jo Kopechne." It was not a description of skin color, but of moral decay; that is, specifically, of Teddy Kennedy, who allowed Mary Jo to die to cover his own sickening ass, and of those battalions of folks who helped him in the cover-up.

Q: The Skeleton Key has been in circulation eighteen years now. Do you see any hopeful signs that any of this information will be made public, or acted upon?

A: I don't know whether you have seen the series on the

JFK assassination which recently appeared on the *A&E* cable network. I see where a number of the surviving witnesses have come forth with bits and pieces which pretty well substantiate how many shooters there really were, where they were standing, etc. Each new retelling adds a little more to the complete picture. This one goes off into the wild blue yonder, however, when a "researcher" sits there with a straight face and tells you the "three shooters" were from the Corsican Mafia, recruited in Marseilles. Surely the good old USA didn't have to go so far to find reliable hitmen, when we have so many home-grown expert Mafioso hitmen, such as Fratianno, Roselli and Brading.

Now that Oliver Stone's movie has come out, and if everyone stays alive, there may be a move throughout the world to get these people out of power, and as I said, it's a slight chance, but if we could all get together, we could do it. Revolutions have happened in the past. When things get bad enough (as they are now), things happen. Whoever thought the Red Splendor would come tumbling down, without a shot, defeated by "free enterprise"? And now that "free enterprise" is far from free, that too may bite the dust. You as an anarchist know what I am talking about, I suppose. Human history may yet take some surprising turns. The thousand year Roman Empire eventually bit the dust.

I recently watched the Oscar ceremonies. Two of the big nominees — Stone's *JFK*, and Warren Beatty's *Bugsy*, came head-to-head. It was fascinating to watch! Both are really about the same subject: Mafia control over the U.S. Stone's, against, we know about. Beatty's, presenting the killer, *Bugsy*, in a sympathetic light, is pro. The absent party, in both, was Onassis, Mayer Lansky's boss. *Bugsy's* "glorious aim," the building of the Flamingo casino in the Las Vegas desert, a great money-milking machine for the Mafia — what a goal! The movie even mentions the power this would give the Mob in Nevada — another dream which came true! Hollywood walked the line between the two sides; *Silence of the Lambs* was the only safe choice! Watching Stone's and Beatty's faces provided a groovy little mini-drama, since both of them knew what was going on! Jack Valenti's scathing denunciation of *JFK* afterward underscored the battle for the hearts & minds of J.Q. Public which is always continuing.

Mae Brussell on the *Gemstone File*

[The following is an edited transcript of Mae Brussell's *Dialogue: Conspiracy* radio program on KLRB FM radio in Carmel, California. It combines programs dated December 25, 1977, no. 302, and January 1, 1978, no. 303.]

Many people have asked me to talk about the *Gemstone File* on *Dialogue: Conspiracy*, and I looked at the index of the shows, and I never have done it with you. So I brought it in and I'm going to read you part of the *Gemstone File*, and explain what it is today, and then next week I'll do more, and it will be a two-or-three part session on *Dialogue: Conspiracy* about the *Gemstone File*.

These pages — there's approximately twenty typewritten pages — I'm not going to read all twenty to you on the air. You can send for it; I can make copies if you want. The cost of copying it is 10 cents a page plus postage, and [I will] mail them to you in case you don't have them. These are circulated... they're in London, they're in Ireland, they're all over the United States, and they were put together by a person named Stephanie Caruana. She came to my house to do an interview with me for *Playgirl* magazine and she saw all the material that I had, and co-authored with me a story on the death of Howard Hughes, being buried off of a Greek island. [It's] a case which I'm still working on, and trying to get the body exhumed in Houston, Texas to prove that it isn't Howard Hughes and our article was the correct one.

She came to my house to work on the Howard Hughes story, because she saw all this material around, and I showed her what is the *Gemstone Files;* it's from Bruce Roberts. I don't know any other person who has the complete set. They were a series of letters that he wrote to his mother, or a diary that he kept for himself, and the whole file is about 300 pages. And, as I said last week on *Dialogue: Conspiracy,* I had it copied and I have three copies put somewhere, each in a different place to be safe, and I believe I'm the only person in the United States that has it.

Stephanie went through the 300 pages and went up to see Bruce Roberts. He was living in San Francisco at the time, but they said he's dead now — he died of a brain tumor about six months ago. She wrote a summary of 20 typewritten pages in essence of what Bruce had to say and what he wanted the world to know, and the summary is called "The Skeleton Key to the Gemstone File."

I met Bruce Roberts when my first article came out, "Why Was Martha Mitchell Kidnapped?" He got in touch with Paul Krassner and myself and he gave us this document. I was staying with some friends at Geary Street in San Francisco, and he came and brought it to me one evening. We were up with him to about one o'clock and kind of shaky and very nervous about the way it was put on us and given to me, and didn't know anything about Bruce at the time.

And so I went with a friend downstairs and we decided we'd go out and get a cup of coffee. When we went out there was a car in back of us with a man standing by the parking meter, near Van Ness and Geary. We got in our car and he got in the car behind us and followed us. We looked in our car and the whole car had been pilfered. Documents and letters of the party I was with [were] taken out of the car and the suitcases in there taken away, and the radio was taken. It looked like a burglary but everything was thrown around inside the car, and we had a chase in San Francisco up and down the streets. By then it was 2:00 or 2:30 and everything was empty and we couldn't find a place to pull up. There were 2 cars that zeroed in on us and followed us and then we finally went to — about 3:30 or 4:00 in the morning. We went to an all-night restaurant that was open on Geary and said "to heck with it if they're following us." I didn't know what to do. We went in, got something to eat; we went back to where we were staying, and we were locked out and I didn't have the key. Finally we went to KSAN radio station, and, just as luck would have it, we went upstairs and I remembered they had a waterbed in the lobby which they didn't have any more. We fell asleep on some beanbag chairs until the morning. I had a radio show around 9:00 or 10:00.

So I was carrying these *Gemstone Files* with us all night through this wild chase. I was really up all night and [couldn't] concentrate on them and didn't have a chance to go through it. I was wondering what in the world was here? And it was a funny scene — sort of funny now, but it wasn't funny then. I have the large set of files, as I say, all of the documents, and what he wrote about them, so they were at my house. I'll read you some of the points about them that are pertinent to you, and I'll read you some of the places where I differ. This is why I haven't used it in terms of writing yet or getting it published, and I hope the people that want to make the movie in England will seriously go over the material with me because some of it is in error and some of it is correct.

I'll start just by reading you sections of it, and you will know what it is because many of you have heard it by name and are not familiar with the works. It begins by saying "It is dangerous to transmit or even to possess this information. There is no copyright on this material. Anyone who wishes may reproduce it. Credit will go where credit is due after the mess has been cleaned up. The *Gemstone File* was written in many segments over a period of years by an American named Bruce Roberts. Parts of the File were released to certain Americans starting in 1969. The number of pages is well over a thousand..." I have about 350, it says there are a thousand. "I have been able to verify some of the statements but research facilities required to verify the entire story would be monumental. Although parts of it seem improbable, in general it rings true. Since the scope is so large, and the events described are so complex and interlocking, the Skeleton outline of the Gemstone thesis is merely a guide."

It begins with the year 1932: "Aristotle Onassis, a Greek ship owner who made his first million dollars was selling 'Turkish tobacco' (known as opium) in Argentina. He worked out a profitable deal with Joseph Kennedy who is into the whiskey business in Ireland, transporting to this country, and Eugene Meyer who is the father of Mrs. Graham, who owns the *Washington Post* and Meyer Lansky. They imported bootleg liquor into the United States and also, when Prohibition was over, in the liquor bottles with opium and heroin and cocaine disguised as liquor."

"In 1934 Aristotle Onassis, the Rockefellers, and the Seven Oil Sisters (the major oil companies) signed an agreement, where they outlined an oil cartel memo, which in essence said screw the Arabs out of their oil, transport it on Onassis's ships. This was done and those who did it considerably increased their already vast wealth."

Now the *Gemstone File* was given to me in 1972, since that time we have learned that Robert Maheu of the Hughes Organization worked with Mr. Niarchos, the competitor of Aristotle Onassis, to get the oil contracts from Saudi Arabia. So it wasn't Onassis who had the power. The Hughes oil contacts had more power because Onassis, who is made the fall-guy of the entire Gemstone, had his son murdered and his ex-wife murdered. He died then, all alone, and it seems that he didn't have the power; it's in the power of other people.

That's one of my objections to the Gemstone — that Onassis keeps seeming to be the fall-guy, but he in turn was done in, just like Nixon. [He] worked with them a long time and then they took Nixon and did him in. Onassis and Nixon had the power up to a point and then each of them was expendable.

There's an article last week that the reason we're arming Iran is to take over Saudi Arabia. That's consistent with the *Gemstone Files* of the Seven Sisters because John J. McCloy, the lawyer for the Rockefellers and a member of the Warren Commission, started the organization of Seven Sisters. They did form an oil cartel, and they do intend to take the oil from the Arabs, if they need to, militarily.

"Bruce Roberts studied journalism and physics at the University of Wisconsin. He studied crystallography, synthetic rubies, and made the original Gemstone experiment, and this is why it's called the *Gemstone File*. In 1936-1940, Eugene Meyer, part of the Syndicate with Onassis and Rockefeller, bought the *Washington Post.*" Later Eugene Meyer is killed and a suicide is forged[?]. "Meyer bought the *Washington Post*. Other Mafia members bought newspapers, radios and magazines to control the news media. As the war approached, new censorship of all major media went into effect.

"1941-45 was World War II which was profitable for Aristotle Onassis, the Rockefellers, the Kennedies, the Roosevelts and I.G. Farben. Onassis was selling oil and arms to both sides," as were ITT, American Corporations and General Motors. They were selling tanks and airplanes to Hitler and to America at the same time. He says, "These people went through the war without losing a single ship or man." At the end of the war the Nazi experts assimilated into the Pentagon and infiltrated the highest levels of government.

And that is what I published, also through my research. Before I knew Bruce Roberts I had published that in my first article in *The Realist*.

He says, "Allen Dulles went in partnership with ex-Nazi Reinhard Gehlen and formed a new agency to be called the Central Intelligence Agency. In 1949 Aristotle Onassis bought U.S. surplus Liberty Ships in questionable (illegal) purchases, and lawyer Burke Marshall helped him."

Burke Marshall is important, because in the case of the Kennedy assassination, he has been the man to lock up the National Archives to any of the researchers and he was working with this team way back when. He also was in the Vera Foundation of WBAI in New York, which is supposed to be a liberal radio station. Burke Marshall has been in control of bottling up the conspiracy truth ever since John Kennedy was killed. John Kennedy wasn't the man that they thought he was going to be and Burke Marshall and the team that I mentioned above has continued to suppress the murder of this president.

"In 1956," according to Bruce Roberts, "Howard Hughes, the Texas millionaire, was buying his way into control of the United States. He bought senators and governors. He bought his last politician, his newly-elected Vice President Nixon, via a quarter million dollar non-repayable loan to Nixon's brother, Donald."

Now, there's one error in this that I differ with Bruce and the *Gemstone File*, and I'll interject my opinions as we go on. Howard Hughes and this group bought Richard Nixon in

1946 when he ran against Mr. Voorhis in California. Nixon was still in the Navy, and I wrote about that on how Nixon gets to power and Nixon met Howard Hughes in a bungalow at the Beverly Hills Hotel. And when he was just a member of the House of Representatives, and then a senator, and then a vice president, he was being funded by this Committee of 100 and the neo-Nazis at California, the agriculture business and the aerospace business. Howard Hughes was buying Richard Nixon as a front man in '46, not '56.

He goes on to say, "Early in 1957, Richard Nixon then repaid the favor to Howard Hughes for giving his brother this quarter of a million dollars, by forming Internal Revenue's tax free foundation, called the Hughes Medical Institute. With Hughes Aircraft being sole owner it was a tax-free non-accountable money funnel or laundry for whatever Howard Hughes wanted to do. The U.S. government anti-trust suits against Hughes, TWA and other enterprises were shelved." The medical institute in Florida was a funnel for funding members of congress, all those very congressmen that won't open up the assassination now or the conspiracy. Gerald Ford was one of the recipients of that money, and he was the one who put Richard Nixon; he was selected by Richard Nixon to be on the Warren Commission and Richard Nixon then selected him to become president of the United States.

"The Hughes Medical Institute down in Florida goes into a lot of questionable operations. It's simply an office building with a handful of people." And goodness knows where the money goes, but some of it has been pinpointed, like the Korean CIA to the members of Congress. Richard Nixon formed this institute which funded other members of Congress that would vote for him later to put him into power. It not only saved tax money for Howard Hughes, but by paying Richard Nixon several hundred thousand he got what he wanted. Nixon formed this institute for Howard Hughes, and then it funded the politicians that kept Richard Nixon going until he became president of the United States.

The Gemstone goes on, "In March 1957 Aristotle Onassis carried out a carefully-planned action. He had Hughes kidnapped from his bungalow at the Beverly Hills Hotel, using Hughes's own men (such as Chester Davis, who was born

Mr. Cesare in Sicily, and the other Hughes men either quit, or fired, or stayed on in the Onassis organization."

Now the Gemstone has an area here which should be cleared. People I know have copies of this Skeleton Gemstone, and I can answer these questions for you on the air and share some of the facts with you, against what Bruce wrote.

In March '57 Howard Hughes was kept in the bungalow of the Beverly Hills Hotel. He wasn't kidnapped, but he was isolated. He was as good as kidnapped, but he wasn't taken down to the Bahamas like he said. He was kidnapped from his hotel; that is a fact that is in error. He was kept in the bungalow from '57 to '66, and he never saw any of his old aides. Noah Dietrich was fired, Robert Maheu of the CIA was taken over, he was also in the FBI. The assassination teams were incorporated in the Hughes Organization and the Hughes Organization at that point became the Hitler Organization, the Nazi organization, the secret government.

Hughes's body didn't matter anymore. They could give him the heroin and cocaine, and the injections, and drug him out of his mind. He was taken on a train from Los Angeles to Boston in 1966.

So, '57 to '66 he was kept in the bungalow by the Los Angeles Police Department and the Beverly Hills Police Department — Captain Jack Eggers. That is important because the kidnapping of Hughes, or the care of Hughes didn't just involve Aristotle Onassis.

In the *Gemstone File* Bruce Roberts keeps pinpointing the Mafia and Onassis, as if these were the two culprits, but it goes much bigger. It infiltrates the police department at the local level; Beverly Hills Police, Los Angeles Police, the Dallas Police, down in the Bahamas, in Texas, and the Central Intelligence Agency and the FBI. It's true that narcotics trafficking is involved but here it's also the satellite control of the world: the communications media that's involved, and the Hughes company are making the satellites for space stations and communications, and for weapons. And they can use it for agricultural surveillance or for oil surveillance or minerals and effect our whole lives by these satellites. And the satellites are made by the Hughes organization and the CIA.

So Howard was kept in that bungalow and then taken, literally kidnapped, after he was zonked, he was kept around for enough people to say oh, he's irresponsible or mentally sick or queer, or he talks crazy, and then from Boston there isn't a trace of a hair or a fingerprint or a sign of the real Howard Hughes.

The Gemstone papers go on to say that "a few days later," this is after March '57, in April, "Mayor Cannon, the new Senator Cannon from Nevada, arranged a fake marriage to Jean Peters to explain Howard's sudden loss of interest in women, and this brain-damaged person was taken to the Emerald Isles Hotel in the Bahamas, where the top floor was rented." Later, it said, "after he was injected with heroin for thirty days, he was taken to a cell on Onassis's island in Skorpios, where he spent the rest of his life. Onassis then has a much larger power base in the United States, the Hughes empire. Wayne Rector, acting as Hughes's double since 1945, then became Howard Hughes."

Now, to correct the Gemstones, I have been told that what Brooks Randall said on *Good Morning America* [was] that Brooks Randall and not Wayne Rector is the double that was buried, but we haven't seen a picture of Wayne Rector, or he hasn't surfaced, so it could be one of the two. It wasn't after a few days the marriage to Jean Peters was faked. There was no fingerprints, of an application for the wedding, or a wedding certificate, nobody saw the groom, the judge is dead, the woman at the office there in Nevada is dead. The circumstances of that wedding would prove without any doubt that there was no marriage to Jean Peters and that this was an excuse to get everybody off of the tail of Howard Hughes.

[Bruce Roberts] died of a brain tumor about a year ago. Bruce lived in San Francisco and he gave me his research at the time of Watergate because he wanted me to know what he thought was the story behind Watergate and what led up to it, and because he had been at a certain bar in San Francisco on Geary Street, where the Watergate defendants used to hang around right after the Watergate arrest. The bartender there was killed, and I did go into that bar a couple of times to see what was going on.

He claimed that G. Gordon Liddy and E. Howard Hunt, and John Erlichman and most of the Watergate defendants had an active role in their CIA intelligence work in San Francisco and hung around this bar, and he gave me a lot of information which has been circulating around the world. Many people have it, and as I say they want to make a movie about the Gemstone Key-File in England.

Parts of this file are true, parts of them are absolutely untrue, some of it is difficult to check, some of it I have used for my own research and writing. It's a very controversial document because it's filled with a lot of misinformation.

There is one section of the *Gemstone File* that is particularly interesting and controversial, and it has to do with the role of the present Pope, Cardinal Montini, who he had made the allegations [about]. Bruce Roberts said that the Pope was part of the international narcotics traffic with the Mafia and the CIA since his early days as a cardinal.

"The battle of the Mafia narcotics traffic has been tangled with the hierarchy of the Catholic Church, specifically the Vatican and the Pope." It was Bruce Roberts who told me in 1972 that this current Pope was in the OSS and that he was linked to the Golden Triangle narcotics traffic in Southeast Asia that particularly escalated during the Vietnamese War. A year later, after he told me this information, a book came out on the history of the OSS and it did link Cardinal Montini, who then became the Pope, as being in the OSS for the United States. Many people know that almost every agent in the OSS then became an officer or an agent of the CIA.

Recently there is a new book out that I quoted on *Dialogue: Conspiracy* called *Treason For My Daily Bread*, which has to do with Cardinal Montini, naming him as the person who assisted Martin Bormann, the Nazi, and other Nazis to leave Italy and to go to South America. They went from Austria to Brenner Pass disguised as monks and this information is new about the Cardinal, Montini, the Pope working with Martin Bormann, the Nazi.

In addition, the *Gemstone File* refers to Cardinal Tisserant. He was the head of the College of Cardinals at the Vatican, and Bruce Roberts claimed that he was murdered with sodium morphate. He said Tisserant had followed the career of this present Pope, Montini, and that's the reason that he was murdered. He said that Montini had also poisoned Pope Pius XI in order to become the Pope, and that he was banished from Rome for a time being by Pope Pius XII, and then returned and became the present Pope in 1963, the year that Diem was murdered and John Kennedy was murdered.

Bruce Roberts wrote in the *Gemstone File* that Tisserant wrote all of this down in his diaries, and at the time he called the present Pope, that was Cardinal Montini then, "The Deputy of Christ at Auschwitz," meaning the extermination camp. And he said that Montini was the fulfillment of the Fatima prophecy, that "The anti-Christ shall rise to become the head of the Church." Now, this is pretty heavy stuff for a person to put in your hands, these allegations of the cardinal. It has been confirmed, the role of the present Pope in helping Martin Bormann and the Nazis escape, but the murder charges were never written up or discussed until just 1977.

A new book came out two months ago called *The Assassination, Theory and Practice*. It's put out by Richard Chameleon, by Paladin Press, in Colorado, a 1977 publication. And I'll just read you a couple of sentences from this book, which is the first book that I've seen or owned that would back up Bruce Roberts' allegations. And these are quotations from the book.

It says, "A suggestion of intrigue surrounds the death of Pope Pius XI. He died in bed in the Vatican at the age of 81. To his very last, Pope Pius XI was the deadly enemy of fascism, Benito Mussolini, and Adolf Hitler. Shortly before he died, Eugene Cardinal Tisserant was directed to convene a meeting of all Italian bishops to hear what His Holiness had to say, and what he had to say was against Nazism and Fascism. Just before the meeting was to take place, Pope Pius XI was given what they called a stimulant, it was an injection, and an hour later His Holiness was dead so that he couldn't meet with the bishops to object to Hitler's Fascism or Mussolini's Fascism."

And the author asks in this book, "Where is the evidence for assassination?" He said, "It is historical fact Claretta Petacci was Benito Mussolini's mistress for eight years. Along with Mussolini, she was executed. Petacci happened to be a fanatical pro-fascist, pro-Mussolini follower. Is it purely by chance or sheer coincidence that the father of Claretta Petacci, the woman who lived with Mussolini, his name was

Dr. Francesco Pettacci, was the senior Vatican physician who gave Pope Pius XI the injection, allegedly the stimulant, the hour before he died? Pope Pius was to meet and discuss with the bishops the evils of fascism, both German and Italian. Was Pope Pius XI murdered?"

This is in this new book on assassinations, and it is an excellent book. It just came out and it goes into the origin of assassinations from the various countries and the way they're done. It's the first book that I've read in print that has linked Marina Oswald to the CIA and that is a big jump in terms of information. That her uncle wasn't necessarily with the KGB, but branches of the CIA, was in fact true.

So Richard Chameleon asks the question, "Was the Pope murdered?" And in the *Gemstone Files*, Bruce Roberts had said in 1972 that both Tisserant and Pope Pius XI were murdered, and that would make sense if Cardinal Montini was working with the Nazis, if he was described as the "[anti-]Christ at Auschwitz," if he was in favor of letting Martin Bormann and the head Nazis go out of Italy, out of Austria to Italy to South America, and if this man was in charge of the Pope's health. His daughter lived with Benito Mussolini, and they were confirmed Fascists and the Pope was objecting to Fascism. It's a good question coming out in literature now: was the Pope murdered for his anti-Fascist stance, and why would the father of this woman who lived with Mussolini all these years be the one giving the injection to the anti-Fascist Pope? So, putting that together, the *Gemstone File* has certainly some provocative questions to ask, and I'm not putting it all down, because it's that kind of information that does wet your appetite.

There's another section of the *Gemstone Files* where he makes the statement, "Two murders had to occur before John Kennedy was killed in order to get away with this killing." And he cites Senator Estes Kefauver. He said, "His crime commission had uncovered the original deal in 1932 between Aristotle Onassis, Joe Kennedy, the father of John Kennedy, and Meyer Lansky, for the international narcotics swindling that they were doing. And Kefauver was planning a speech on the Senate floor to denounce these Mafia operations. Instead, he ate a piece of apple pie laced with sodium morphate, had a sodium morphate-induced 'heart attack' on the Senate floor."

The second murder that he says had to take place was "Phillip Graham, the editor of the *Washington Post,* who was married to Katherine Meyer." Bruce Roberts says in the *Gemstone File* that "Eugene Meyer's daughter Katherine was to take over the Mafia-controlled *Washington Post,*" and they also owned *Newsweek.* And "Graham was a very strong John Kennedy worker, he put together the John Kennedy-Lyndon Johnson ticket. He was Kennedy's best friend in a struggle against the power of Onassis and the Mafia."

He said, "Katherine Meyer Graham bribed the psychiatrist to certify that her husband was insane. He was allowed out of the asylum for the weekend. He died of a gunshot wound in the head, and the death was ruled as a suicide."

I don't know and have no way to check out the links of Eugene Meyer and his links to the Mafia. This was an allegation made by Bruce Roberts that I cannot support. I do support the belief that Phillip Graham was murdered. This suicide was like the death of George de Morenschildt. I believe that he did have to die at that time and the circumstances of his death gave Katherine Graham tremendous power which she has wielded, even [in] the role of the *Washington Post* getting Richard Nixon out of office.

In their one-sided investigation, the power of the *Washington Post* and *Newsweek* combined with Henry Luce's power in *Time* and *Life* and their syndicate fortune is overwhelming. With the assassins, they work hand-in-glove with the CIA-Mafia-connected links.

I don't know how much Senator Estes Kefauver knew. I know that the man who worked with him, who would have been controlling his campaign if Kefauver ran for vice president, was Bernard Fensterwald of the CIA, one of the dirtiest dogs to walk the face of Washington. He's a Senate lawyer; he turned up at the time of Watergate and became the attorney for James McCord. I've known Fensterwald, unfortunately, for quite a few years, at least 8 or 9, and I have utmost contempt for him. I can link him at least physically in the presence of situations where people died in 2 cases just weeks, 7 or 8 weeks, after he was present. I don't trust Fensterwald, and I don't know what role he had at the time going way back with the Kefauver death, but in the *Gemstone Files*, two deaths are necessary, according to Bruce Roberts, and those were Kefauver and Phillip Graham.

I think the death of Marilyn Monroe that took place just a month or so before John Kennedy was killed was the primary death or murder that had to take place. With her relationships with John and Robert Kennedy it could hush Robert Kennedy up and they could blackmail him for not investigating his brother's murder. I think the Marilyn Monroe death was more important in my research, but for reasons that he never documents or goes into detail, Bruce Roberts said that Kefauver's death and Phillip Graham's were primary before the Kennedy assassination took place.

Where Bruce Roberts gets way off base, I believe, is in the story of the Kennedy assassination. And because that's the area that I know the best, I have to use it as a yardstick to base the value of some of the other information which I can't get into.

His account of the Dealey Plaza killing of John Kennedy goes this way: he says there were four shooters: Lee Harvey Oswald, Eugene Brading, Jimmy Fratianno and John Roselli. E. Howard Hunt and James McCord were at Dealey Plaza and Frank Sturgis was in Miami. It's the other way around. There's no proof that Lee Harvey Oswald shot any gun November 22, 1963. I don't believe that Oswald was one of the shooters at all.

There's no evidence that McCord and Hunt were at Dealey Plaza. There are no photographs of them that confirm that, but there's reason to believe Frank Sturgis was there, so I believe that Bruce Roberts has turned this around.

He goes on to say that Jimmy Fratianno shot from the Dal-Tex Building. Now, I can't say that Fratianno did or didn't shoot at the time of the Kennedy assassination. He's been called before the House Select Committee to testify about where he was, except for the fact that he did publicly say that Kennedy should be killed, and he did work with Robert Maheu and the CIA-Mafia assassination teams.

There has been no photograph of Fratianno in the Dallas-Fort Worth area, up to or after the assassination. Nobody said they saw him there or registered as any alias. That doesn't mean he wasn't there, but up until now there has been no proof that Fratianno was there at all, and I have the feeling that the assassins were better trained, as I said before on this program, in Mexico, by Albert Osborne, and that they were not this assassination team. This team may have picked up some shells at Dealey Plaza.

He says Fratianno shot from the Dal-Tex Building, but has no supportive document or photograph to prove it. Bruce Roberts said that John Roselli shot John Kennedy once on the right side of the head; blew his brains out from behind the fence. Again, this is questionable. Nobody saw John Roselli at Dealey Plaza. He was a well-known Mafia man in 1963. That doesn't mean he wasn't there. But he says categorically that Fratianno shot one shot from the Dal-Tex and Roselli did the fatal shot.

"The third point of triangulation," he claimed, "was supplied by Eugene Brading from that small pagoda at Dealey Plaza." Now, Brading is a Mafia member who later went on to join the early LaCosta gang down in San Clemente when that resort opened. Brading was seen at Dealey Plaza and he was given aliases, and he did walk over to the Dal-Tex building afterwards to make a telephone call. He could have left a gun in the bushes that one of the other men picked up.

I know Oswald didn't shoot a gun November 22, 1963. I don't know where Fratianno was. John Roselli is dead, killed right after he testified before the Senate House Select Committee. And Eugene Brading has never been called to testify before anyone, so I just give you the allegations and what I think of them.

I also have this statement here, from the *Gemstone File*. Bruce Roberts said "Lee Harvey Oswald shot John Connally twice from the Texas School Book Depository. He left the front door of the building with his rifle in the building. There was a back up man. Instead of taking it out, they left it so that Oswald would be the patsy."

I don't believe that Lee Harvey Oswald shot John Connally twice, at all. If he were going to be the patsy they would have left the bullets around the car that they were in, or in the hospital to positively link them to Lee Harvey Oswald's gun. There were no bullets found except a pristine bullet numbered "Commission Exhibit 399," and that doesn't link to Lee Harvey Oswald in any sense. There were no fingerprints on the rifle that was supposed to be Lee Harvey Oswald's and the direction of the shots couldn't have come from the sixth floor window the way that John Connally was shot.

The paraffin tests on Lee Harvey Oswald were negative on his head and hands. He couldn't have fired a weapon that day without holding the gun. There is no way to link Lee Harvey Oswald to any weapon. Therefore, I don't believe that he shot John Connally twice, and I think that Bruce Roberts is filled, in this case, with disinformation.

Marina Oswald was recently on a national television show saying that Lee Harvey Oswald wrote a letter from USSR to John Connally, saying that when I come home I want to work for you. Well, John Connally was Secretary of the Navy when Oswald was in the Navy. He was the governor of Texas at the time. And being as he [Oswald] was an important agent, when the U-2 flight was downed and Oswald was in Russia, I think that his contacts to Connally were more friendly than people believe. And I don't believe he shot anybody, and I don't believe what Bruce Roberts said about Oswald shooting John Connally.

The *Gemstone File* also says that three men were dressed as tramps, then picked up shells from the ground at Dealey Plaza, and one of the men was Howard Hunt. He said a Dallas police officer ordered two Dallas cops to go over to the boxcar and pick up the tramps. They were released without being booked. Well, many people know the book *Coup d'Etat* by A.J. Weberman, where he makes the allegations that two of the three men that were taken away were E. Howard Hunt and Frank Sturgis, and many of you have the book and you've seen the picture of the tramps.

We know that three men were paraded off and have been described as "the tramps." There is no picture of these three men picking up any shells at Dealey Plaza. He says that they were picking up shells, but there's no evidence that these three men leaned down and picked up a shell.

I've seen all of the pictures of Dealey Plaza that are available, but I've never seen a picture of these men picking up the shells. The only photograph we have is the three men being led away by men disguised as Dallas police. In the

Gemstone File he says the Dallas police ordered the cops to go over to the boxcar, but there's no tape recording of it.

There's no proof that the Dallas police were ordering anybody. There is evidence that men wearing the uniforms of the Dallas police department were escorting three men away from the scene, but later they couldn't be identified as Dallas policemen.

So this kind of reasoning or misinformation that's in the *Gemstone File* should be broken down very seriously, and you should ask for your evidence, and realize that not all of it is true, and that it's very dangerous to go by this file.

I'll read you some more quotes. He said, "The rest is history, after John Kennedy was killed. Aristotle Onassis was so confident of his control over the police, the media, the FBI, the CIA, the Secret Service, and the United States judicial systems, that he had JFK murdered before the eyes of the nation, then systematically bought off, killed off, or frightened off all witnesses, and then put a 75-year seal of secrecy over the entire matter." Now, if you think seriously about that statement, you realize that Aristotle Onassis didn't have that kind of power. He didn't control Earl Warren, he never was around the United States to control the Dallas police department. People like Niarchos, his competitor, or Tom Pappas, the Greek shipping oil clerk who had entree into the White House with Spiro Agnew and Richard Nixon and the Rockefellers had more political clout than any Aristotle Onassis had in this country.

And it seems that the whole *Gemstone File* has two scapegoats: one is Onassis and the other is the Mafia. Onassis had some kind of information. But I think that Onassis was a victim. I think that Jacqueline Kennedy was sent to Onassis to babysit him. He put up a large amount of money to try and find out who killed John Kennedy and there's been stories that that's the reason his own son was murdered.

And then Niarchos murdered Onassis's ex-wife. She was murdered and the man wasn't even held for charges. And Onassis then died alone and had to kick out Maria Callas and make way for Jackie. I think that Onassis was curious and wanted to know the way that the narcotics traffic was going to flow; he has a big investment here and so forth, but I can't believe that Onassis has this clout over the entire

Warren Commission or Lyndon Johnson. He dealt with a different ball of wax at a different level, and he didn't have the control over the system.

Furthermore, Onassis is dead and all of these witnesses now that are being killed off are escalating: people like George de Morenschildt and Gary Powers and William Sullivan of the FBI, Charles Nicoletti, all these deaths, the last six FBI men that died in six months that I've talked about. The witnesses are dying like flies, and Onassis isn't around to reap the benefit.

So, for some reason or other, Bruce Roberts had a fixation about the power of Aristotle Onassis. And I think, in the end, when the power control group took over, Onassis was a victim like Richard Nixon and he was under the control of people. He became victimized, and it was not Onassis who had the power.

Now the Gemstone goes into various payoffs that people involved in the assassination had, and I tend to agree with him on that point. He talks about John Roselli who got a $250,000 finders fee for bringing Howard Hughes to Vegas in '67 — that was just a clear-cut payoff and may have had something to do with his links to Jack Ruby, and having Ruby kill Lee Harvey Oswald. He cited Jimmy Fratianno getting a $109,000 loan, a non-repayable — California — and started a trucking company in the Imperial Valley. Eugene Brading became a charter member of LaCosta Country Club, the Mafia heaven. Gerald Ford was appointed president of the United States by Richard Nixon. John McCone, who covered this up, former head of the CIA, became a member of the ITT board of directors. Richard Helms became CIA director. Leon Jaworski became the special Watergate prosecutor. He calls that "government in theater."

And then two people who got their reverse payoffs, who were hurt by some of this assassination inquiry, was a Doctor "Red" Duke he cites, who dug two bullets out of John Connally and saved his life, and then was shipped to Afghanistan by the CIA to hush up the information about the bullets in John Connally. And then he cites Jim Garrison, who had all his witnesses shot out from under him, and was framed and charged with bribery and extortion.

There is no doubt that there was a lot of payoffs for people that covered up the Kennedy assassination.

Bruce Roberts goes into Daniel Ellsberg. He said, "In May 1971, folk hero Daniel Ellsberg, the war hawk from Rand Corporation who designed the missile ring around the Iron Curtain, released the fake *Pentagon Papers*. It distracted attention from John Kennedy's death, Robert Kennedy's death, Martin Luther King's murder and Howard Hughes's disappearance." He said, "The *Pentagon Papers* were designed by Ellsberg and Rand chief MacNamara who became the World Bank head to make the Vietnamese War look like one of those incredibly dumb mistakes." Now, I take issue with the *Gemstone File* on this and many other points. I'll explain why on this issue. If the purpose of Ellsberg's coming forward was to hide the assassination information, it had the opposite effect. The very first broadcast I had on KLRB was in May, 1971, and I was asked to analyze the *Pentagon Papers* and what it meant at the time. I said that the *Pentagon Papers* was maybe a moment of truth coming through, and that the real truth to go over the air would be the killing of John Kennedy and Robert Kennedy and Martin Luther King, and that's when I began my programs here on this station and we've been on six and a half years.

The *Pentagon Papers* hardly hushed up the political assassinations, but opened up a Pandora's box. Another point is that I have read the *Pentagon Papers* very carefully, and in them Daniel Ellsberg makes it very clear by printing the State Department papers that the death of John Kennedy began the escalation of the war in Vietnam; that November 24, 1963, for no noticeable reason, the Northern Vietnamese came down, just the exact place where they had been up to the time of the death of Kennedy, but the South Vietnamese escalated the war with the American troops.

And he showed in the *Pentagon Papers* that we had been planning this war for a long time. Evidently we had to have Kennedy dead before they could escalate and begin the war, and Lyndon Johnson was their man. So Bruce Roberts is very unfair about that.

I think that the *Pentagon Papers* also showed our American assassination team for what it was. It showed very clearly the murder of Diem and his brother-in-law, implicated

Henry Cabot Lodge in Washington, the powers that be in Washington. It was the first glimpse of the assassination teams running from Washington, D.C. that we're spreading all over the world.

The *Pentagon Papers* was a major contribution. And Bruce Roberts has put it down as being fake. A lot of people have tried to discredit Daniel Ellsberg. If they do, they haven't read the papers. I've read them and I believe that they were a major contribution.

After they were published, Lewis Tackwood of the Los Angeles police department came forward and told about Squad 19 and the plans to kill Nixon, and about the Watergate team in the White House. He identified with Daniel Ellsberg and began to spill stories. Tackwood came forward because Daniel Ellsberg did, and then a man named Larry Shears came forward and talked about how Alcohol, Tobacco and Firearms were going to kill Cesar Chavez. They saved the life of Cesar Chavez by exposing the assassination teams — the Treasury Department. And then Mr. Martinez came into the Chicano riot in Los Angeles — and agent provocateurs. Ellsberg was a source of inspiration to Colonel Hebert over Vietnam. He was a major contributor to getting some truth out. Sure, there's things he knows that he didn't tell, and he could tell us a lot more, but I don't think the burden was on Daniel Ellsberg. I think he did a magnificent job.

There are many things about the Gemstone papers which I like, there are many which I know are absolutely wrong. You have to read history, you have to read seven or eight hundred books like I've done to make an analysis, but I did promise you I would go into it and you can get a copy of the Skeleton Key yourself and read it. I think that's enough for me to cover on *Dialogue: Conspiracy,* and I hope it's clear to you, and the best thing you can do is then read it for yourself.

The Kiwi Gemstone

The *Gemstone File* was written in many segments over a period of years by an Amerikan named Bruce Roberts. Parts of the File were released to certain Amerikans in 1969. The number of pages is well over a thousand. It has been possible to verify some of the statements made, but the research facilities required to verify the entire story would be monumental. Those who transmit the story do so because it makes sense in the light of current events. Although parts of it seem improbable, in general it rings true. Readers will have to make up their own minds as to it's authenticity.

Since the scope of the work is so large, and the events described are so complex and interlocking, it may be more easily understood with this skeleton outline of the Gemstone thesis. Individual papers can then be read with greater comprehension. Following are some of the major points from the early pages of the book, then we jump ahead to take excerpts from the extensive section dealing with the Mafia takeover of Aotearoa in recent years.

1932: Onassis, a Greek ship owner, who made his first million selling "Turkish tobacco" (opium) in Argentina, worked out a profitable deal with Joseph Kennedy, Eugene Meyer, and Meyer Lansky importing bootleg liquor into the U.S.

1934: Onassis, Rockefeller and the Seven Sisters (major oil companies) signed an agreement, outlined in an oil cartel memo: Screw the Arabs out of their oil, transport it on

Onassis's ships. This was done, and those who did it considerably increased their already vast wealth.

Roberts, studying journalism and physics at the University of Wisconsin, learned these things via personal contacts. His special interest was crystallography: the creation of synthetic rubies, the original Gemstone experiment.

1936-1940: Eugene Meyer buys the *Washington Post* and other Mafia buy other papers, radio stations, etc. to gain control of news media. As the war approaches, news censorship of all major media goes into effect.

1941-1945: World War II, which was very profitable for Onassis, Rockefeller, Kennedy, the Roosevelts, I.G. Farben, ITT, etc. Onassis and Rockefeller barter oil for German oil tankers. ITT Focke-Wulf planes bomb the Allies and it's telephones pass information to German submarines. I.G. Farben builds synthetic fuel & rubber plant at Auchwitz. Onassis & Rockefeller sell arms and oil to both sides. At the end of the war, Nazi "experts" assimilated into the Pentagon infiltrate to highest levels. Allen Dulles, in partnership with "ex-Nazi" General Reinhard Gehlen, forms a new agency: the Central Intelligence Agency (CIA).

1946: Eugene Meyer becomes head of the World Bank. "Ex-Nazi" Klaus Barbie (the Butcher of Lyons) smuggled to Bolivia by CIA helps set up P2 Lodge and Ordine Nuovo with Italian neo-fascist Licio Gelli.

November, 1948: Onassis and Rockefeller form a new company, Aramco, and devise the 'Golden Gimmick' - oil royalties deducted from companies' tax bill.

1949: Onassis buys U.S. war surplus "Liberty Ships" in questionable (illegal) purchase. Lawyer Burke Marshall helps him. Rockefeller protege Eugene Black takes over the World Bank and later appointed to the Board of ITT.

1953: Seven Sisters' oil profits in Iran threatened by Mossadeq. CIA's Kermit Roosevelt organises coup with money funneled through CIA's Deak Bank. Shah installed and secret "participant's agreement" drawn up by Seven Sisters' lawyer, John McCloy.

1954: Onassis uses I.G. Farben's Prince Bernhard to preside at first secret meeting of Bilderberg group held at Oosterbeck, Holland. Members include U.S. and European financiers, government officials etc. Bilderberg to play a key role in setting up EEC, NATO, Cold War strategy, and the Trilateral Commission.

1956: Howard Hughes, Texas millionaire, is meanwhile buying his way into control of the U.S. electoral process with a view to his own personal gain. He buys senators, governors, etc. He finally buys his last politician: newly-elected Vice-President Nixon, via a quarter-million dollar non-repayable loan to Nixon's brother, Donald.

Early 1957: Nixon repays the favour by having Internal Revenue Service and Treasury grant tax-free status (refused twice before) to Hughes Medical Foundation, sole owner of Hughes Aircraft, creating a tax-free non-accountable money funnel or "laundry" for whatever Hughes wanted to do. U.S. government anti-trust suits against Hughes's TWA airline and other enterprises also shelved.

March 1957: Onassis carries out a carefully planned action. He has Hughes kidnapped from his bungalow at the Beverly Hills Hotel, using Hughes's own men (Chester Davis et al.) The other Hughes men either quit, get fired, or stay on in the new Onassis organization. A few days later, Mayor Cannon (now Senator Cannon) of Nevada, arranges a fake marriage to Jean Peters to explain Hughes's sudden loss of interest in chasing movie stars. Hughes, battered and brain damaged by Mafia treatment, is taken to the Emerald Isles Hotel in the Bahamas, where the entire top floor has been rented for the "Hughes party." Hughes is shot full of heroin for 30 days then taken off to a cell on Onassis's Skorpios Island, where he spent the rest of his life. Onassis now has a much larger power base in the U.S.: the Hughes empire, as well as control over Nixon and other Hughes-purchased politicians. L. Wayne Rector, who had been acting as Hughes's "double" since 1955, now becomes "Hughes."

September 1957: Onassis calls the Appalachin meeting to inform U.S. Mafia leaders of his control of Hughes, and his adoption of Hughes's method of acquiring power: buying high-ranking politicians en masse to gain control of the U.S. government "legally."

Also in 1957: Joseph Kennedy takes John F. & Jackie to see Onassis on his yacht, introduce John, and remind Onassis of an old Mafia promise: the presidency for a Kennedy. Onassis says sure.

And so it goes! To jump ahead to the Kiwi connections, by which time Onassis has died and been replaced by Rockefeller as Mafia supremo, we cross to the ocean near the Chatham Islands - the Great South Basin:

18th May 1967: Texas oil billionaire, Nelson Bunker Hunt, using a sophisticated satellite technique to detect global deposits, discovers a huge oil source near Aotearoa in the Great South Basin.

10th June 1967: Hunt & Kiwi Finance Minister reach an agreement: Hunt will receive sole drilling rights, and Muldoon will receive a $100,000 non-repayable loan from the Placid Oil Co. (Hunt's).

8th September 1967: Placid Oil granted drilling rights to the Great South Basin.

10th May 1968: Hawaiian meeting between Onassis and top lieutenants, William Colby & Gerald Parsky, to discuss establishment of a new front company in Australia - Australasian & Pacific Holdings Limited - to be managed by Michael Hand. Using Onassis-Rockefeller banks, Chase Manhattan and Shroders, Travelodge Management Ltd. sets up another front to link the operation to the U.S.

Onassis now crowned head of the Mafia; Colby (head of C.I.A. covert operations in S.E. Asia) ran the Onassis heroin operations in the Golden Triangle (Laos, Burma, Thailand) with 200 Green Beret mercenaries - i.e. the Phoenix Programme.

Gerald Parsky, deputy to ex-CIA/FBI Robert Maheu in the Howard Hughes organisation took orders from Onassis and was made responsible for laundering skim money from the Onassis casino operations in Las Vegas and the Bahamas.

Mid-July, 1968: Placid Oil Co. and the Seven Sisters (major Oil companies) begin Great South Basin oil exploration - Hunt finances 45.5% of exploration costs, Gulf Oil 14.5%, Shell (U.S.) 10%, B.P. Oil 10%, Standard Oil California 10%, Mobil 6.5%, and Arco 6.5%

12th October 1968: Hunt & Seven Sisters announce confirmation of new oil source comparable to the Alaskan North Slope - gas reserves estimated at 150 times larger than the Kapuni Field.

Early 1969: Mafia consolidates it's banking operations: David Rockefeller becomes Chairman of Chase Manhattan; Wriston at Citibank, & Michelle Sindona captures the Vatican Bank. Partnership Pacific launched by Bank of America, Bank of Tokyo, & Bank of New South Wales.

24th February 1969: Onassis calls Council meeting in Washington to discuss strategy to monopolise the Great South Basin discovery. Council members included Nelson Rockefeller and John McCloy, who managed the Seven Sisters, and David Rockefeller, managing the Mafia's banking operations. McCloy outlines the plan to capture all oil and mineral resources in Australia & Aotearoa.

10th March 1969: Parsky & Colby use Australasian & Pacific Holdings to set up a 'front' company in Australia. Using own banks - Mellon Bank and Pittsburgh National Bank, they buy control of near-bankrupt Industrial Equity Ltd (IEL), managed by Kiwi, Ron Brierley. A'asian & Pacific Holdings' consultant Bob Seldon helps Michael Hand set up the new organisation. Seldon took orders from Mellon & Pittsburgh National Banks, while Hand was directly responsible to Gerald Parsky & William Colby. Ron Brierley would take orders from Hand.

24th July 1969: New board established for IEL included Hand, Seldon, Ron Brierley, plus two Brierley associates - Frank Nugen & Bob Jones. Both are appointed consultants to A'asian & Pacific Holdings Ltd. Jones will help Brierley launder funds into real estate (Brierley/Jones Investments) while Seldon & Nugen will channel funds into oil and mineral resources through IEL.

October 1969: Chase Manhattan begins a new operation in Australia with National Bank Aust. & A.C. Goods Associates - Chase-NBA. J.C. Fletcher appointed chairman of Seven Sisters' company - British Petroleum (NZ).

17th February 1970: Gerald Parsky sets up a new heroin-dollar laundry in Australia - Australian International Finance Corp., using the Irving Trust Co., New York.

April 1970: Onassis, Rockefeller, & the Seven Sisters begin setting up the Shadow World Government using the Illuminati-controlled banks and the transnational corporations. In Melbourne, they set up the Australian International Finance Corp. using:

*Irving Trust Co., N.Y. - linked to Shell Oil, Continental Oil, & Phillips Petroleum.

*Crocker Citizens National - linked to Atlantic Richfield (Arco), & Standard Oil of California, which is Rockefeller-controlled.

*Bank of Montreal - Petro Canada, Penarctic Oils, Alberta Gas, Gulf Oil.

*Australia & New Zealand Bank (ANZ).

Meantime, Japanese members of One World Government move into Aotearoa, helped by finance minister R. Muldoon; Mitsubishi & Mitsui make a profitable deal buying up rights to iron-sands, helped by Marcona Corp. (US) and Todd (Shell, BP, Todd). Todd rewarded with sole Kiwi franchise for Mitsubishi vehicles. Muldoon helps Mitsui (Oji Paper Co.) obtain a lucrative 320-million cubic foot Kaiangaroa Forest contract with Carter Holt.

November 1970: Fletchers extend the Rockefeller Travelodge operation by buying control of NZ's largest travel company - Atlantic & Pacific Travel.

Early 1971: Onassis & Rockefeller begin global operation to buy influence for the One World Government concept. They use Lockheed, Northrop, & Litton Industries' agent Adnan Khashoggi, to organise operations in the Middle East, Iran, & Indonesia. I.C.I. set up $2.5 million slush fund for Australia & Aotearoa.

Finance Minister Muldoon changes law to allow Mafia-controlled banks to begin operations in NZ. Links also made by N.Z.I. (in preparation for Paxus control) with Hong Kong & Shanghai Bank; Wells Fargo with Broadbank; Chase Manhattan with General Finance; Bank of America & Barclays with Fletchers and Renouf in NZ United Corp. All members of the Business Round Table org.

Late 1971: Gulf Oil & their man Brierley begin organising chains of Shell companies and dummy corporations to conceal their takeover operations of oil, gas & mineral resources, and related industries such as vehicle franchises, vehicle spare parts, & finance services - all part of the Seven Sisters' controlled car culture. To extend links to the U.S. banking operations, they buy control of I.S.A.S. (NSW) & I.S.A.S. (Qld.) which hold sole franchise for construction & mining equipment produced by International Harvester Credit Co. which is part of Chase Manhattan Bank and associated with First National Bank Chicago (Chairman Sullivan also Exec. Vice-President of Chase Manhattan), Continental Illinois (linked with CIA and Michele Sindona of Vatican Bank), & Rockefeller's Standard Oil of Indiana (AMOCO). I.S.A.S. (Qld.) also has strategic holdings in North Flinders Mines, Flinders Petroleum, and Apollo International Minerals.

February 1972: Onassis & Rockefeller help their associate Adnan Khashoggi buy the Security Pacific National Bank in California and take control of the United California Bank through CIA-linked Lockheed Aircraft Corp. Both banks used by Onassis & Khashoggi to funnel bribes & payoffs to captive

Japanese and other crooked politicians, via the CIA's Deak Bank. Security Pacific also used to launder over $2m for Nixon's re-election campaign. Khashoggi buys 21% of Southern Pacific Properties, which is the majority stockholder in Travelodge (Aust.), thereby establishing direct links to Aotearoa, & UEB and Fletchers through its equity links with Travelodge (NZ).

April 1972: Mafia banking operations expanded through New Hebrides (Vanuatu) with establishment of Australian International Ltd to finance Pacific development by the oil companies (Seven Sisters). Banks involved include Irving Trust, N.Y., Bank of Montreal, Crocker Intl, ANZ Bank, and the Mitsubishi Bank, whose president, Nakamaru, is appointed Chairman.

26th May 1972: Gerald Parsky installs Michele Sindona as 'owner' of Franklin National Bank, helped by the Gambino Mafia family and David Kennedy, chairman of Continental Illinois Bank and Nixon's Secretary of the Treasury.

Pacific Basin Economic Council conference in Wellington. Vice-President Shigeo Nagano also chairman of Nippon Steel and a member of Onassis and other World Government organisations. Chairman of the NZ sub-committee J. Mowbray is also general manager of the National Bank (NZ).

Meanwhile, Michele Sindona, acting as the go-between for the Mafia and the CIA, was the conduit between U.S. and European banks. Sindona's Vatican Bank and associates Calvi's Ambrosiano Bank were used to finance CIA neo-fascist Italian/Latin American operations through Licio Gelli's P2 Lodge, which helped to organise the 'death squads' in Argentina, Uruguay, & Chile. They were aided by P2 members such as Klaus Barbie (the Butcher of Lyons) and Jose Rega, organiser of the AAA in Argentina.

16th August 1972: Gulf Oil associate Bob Seldon helps establish new banking operation; first Kiwi international banks include Bank of NZ, D.F.C. (Aust.), NZI, Morgan Guaranty Trust, Morgan Granfel, and S.F. Warburg.

Fletchers begin expansion overseas with deals signed in Indonesia, Fiji, and New Guinea.

December 1972: Norman Kirk elected Prime Minister of Aotearoa.

February 1973: Gerald Parsky, William Colby, Michael Hand, Frank Nugen, & Bob Seldon move to further consolidate the Mafia banking operations. In Aotearoa, they acquire 20% of Fletcher subsidiary Marac, using the Security Pacific National Bank and helped by Marac corporate secretary Alan Hawkins. Frank Nugan & Michael Hand use Fletcher and Renouf and their NZ United Corp. to link with IEL and Brierley Investments through cross-shareholding agreement. In Australia, the Nugan Hand Bank begins operations, with 30% of the stock held by A'asian & Pacific Holdings (100% Chase Manhattan Bank), 25% by CIA's Air America (known as Air Opium), 25% by South Pacific Properties, and 20% held by Seldon, Nugen, and Hand.

The Irving Trust Bank's New York branch establishes U.S. links between the CIA and Nugen Hand Bank - a worldwide network of 22 banks set up to:

(a) launder money from Onassis heroin operations in the Golden Triangle and Iran;

(b) as a CIA funnel to pro-U.S. political parties in Europe and Latin America, including P2;

(c) a spying conduit for information from Cambodia, Laos, Vietnam, & Thailand;

(d) finance arms smuggled to Libya, Indonesia, South America, Middle East, & Rhodesia, using the CIA's Edward Wilson.

Heroin flown into Australia by CIA's Air America and trans-shipped to Onassis lieutenant in Florida, Santos Trafficante Jnr., assisted by Australian Federal Bureau of Narcotics officials and co-ordinated by CIA's Ray Cline.

14th June 1973: Inauguration of the Onassis's shadow world government - the Trilateral Commission. Includes over 200 members from the U.S., Europe, and Japan - bankers, government officials, trans-national corporations' top executives, trade unionists, etc. Of the world's largest corporations, 24 directly represented, and dozens more through interlocking directorships.

*Trilateralist strategy: monopolisation of the world's resources, production facilities, labour technology, markets, transport, and finance. These aims backed up by the U.S. military & industrial complexes that are already controlled and backed up by the CIA.

18th August 1973: Ray Cline & Michael Hand meet in Adelaide to discuss CIA plans to establish a spying operation in Aotearoa.

September 1973: Seagrams, with strong links to Chase Manhattan Bank of Montreal and Toronto Dominion Bank, buys 2,800 acres of prime land in Marlborough, helped by Peter Maslen.

26th February 1974: Michael Hand meets Bob Jones in Wellington to implement plans for the CIA's new spying operations - countries targeted include France, Chile, West Germany, & Israel. Using the Brierley/Jones investment funnel, Jones buys building in Willeston Street which will be rented to France and Chile, another at Plimmer Steps to house West Germany and Israel. CIA will set up eavesdropping communications center inside the Willeston Street building and another at 163 The Terrace which will link with equipment installed in the Plimmer Steps building. Four CIA technicians will run the whole operation.

April 1974: Finance Minister Rowling appoints Ron Trotter to the Overseas Investment Commission, whose chairman, G. Lau, is also a member of the Todd Foundation (Shell/BP/Todd) investment board.

Mid-1974: Goff Whitlam & Norman Kirk begin a series of moves absolutely against the Mafia Trilateralists. Whitlam refuses to waive restrictions on overseas borrowing to finance Alwest Aluminium Consortium of Rupert Murdoch, BHP, and R.J. Reynolds. Whitlam had also ended Vietnam War support, blocked uranium mining, and wanted more control over U.S. secret spy bases, - e.g. Pine Gap, Northwest Cape. Kirk had introduced a new, tough, anti-Monopoly Bill and had tried to redistribute income from big companies to the labour force through price regulation and a wages policy. Kirk had also rejected plans to build a second smelter at Aramoana near Dunedin, and was preparing the Petroleum Amendment Bill to give more control over Kiwi oil resources. Kirk had found out that Hunt Petroleum, drilling in the Great South Basin, had discovered a huge resource of oil, comparable in size to the North Sea or Alaskan North Slope. Gas reserves alone now estimated at 30 times larger than Kapuni and oil reserves of at least 20 billion barrels - enough for Aotearoa to be self-sufficient for years. Oil companies completely hushed up these facts. To have announced a vast new oil source would probably have meant a decline in world oil prices, which would not have allowed OPEC's and Onassis's plans for the Arabs to eventuate. Aotearoa could be exploited at a later date, particularly since the North Sea operations were about to come on stream - Kirk was the last to hold out.

September 1974: Death of Norman Kirk. According to CIA sources, Kirk was killed by the Trilateralists using Sodium Morphate. Rowling's first act as Prime Minister was to withdraw Kirk's Anti-Monopoly Bill and the Petroleum Amendment Bill. Later, Rowling was to be rewarded with ambassadorship to Washington. Incidentally, the Shah of Iran was murdered the same way as Kirk on his arrival in the U.S.A.

6th October 1974: Ray Cline implements William Colby's plan to oust Australian Prime Minister Whitlam, Nugen Hand Bank finances pay-offs to Malcolm Fraser and other pro-U.S. politicians. A joint bugging operation commences between the CIA and ASIO'. Rupert Murdoch, playing his part, uses his newspapers and TV network to spread lies and misinformation. Whitlam, as well as refusing to waive restrictions on overseas borrowing to finance the aluminium consortium, had plans to ensure that all corporations were at least 50% Australian-owned. This interfered with the Seven Sisters' plans to build three oil refineries at Cape Northumberland in South Australia to exploit the Great South Basin discovery.

December 1974: Australian Governor-General John Kerr joins Ray Cline's payroll, and received his first pay-off of

US$200,000 credited to his account number 767748 at the Singapore branch of the Nugen Hand Bank.

18th February 1975: Governor Kerr sacks the Whitlam government.

August 1975: Rowling re-introduces unrecognisable Commerce Bill, designed to aid monopolisation of the Kiwi economy and repeals the News Media Ownership Act, allowing for more foreign ownership of Kiwi media. The new legislation does not define monopoly, competition, or stipulate permissable maximum market share, or even ascertain what the public interest is - resulting in a sell-out to big business and the Mafia.

December 1975: Election battle between Rowling and Muldoon. Oil companies pour thousands of dollars into Muldoon's campaign via National Bank (NZ), whose General Manager Mowbray is also a member of Todd Foundation's investment board. Director Tudhope also managing Director of Shell Oil and chairman of Shell/BP/Todd. Muldoon wins.

February 1976: Muldoon implements pre-election secret agreement with the NZ Seven Sisters' oil representatives from Shell/BP/Todd for helping to finance the National Party campaign. Muldoon removes the $3/barrel oil levy for the NZ Refining Company, which increases the oil companies' profits by 100% at the taxpayers' expense, and with all future oil prospecting licences, the government has the option to take 51% of any discovery without meeting exploration costs. This is designed to discourage further exploration, thereby keeping the lid on the Great South Basin discovery. Meanwhile in Australia, the new Prime Minister Malcolm Fraser resumes uranium mining and opens the way for takeover of mineral resources with big tax breaks for oil exploration, coal, and mining. Muldoon returns a favour to the oil companies by arranging a loan of US$200-million for Maui Gas Development for Shell/BP/Todd.

September 1976: With captive politicians in place in both Australia and Aotearoa, the Trilateralists can now proceed with their strategy of takeover of the economy and exploitation of natural resources. "In New Zealand, the elimination of unnecessary competition is fundamental to a sound economy," says Brierley. Parsky and Colby use Brierley/Jones Investments as a vehicle to buy into A.B. Consolidated Holdings in Aotearoa. An associate of Jones, Pat Goodman, is appointed consultant of A'asian & Pacific Holdings.

November 1976: The Mafia set up a Kiwi money funnel using Brierley's City Realities. National Insurance Co. acquires 33% of the stock. Largest stockholders in National Insurance are the U.S. Firemen's Fund - whose chairman Myron du Bain is also Vice-Chairman of American Express (Amex). Chairman of IEL-linked International Harvester, Archie McCardell, is also an Amex director. Amex linked with Chase Manhattan and Seven Sisters' Texaco and Mobil. Du Bain also director of CIA-linked United California Bank, which is a partner in Commercial Pacific Trust. To complete the money funnel, National Insurance becomes a stockholder in Chase Manhattan's Chase-NBA. Brierley's declared assets reach $100-million, with shareholders' capital of only $2.5-million - all cash acquisitions.

3rd February 1977: Parsky & Colby close down the Brierley/Jones Investments and open up separate channels for Brierley and Jones. Jones will be supplied with laundered funds via Sydney branch of the Nugen Hand Bank, while for Ron Brierley, Gerald Parsky uses Myron du Bain's United California Bank. Funds to be laundered via Chase Manhattan Bank through National Insurance to City Realties, and via United California Bank through COMPAC (Vanuatu) to National Insurance and City Realties. To expand the Brierley-IEL front, Parsky establishes Industrial Equity Pacific (Hong Kong).

September 1977: Brierley's new holding company begins operations - A.B. Consolidated, with B. Hancox General Manager, while newly-appointed directors include S. Cushing, B. Judge, O. Gunn, and P. Goodman. Linked with Renouf, Fletcher, and Papps through IEL/NZ United Corps.

*Strategy: To target and divide key sectors of the economy for takeover, exploitation and monopolisation. Operations to extend to use Hong Kong facility, IEP. Fletchers to extend the Khashoggi/Rockefeller Travelodge operation by taking holdings in Vacation Hotels and Intercontinental Properties (chairman is Renouf).

October 1977: Muldoon and John Todd (Shell/BP/Todd) sign an agreement: NZ government would take 24.5% holding in the Great South Basin for $1.65 billion. Hunt would reduce his holding from 45.5% to 27.5% and Arco would sell its 6.5%.

*Reason: Hunt did not possess the technology to pump oil from deep water; Gulf possessed the technology but did not tell Hunt. Arco was not told anything and were swindled out of its concession.

November 1977: Muldoon introduces the S.I.S. Amendment Bill, designed to keep the economy free of obstruction and to uncover obstructive elements. Telephone taps, mail tampering and other surveillance methods approved after the CIA input on the contents of the legislation.

Late 1977: Muldoon travels to the U.S. to meet top Rockefeller officials, including Trilateralists' Deputy Secretary of State, Warren Christopher, and Richard Holbrooke, who were in charge of the new South Pacific Desk at the State Dept. established by Rockefeller to target exploitation of both Aotearoa and Australia. In Los Angeles, Muldoon meets top Rockefeller officials Robert Anderson (Rockwell chairman, also Director of Khashoggi's Security Pacific National Bank) & P. Larkin (Rockwell director, also chairman of Executive Committee of Security Pacific National Bank and director of Marac).

April 1978: Muldoon sets up Petrocorp. Kiwi taxpayers pay for the exploration costs but the oil companies control all distribution outlets. Muldoon blocks development of Maui B as restructured supplies mean higher prices and bigger profits for Shell/BP/Todd. South Island gas market not developed as Great South Basin fields are closer than Kapuni.

Plans develop for re-opening of National Parks for mineral exploitation.

22nd July 1978: Director of Australian Federal Bureau of Narcotics suspends investigation into the Nugen Hand Bank after pressure from CIA & Australian politicians, particularly Malcolm Fraser. Brierley's declared assets reach $200-million, with shareholders' funds only $17-million.

May 1979: Trilateral Commission secretary Zbigniew Brzezinski appoints Muldoon as chairman of Board of Governors of IMF/World Bank, on orders from David Rockefeller. Muldoon would head three-man administration committee which included Canadian finance minister Mitchell Sharp, key figure in the Mafia Council and the Trilateral Commission. Australian Treasurer McMahon is also involved.

9th June 1979: Michael Hand, Frank Nugan, Brierley, and James Fletcher meet in Hand's Sydney penthouse to discuss the establishment of the New Zealand Mafia organisation.

Mid-1979: Gulf Oil, using its man Brierley, begins operations designed to capture key sectors of the economy. A.B. Consolidated restructured into the Goodman Group and Goodman to run operations but with the majority of the stock held by IEL and Brierley using Shell companies plus dummy corporations.
*Strategy: To take over food and produce resources. Brierley and Fletcher restructured a small private company, H.W. Smith, using Cyril Smith as Chairman but with key executives Judge, Collins, and McKenzie. Bob Jones helps. Private company used, as no commerce commission control, accounts not published, and no public disclosure of transactions.
Bunting is established as a Shell company, and the South Island is targeted for asset-stripping and takeover, as well as key sectors of the automobile industry. Unlimited funds channelled through City Realties, NZUC, and Marac. UEB extends Travelodge operations by buying control of

Transholdings, which has strategic holdings in Vacation Hotels and Tourist Corp. Fiji Holdings.

17th August 1979: NZ Mafia inaugural meeting in Sydney including Hand, Brierley, Fletcher, Goodman, Ron Trotter, Alan Hawkins, and L. Papps. Key sectors of the economy would be taken over - food, using Goodman; forestry and farming, using Fletcher and Trotter; property, using Brierley and Jones. Brierley, Hand, and Papps would be responsible for banking, insurance, and finance, while Hand and Hawkins would be responsible for setting up new laundry channels into Aotearoa. The economy would be taken over using cheap loans of less than 5%, while consumers would pay 28%.

October 1979: BP Oil begins $100-million joint venture deal with Fletcher and Trotter at Tasman. Muldoon makes secret deal with oil companies which effectively robs Kiwi taxpayers by giving Shell/BP/Todd the Maui Gas deal. Normally the granting of drilling rights on public land is done using a worldwide system which incorporates an auction tender system. Muldoon bypassed this. Also Shell/BP/Todd pays no tax on Kapuni profits, while putting funds into Maui development.

19th November 1979: Secret meeting in Auckland between Muldoon, Fletcher, and Trotter to transfer 43% Tasman Pulp & Paper shares held by NZ government to Challenge Corp. (chairman is Trotter) and Fletchers. Tasman has lucrative 75-year contract for cheap timber signed in 1955. Muldoon paid off with a $1-million non-repayable loan of $500,000 to be paid into account number 8746665 at New Hebrides branch (Vanuatu) of the Australian International Bank.

November 1979: Muldoon drops restrictions on foreign investment. AMAX (subsidiary of Standard Oil of California) captures the Martha Hill gold mine at Waihi. Muldoon (instructed by Rockefeller) unveils the government's plans to form Aotearoa into an offshore production base for the multinational corporations, as benefits include government export incentives, stable government, cheap labour, and so on.

27th November 1979: Gerald Parsky's lieutenant, David Kennedy, meets Muldoon to deliver US$100,000 cash to Muldoon for implementing Mafia Think Big plans. Muldoon introduces the National Development Bill with fast-track legislation, to keep the economy free of obstruction for long-term monopolisation. C.E.R. plan introduced, designed to integrate the economies of Australia and Aotearoa with the Trilateral Commission for the purpose of exploiting the South Pacific countries and as a back-door entrance into China - the world's largest untapped consumer market. Aotearoa is also the closest country to Antarctica, which has a vast mineral resource for future exploitation.

17th January 1980: $500,000 deposited in Muldoon's account number 8746665 at the Australian International Bank, being the final payment for the Tasman deal.

May 1980: Mafia's Nugen Hand banking operation crashes after Frank Nugan killed. Death ruled as a suicide, even though no fingerprints found on the rifle. Maloney, Houghton, Yates and Hand shred important documents, but miss some. CIA helps Hand and bank president Donald Beasley escape to the U.S. The CIA and ASIO cover everything up. Beasley appointed president of Miami City National Bank, run by Alberto Dugue for 'laundering' profits from the CIA Columbian cocaine operation. There is a probability that Michael Hand killed Frank Nugan because of his involvement with Hand's fiancee.

23rd June 1980: NZ Mafia, including Brierley, Fletcher, Trotter, Jones, Hawkins, Goodman, and Papps, meet in Wellington to discuss merger of Fletcher Challenge and Tasman. In order to replace Nugan Hand Bank's 22 worldwide branches, quick moves are made to buy control of NZ Insurance (NZI) by NZ Mafia, using Brierley, thereby capturing an established worldwide organisation with strong links to the Rockefeller organisation through the Hong Kong & Shanghai

Bank, which is also linked to the CIA through it's subsidiary, World Finance Corp.

Late 1980: Fletchers, with strong Rockefeller links, obtains lucrative contracts on U.S. bases in the Pacific and joint ventures in Saudi Arabia & Iraq. Control extended over Kiwi natural resources - Fletcher Challenge & Tasman Pulp & Paper merged. NZFP takes control of MSD Spiers & Moore Le Messurier (Aust.) Brierley begins joint venture with NZFP through Williamson Jeffrey. IEL, through Goodman, buys 20% of Watties & begins cross-shareholding agreement. Goodman continues buying up control of NZ bakeries & flour mills.

February 1981: TNL, Brierley, AMOIL, and MIM Holdings begin joint gold-mining operation. MIM major shareholder is ASARCO (U.S.) whose chairman, Barber, is also a director of Chase Manhattan Bank. NZ Insurance and South British merger. Parliamentarians for World Order - Richard Prebble elected one of 12 councillors.

12th March 1981: Brierley calls secret meeting in Auckland, which includes Jones, Hawkins, Papps, & Burton Kanter, to discuss transfer of the Fletcher Challenge and UEB hotel operations to the Singapore front company controlled by the Pritzker family.

20th July 1981: Parsky, Brierley, & Seldon meet in Sydney with two new members, Kerry Packer and Alan Bond. Chase Manhattan and Security Pacific National Bank will acquire 60% of Packer's company, with the stock being held in Australia, and 35% of Bond's company, with the stock being held in Hong Kong.

August 1981: Gulf Oil, using Brierley, strengthens it's hold over Kiwi natural resources. Cue Energy launched, starring Lawrey and Gunn. NZOG is launched, with strategic holdings by Jones, Renouf, and Brierley with licences in PPD 38206 and 38204 - both next to Hunt's Great South Basin discovery. NZOG also controls 80-million tonnes of coal through the Pike River Coal Co. Brierley-controlled Wellington Gas, Christchurch Gas, Auckland and Hawkes Bay Gas, and Dual Fuel Systems (A'asia) which controls the vehicle gas conversion market. Liquigas Ltd set up to distribute LPG, controlled by Shell/BP/Todd and Fletcher Challenge.

15th February 1982: Brierley calls NZ Mafia meeting of Jones, Fletcher, Trotter, Hawkins, Goodman, and Papps. New members include Bruce Judge, J. Fernyhough, and Frank Renouf. With Muldoon about to deregulate the liquor industry, Brierley and Fernyhough plan to buy up the Kiwi liquor industry, along with it's outlets. Lion Breweries & Rothmans to help. Brierley will do the same in Australia. J.R. Fletcher becomes managing director of Brierley's Dominion Breweries to oversee operations. Rothmans and Brierley (through Goodman) have equal holdings in Saudicapital Corp. Lion director Scott also chairman of Chase-NBA. Lion directors Fernyhough and Myers also stockholders in NZPOG. Fletcher and Brierley begin their takeover of the freezing works industry. FCL buys into South Island works, while Brierley begins takeover of Waitaki NZR through Watties with the help of Athol Hutton. With Think Big projects beginning, Fletcher and Trotter plan to take strategic holdings in NZ Cement, Wilkins Davies, Steel & Tube, etc. and Brierley would use Renouf to take 3% stake of the Martha Hill gold-mine. Also targeted are clothing, footwear, carpet manufacture and more of the auto industry for takeover and monopolisation.

July 1982: Media takeover begins. Brierley takes 24% of NZ News Ltd and begins buying up private radio. Rupert Murdoch helps.

September 1982: Goodman now helps establish the Japan/NZ Council with the Bank of Tokyo & the Industrial Bank of Japan. Tokai Pulp Co. buys shareholding in NZFP, which also begins joint venture with Shell Oil. Fletcher Challenge strengthens links with the Rockefeller organisation by acquiring the Canadian operations of Crown Zellerbach, whose chairman is also director of Gulf Oil. Crown Zellerbach Corp. has direct connections to Rockefeller through directors Mumford, Hendrickson, and Granville, to United California Bank through Roth, and to the Bank of America through chairman C.R. Dahl. Meanwhile, Robert Jones Investments floated to extend operations of City Realties, Ijmond Properties, Chase Corp., etc. The Commerce Building in Auckland sold to Robert Jones Investments by Robert Jones Holdings for $950,000, when it was recently offered on the market for $200,000. A quick $750,000 profit for Jones. Robert Jones Investments was set up by Brierley, Jones, and Hawkins.

8th December 1982: Mitchell Sharp heads top-level Mafia meeting in San Francisco. Among those present are Parsky, Dahl (Chairman of Crown Zellerbach), Perkins, Woodcock, Brierley, Trotter, Fletcher, and Seldon. Meeting discusses Great South Basin exploitation strategy with first priority being monopolisation of the economy; second priority to establish oil refineries and related industries; third, to integrate Kiwi economy into Trilateral economy, & fourth, to concentrate power back to the U.S. through the Seven Sisters, Chase Manhattan, and Security Pacific National Bank. NZ economy linked directly to the U.S. by Fletcher Challenge merging with Canadian subsidiary of Crown Zellerbach, with funds provided by Security Pacific National Bank and United Californian Bank. Brierley, Fletcher, Trotter, & Sheldon will be NZ Ruling Council, headed by Brierley, who would take orders from Parsky.

Mid-1983: Brierley's Ariadne (Aust.) takes control of Repco (NZ) through Repco (Aust.), thereby taking control of key auto-related industry, helped by Borg Warner and Honeywell - which are closely associated with IEL through International Harvester, Continental Illinois Bank, & First National Bank of Chicago. Toyota & Nissan also help so that Brierley now largest distributor of auto & industrial parts, largest manufacturer of pistons, filters, & engine bearings, as well as biggest supplier of forklifts, tractors, and agricultural equipment. Meantime, control is extended over the Great South Basin Oil source with Hunt, after big losses resulting from trying to corner the world's silver market, being forced to sell out some of his concession to Gulf Oil, which uses Brierley to set up a new company - Southern Petroleum - which takes a 14.5% interest. Hunt retains control with 45.5%, Petrocorp has 40% and chairman F. Orr, also a director of Brierley-controlled Watties. Brierley through Goodman takes control of TNL Group and it's subsidiaries, NZ Motor Bodies and L & M. Mining, which has 15% interest in the Chatham Rise, right next to the Hunt concession.

11th-12th May 1983: NZ Mafia meets in Cook Islands. Included are Brierley, Trotter, Fletcher, Jones, Hawkins, Goodman, Papps, Judge, Renouf, & Fernyhough. New members include A. Gibbs, McConnell, H. Fletcher, and O. Gunn. Japanese Trilateralists Takeshi Wataneve and Daigo Miyado discuss integration of Aotearoa into the Pacific Rim economies. A new political party would be established using Jones and financed by the NZ Mafia Council.

*Reason: Parsky & Colby wanted Muldoon out because he had welched on a deal to set up two U.S. military deep-water submarine bases planned for Dusky Sound & Guards Bay in the South Island.

Parsky, Brierley, & Ray Cline hold a separate meeting to discuss the purchase of Kiwi politicians including Langue, Douglas, & Bolger. Cline was a consultant to the CIA's Deak Bank, took orders from Colby, & was responsible for the 10 Australian politicians on the CIA's payroll, including Bjelke-Petersen, I. Sinclair, Keating, McMullen, M. Fraser, D. Anthony, K. Newman, J. Carrick, B. Cowan, and R. Conner. Cline outlines CIA plan to begin subliminal television advertising.

22nd June 1983: Kiwi politician J. Bolger meets Ray Cline in Sydney and agrees to join the organisation for a monthly fee of US$20,000, to be paid into account number GA1282117 at the Geneva branch of Credit Suisse.

20th July 1983: Kiwi politician R. Douglas meets Ray Cline in Wellington and agrees to join the organisation for a monthly fee of US$10,000, to be paid into account number 3791686 at the Sydney branch of the Deak Bank.

July 1983: Parsky launches a new front company, Chase Corporation, with 25% of the stock being held through Security Pacific National Bank in Australia and 25% held in Hong

Kong by Chase Manhattan. Brierley and Hawkins set up a back-door listing to cover up true ownership.

August 1983: Muldoon imposes withholding tax on all offshore borrowing. Renouf sells 20% of NZUC to Barclay's & prepared for expanding of operations with Brierley. Meantime, Murdoch & Brierley expand their close ties by each taking a piece of NZ Maritime Holdings, and with the election imminent, divide up Kiwi media for takeover to increase Mafia control. NZ News buys Hawkes Bay News, Nelson Tribune, Timaru Herald, etc. Brierley increases holding in Hauraki Enterprises and other private radio stations. Brierley and Murdoch have majority stockholding in NZPA with 48.5%, while in the U.K. Murdoch has a large stockholding in Reuters. Now, the phoney news becomes THE news. Head of the Murdoch operation is Burnett, who is also on the board of Winstones - a Brierley company.

September 1983: With global heroin epidemic, Rockefeller expands operations to recycle profits.

October 1983: Brierley takes over NZ Forest Products through Watties, helped by newly-appointed chairman Papps. Papps also chairman of NZ Railways and presided over transport deregulation, the major beneficiaries of which include Watties and Freightways - managing director Pettigrew and director Lang also both on the NZFP board with Papps. Papps also responsible for the railways' electrification programme with big contracts for Cory Wright & Salmon, whose directors include I.L. McKay - also on the board of NZFP.

Late 1983: AMAX gives Gulf Oil a share in the Martha Hill gold bonanza by selling 15% of it's holdings to Brierley through Goodmans. Oil Co. says that only $870-million worth of minerals in Martha Hill, while true figure is closer to $3-billion.

February 1984: Kiwi politician D. Lange meets Ray Cline in Wellington and agrees to go on the Mafia payroll for a monthly fee of US$40,000, to be paid into account number

5263161 at Commercial Pacific Trust, New Hebrides (Vanuatu).

March 1984: Muldoon knighted with G.C.M.G. for keeping the economy free of obstructions for easy takeover and exploitation.

24th May 1984: Four-man CIA team coordinated by Ray Cline arrives in Aotearoa to begin installing equipment for subliminal television advertising at five sites - Waiatarua, Mt. Erin, Kaukau, Sugarloaf, and Obelisk. Sophisticated equipment can be installed within one kilometre of TV relay aerials and all linked to one IDAPS computer bureau in Auckland. Same equipment installed in Australia in August 1985; Japan in September 1986, U.K. in February 1987; New York in 1987.

Amax geologists now estimate Martha Hill gold source could be worth up to $30-billion on the strength of high gold/tonne ore assay.

17th July 1984: In Aotearoa, subliminal advertising beings on Channel Two between 6 p.m. and midnight - hours later extended to begin at noon. Subliminal messages prepared in the U.S. by the CIA, and with the Kiwi election imminent, tell voters to support the Labour Party, the New Zealand Party, and to buy Mafia company products.

The NZ Party was formed to ensure that Muldoon would lose, as Big Business was unhappy with controls over economy. Big campaign contributions from Brierley, the oil companies, & the Business Round Table ensure a Labour victory. Later, Lange agrees to repay the favour to Brierley by selling the government building in the Karioi Pulp Mill to Winstones. Kiwi taxpayer loses $100-million. Government now becomes an arm of Big Business, using economic policies provided by the Business Round Table, implemented by Finance Minister Roger Douglas, and the package being sold by David Lange, who also keeps up a noisy CIA-directed ANZUS withdrawal campaign.

*Reason: (1) ANZUS Treaty did not cover Mafia requirements over the Great South Basin discovery; (2) To identify any opposition or threats within Aotearoa who align themselves with supposed government policy. Lange increases the SIS budget and strengthens links with the CIA.

Brookings Institute is the actual designer of the Kiwi government economic policies, provided by the Business Round Table (NZ Mafia front) and implemented by the government.

Douglas devalues the dollar and deregulates interest rates, which means cheaper labour, cheaper capital assets and high mortgage rates, thereby implementing Big Business policy of driving farmers off the land, establishment of the corporate farm, and eventually remove viability of small business sector, etc.

27th September 1984: NZ Mafia meets at new 'safe house' registered under Fernyhough's name, in Auckland. Those present include Brierley, J. Fletcher, Trotter, Jones, Goodman, Gunn, Papps, Hawkins, Judge, Renouf, Fernyhough, Gibbs, McConnell, and H. Fletcher. Daigo Miyado announces appointment of Trotter as international vice-president of the Trilateral Commission Pacific Basin Economic Council. Brierley outlines strategy for privatisation of Kiwi government and the establishment of the NZ Centre for Independent Studies which will be chaired by Gibbs, aided by Fernyhough and controlled by Cline, which will advise Treasury on privatisation. Parsky, Brierley, and Seldon hold a separate meeting with Parsky, outlining plans for an expanded laundry operation which will coincide with the launch of 'crack' - a new addictive product developed by CIA chemists for the world market.

26th October 1984: Trotter, Hawkins, Lange, & Douglas meet in Wellington to implement Mafia plans to privatise the government and to deregulate the banking system.

Early 1986: CIA's Deak Bank, with it's 22 worldwide branches, merges with Brierley's Ariadne & Paxus NZI. In the Cook Islands, Brierley sets up the European Pacific Banking Corp. with Fay Richwhite, which is closely linked to the Mafia's United California Bank through the European Pacific Finance Corp.

16th February 1986: The Mikhail Lermontov was sunk near Picton (not by accident).

22nd February 1986: Parsky, Brierley, & Trotter oversee the second launder of Mafia dollars to the Kiwi government, US$300-million, with a commission of $20-million.

26th February 1986: Preliminary inquiry into Mikhail Lermontov released by Minister of Transport Prebble, disobeying all Marine Division instructions on holding preliminary inquiries into shipping casualties.

10th December 1986: Geoffrey Palmer's Constitution Bill removes the power of the NZ Governor-General to refuse assent to legislation: he must now sign in token of his assent.

17th December 1986: National M.P. Peters reveals the Maori loans affair and mentions the Fletcher connection. This fact and many other details were never mentioned in the media after pressure from Trotter using Burnett at Independent News Ltd., Hancox at NZ News, and through CIA-funded sub-editor at the NZ Herald.

27th February 1987: New subliminal messages appear on Kiwi TV screens - "Hello Friends. Make More Money. Vote Labour." Other messages include: "Greetings My Own. Buy Cars. Buy Now," and the most sinister of all, "Smash. Hate. Rape. Punch. Kill. Use Violence." With an election imminent in Aotearoa, frequency of messages increases to average of four per hour.

10th March 1987: Parsky, Colby, Brierley, & Cline meet in the Gibbs safe house in Auckland. Parsky outlines the expansion of the European Pacific banking operation with 12 new subsidiaries to be set up in South America to replace the United Fruit Co. front and which will:

(a) launder heroin dollars from the Rockefeller operations in the Golden Triangle and Pakistan;

(b) launder coke & crack dollars from Columbia, Peru, Bolivia, Ecuador, & Venezuela;

(c) CIA funnel to pro-U.S. political parties in Europe and Latin America;

(d) financial conduit to Colby's P2 neo-fascists in Panama, Argentina, Chile, & Uruguay;

(e) spying conduit for information from Middle East, Latin & South America;

(f) financing arms smuggling to Central & South America and the Middle East, including the Christian Militia in Lebanon;

(g) financial conduit to mercenary army in Kuwait (standing by to conduct CIA invasion of Iran) via CIA's Vinell Corp.

1st April 1987: Business Round Table plan, 'Government Departments to Corporations,' implemented by Lange & Douglas to privatise Aotearoan national assets.

*Reason: You cannot bankrupt a government department, which belongs to the people of Aotearoa. Privatisation means that the whole country can be asset-stripped of all that was Crown-controlled - land, minerals, & energy.

17th June 1987: Kiwi Mafia meet in Gibbs' safe house in Auckland - including Brierley, Trotter, J. Fletcher, Jones, Goodman, & Gunn - to plan strategy for the Aotearoa election, bankrolling of the Labour Party, and post-election agenda for privatisation of the Kiwi government. Included is establishment of a presidential (dictator) system, with Trotter installed as el presidente.

27th July 1987: J.D. Rockefeller, Colby, & Parsky meet in Paris to implement plans for the assassination of David Rockefeller, Rodman Rockefeller, and John McCloy, using Gordon Liddy and his eight man team.

July 1987: Brierley-controlled Newmans/Ansett airline goes into operation. With Douglas, Lange, and Palmer helping with Banking Deregulation Bill, City Bank and Paxus NZI etc. become fully-fledged banks in Aotearoa.

Late July 1987: DFC and Trusteebank merger. End of the last Kiwi-owned bank. The Douglas Administration.

Gemstoner

Len Bracken

This text, reportedly a biographical sketch of the protago-
nist by someone who knew him well, was given to me by a
San Francisco bicycle messenger in 1983. I suspect that it
may have been written by the messenger himself. I am in no
position to verify or dispute the incidents described below.

—Len Bracken

The Opel GT skidded off the Great Highway onto the dirt
parking lot — a Winnabago followed. BR got out of his car as
the whale with diplomatic plates pulled up next to him. He
could hear the lions roar at Fleischaker Zoo over the sound
of the surf. A sunny, windy day in San Francisco.

The camper door opened. What were diplomats doing on
the deserted beach — the only other car in the lot had a
surfer with a broken ankle as a hood ornament. Why wasn't
the guy in Vietnam? Why was he reading a medical text?
Trying to figure out what happened to his Inner Malleolus?

BR zipped up his windbreaker and stood on a piece of
driftwood — straining to see who was in the camper — driftwood, driftwood... He needed a drink.

"You see someone?" one diplomat asked the other in ex-
aggerated Italian.

So they were Italians from the consulate.

"No, I don't see anyone." The guy looked right at BR.

The first one replied: "I also don't see anyone. Hahahaha!"

BR's ears were on fire — he had to talk to someone, anyone. Walking over to the surfer with the cast on his ankle... The Italians definitely had a hand in Onassis's game.

"Nice day. Bet you wish you were out there." BR pointed to the ocean.

"Naahhh. Too windy," the guy replied, shading his eyes to check the surf. "I'm not missing anything."

"Say, I'm looking to rent a room. Know of one?"

"You should try the bulletin board at the Med. School. Everyone wants a doctor in the house."

"Got any weed?"

"If I did, we'd be smokin' it."

BR cupped his hands to light a joint in the wind.

"Columbian." BR held his breath as he spoke.

"Thanks, man. Manna from heaven."

BR gave the guy half the joint. With a little buzz he saw the connections; a big buzz made him paranoid. He needed a safe house — otherwise he'd sleep in his car — no way could he go back to his apartment. Why had he rented a place in North Beach? — HQ of the S.F. mob.

The Italians were still laughing when he wheeled out of the lot, over to the gas station. A rack of pay phones. He dialed a number from the classifieds — here he was patronizing Hearst, while the latter's daughter played revolutionary with the Symbionese Liberation Army. No answer. As he listened to the ring in the receiver, one of the Italians sauntered up to the phone next to him. Why didn't he use the one farther away?

"%$%(&%$#@*00^$##@%*&(%$#@#$#@$#%^"

BR couldn't make out any of it — he doubted the Italian was talking to anyone — just trying to get under his skin. Could bump him off any second — diplomatic immunity.

Sloat Blvd., to 19th Ave., leaving sunny Sunset, to Judah St., to Parnassus Ave.: kids and yids, he had a lid — parked on Clayton and walked down to the Medical School... Imagined making it with a coed; her promiscuity, her disregard for death, her lasers — he was running out of gemstones. The bulletin board was brimming.

"Hello Patty, I'm calling about the room you have for rent."

"Yes," the woman's voice answered, like the squeak of a mouse.

"Can I see it?"

"O.K. — are you a doctor?"

"No, I'm a physicist."

"I guess that's okay. Why don't you come over now; 736 Arlington St. in Glen Park."

"Thank you. See you soon."

The woman sounded strange, but what did he care — all he needed was a place to hide out, to hide his letters and gemstones — maybe he'd get a few rooms around the city, just in case. Time to swing by the post office.

Willard St., to Lincoln Way, to Stanyan, to Haight: bikers, bums, and streakers; he stopped at the light on Masonic Avenue; was it fate? A bearded, barefoot sold love books on the sidewalk: "I read one of these the other night. It said, 'Redheads are better for eating.' Look around you my friend — all you see are redheads (and I don't mean Marxists like they got over in Berkeley). Everyday is St. Patrick's Day..."

Masonic Ave. to Oak St., skirting the Panhandle: drunks, beggars, punks... Oak to Market St. crossing the intersection of Fell and Polk (a lousy pun of a queer joke), Civic Center, U.N. Plaza, the bus depot. He turned down 7th and parked on this skid row. If he had to, he could get a motel room here. It'd been good enough for Koffman — but no "Ancient Rain" could clean these streets of winos, grifters, homos...

A $2 Mission Street whore, possibly transvestite, smiled at him; he was too stoned to notice — stealing glances over his shoulder, walking sideways... He bumped into a beggar: "Can you spare a buck?"

"Fuck off."

"Big shot."

BR'd've cleaned the guy's clock if he wasn't so filthy — crushed the scumbag with one punch to the jaw... From the looks of his face, BR wouldn't have been the first to use it as a target. What'd BR have to fear? He was powerful and intelligent... dangerous, a one man army — they'd better watch out.

One lonely letter in his P.O. Box: addressed in Aegean Blue, postmarked Corfu, ripped open across the top — let 'em have a look, what did he care if they knew that he knew???? He stuffed the letter in the inside pocket of his windbreaker.

Walking down the steps, he looked up to see someone photograph him from the passenger side of a black Pontiac — sped off as BR bounded down the steps toward it. He needed a drink. What did they want from him? A photograph?

"Saw a picture of a guy in the paper," yelled the scarfaced panhandler from behind BR.

"So what," BR said without looking back.

"So... he looked like you. Hey, I know who I am and I know who you are too."

The Latinos who loitered near the carry out shop — high on horse — laughed at the look on BR's face: he'd been had by a bum! He needed a drink. Back in the Opel: Market St., to Powell St. — he cruised California St., looking up at his mother's wooden house (Would the hit men go after his dear old mother? Why was she living so close to the Masonic Auditorium?) — Leavenworth St. over to the 600 block, to Geary St.: The Driftwood.

Slamming shut the bottom half of the Dutch door, he squinted in the dark. There was usually a crew of exiles and mercenaries patronizing the bar. All he saw were the guys from the black Pontiac in wingtips and trenchcoats. It was like they were waiting for him — had he followed them? After all, the Driftwood was a C.I.A. hangout.

"Draught beer and a shot of bourbon," BR said to the bartender who had told BR that he recorded every conversation in the place for the owner of the *Washington Post.*

The suits were at the other end of the bar; they spoke loudly enough for BR to hear:

"We could've used a guy like that."

"Yes, he's clever enough — speaks a few languages without accent."

"Too bad he got mixed up in this conspiracy business..."

BR took the letter from Greece out of the inside pocket of his windbreaker — took a sip of beer, dipped the filter tip of a cigarette in the bourbon and lit up. Through the cloud of smoke he read the letter written in blue in classic Greek.

Dear BR,

I must tell you that my wife and I are very grateful for the gemstone. We fear for our safety and will have to sell it to leave our beloved island. This will be the last letter you will

receive from me for some time. All I can say at this time is that
you are correct. Onassis has kidnapped Hughes and taken
control of all that was the Hughes empire. That includes nu-
merous U.S. politicians...

One of the suits yelled from the other end of the bar:
"Hey you! Who do you think killed JFK?"

"Who do I think killed JFK?" BR responded. "BVD."

"BVD? Why BVD?" the second suit asked.

"Because JFK got too big for his britches — who wants to
know anyway?"

Just then, the bartender motioned for BR to look toward
the door — the two Italian diplomats were grinning at BR
from above the lower half of the Dutch door. BR stared them
down. They left.

"We heard you had some kind of conspiracy theory to
prove who did it. That wouldn't be one of your letters about
the assassination, would it?" one of the suits asked.

"No, it wouldn't." BR didn't feel like taking the stage to-
night — wasn't drunk enough. "Charlie, put this on my tab."

"Right 'O."

BR downed his shot and split. The tule fog was rolling in,
and with it, the smell of fried soy sauce wafting over from
Chinatown — reminded him of the misty day he picked peb-
bles from China Beach to use in lieu of gemstones to symbol-
ize the Golden Triangle.

Back in the Opel — no sign of the Italians — his duffle
bag still in the back seat. Did they want his letters? If so,
why didn't they just get a half-assed repo man to break in
while he was in the bar? No, that wasn't it — they'd arrange
an accident on some deserted stretch of road — be done with
BR once and for all.

He took a roach from the ashtray — just a puff or two —
singed his moustache, like the time a gemstone experiment
failed. His lungs filled with smoke and his mind raced as he
revved the engine. Spinning onto Geary St., 700 to 500 block
through the fog: flashing yellow light of a construction detour
— silhouette of a man crossing his path. Thud.

Before he could get out of the car to see what he'd hit, he
heard the wail of a siren..., two sirens... nearby. Patrol car
lights flashed in the mid-block alley on the left and swirled

around the corner of Taylor St. BR hopped over the construction barricade with his duffle bag, glimpsing the dead man lying in the dirt. He was being framed and the S.F.P.D. was in on it.

The cops converged on the Opel — lost sight of BR in the fog — cut their sirens and heard his boots running down Shannon Alley. BR backtracked on O'Farrell, turned on Jones Street: the squad cars were right behind him. The Stevloe Alley entrance to "Mom's" — BR headed for the can, washed the sweat off his face.

"Give me a beer, Paul," BR said from the stool, his duffle bag slung over his shoulder.

"You know I love you BR, but if the cops are after you, you better get outta here," the bartender said.

"Thanks."

"It's for your own good."

The cops were cruising Jones St. and Antonio Alley — more sirens were approaching... BR skirted the warehouses — garages, chain link, garbage — then turned down a passageway toward Ellis St. to the sound of a Santana clone practicing in a motel room. A squad car spotted him crossing Taylor St. — he ran into a business office, startled the uniformed security guard, sprinted out the back door, threw his bag over a wooden fence and scaled it.

Across a vacant lot — the sound of sirens was deafening. A door on the side of a low building was held ajar by a folding chair. BR entered the chaos of thirty fashion shows going simultaneously in separate booths, runways and carousels. The models stared, either at his rugged good looks, or because he was obviously out of place: strapless silk dresses with sequins; fishnet stockings; hair, lots of hair...

"Excuse me sir, but where is your name tag?" a plain clothes security guard asked.

BR could've clocked him, but didn't. "It's too low class for me to wear a name tag. I am who I am, not my name."

The guard was wearing his name tag, so that line of reasoning didn't go over very well.

"I'll have to ask you to leave."

A bus passed on Taylor St. as BR left via the front door: it slowed to get around the squad cars that were parked in front of the building. The uniformed security guard was gesturing to the cops that BR was inside. His timing couldn't have been better — he strolled across the street behind the bus...

...into the Airlines Terminal. Wiping the sweat off his face with his sleeve he looked out the door over his arm — they hadn't seen him. What to do? A travel agent was closing up for the day.

"Excuse me Miss, but I need to get a ticket right away."

"But it's late. I was on my way home."

BR smiled at the aging Oriental woman, probably a spinster with no one to go home to anyway.

"I need to catch a flight tomorrow. I can pay you cash. O.K.?"

"You want to buy a ticket now? Alright."

As they entered her agency BR scanned the brochures on her desk — Mexico! BR looked out the plate glass window at the cops who were trying to get into the fashion show. It was hopeless — they needed an I.D. or a search warrant. The plain clothes security guard wasn't going to let anything, not even cops, disrupt the show.

"The first flight tomorrow to Mexico."

After a few moments at her computer, the agent said: "Your ticket to Mexico City will be waiting for you at United Airlines. Be there two hours before departure, which is 10:20."

"Thank you very much. Can I call a cab? Hello, Diamond Cab. Pick me up at the Airlines Terminal on Taylor St. That's right, right now."

BR went into the men's room and quickly shaved off his moustache — no soap, just hot water. Outside the can he lit a smoke. With his duffle bag, he looked very natural leaving the Airlines Terminal, hopping into a cab. His heart was still beating wildly — he scarcely remembered the ride.

The taxi dropped him off in front of a rundown house on Arlington Street: a dump old enough to have survived the fire. He was running low on scratch — had to tip the driver though, for being there... He knocked hard, three times.

The mousy-looking lady who answered the door looked up at him with a glow in her eyes.

"Come in, come in. I didn't think you'd show up so I told

Matt here to come over and look at the room. By the way, this is it."

The room was at the top of the stairs: the mattress would serve BR nicely, especially for one night. A long haired medical student with a flute in hand, Matt, was sitting on a run-down armchair — the only stick of furniture in the living room other than the TV.

"I was just telling Matt that I have the shakes because I'm on medication. It's a combination of prolixin and lithium," Patty said.

A mouse scurried along the wall.

"While I was in the hospital," Patty continued, "there were people living here."

BR read the poem scrawled on the wall:

Aubade to the Lady

For three nights under this roof music had a place to live. The sax cracked its notes, breaking the torpor of the night while the guitar responded to the melody and was followed by the incessant beat of a conga. And the chorus — plumbing a deep darkness, the immeasurable depths of darkness with its nameless wildness, like a hiccup after countless sobs or a good drunk — sung with my swollen feet pressing against my boots as if hurling words at each other or a cat fight. My katzenjammer: I'll fuck you till you die/I'll fuck you to death/It is I who dies a little death...
Rick Roderick the Conceptual Lover

"Well Matt, I'll have to let you know. Goodbye," Patty said as she ushered the medical student to the door. "He seems like a nice boy, but I really need a man. I don't want to have anyone break in here."

"They won't break in if they know I'm here," BR lied, "if they know what's good for them."

"Let me show you the rest of the place."

Patty led BR over to the bathroom, through the kitchen —he looked in her room: there was a children's book about a mouse on the dresser. Good thing he'd never have to cook there.

"Well... I didn't get your name."

"BR. For $125 a month, not bad. I'll take it. May even see what I can do about painting over that poem on the wall."

"Good. Glad to have you. How can you pay?"

"Personal check."

Alone in his room, looking out over San Francisco from the lower elevation of Diamond Heights, he fingered his simulated rubies and diamonds that were inside a Chivas Regal pouch. These stones were his alchemy, like making gold from dirt: they were all he had now, other than his letters — ink smeared like snot, piss and shit across page after page; smearing the owners of the world who had taken more than their due.

BR cracked the window to take a few hits of Columbian, gazing at the lights of San Francisco, partially obscured by the fog. Why this thirst for knowledge that risked his life? He stretched out on the bed and felt his mind getting bigger and bigger — he saw the connections. Reaching for the pen...

The Gemstone File and Me

Jonathan Vankin

I first saw the Skeleton Key to the Gemstone File in the winter of 1988. At the time, I didn't know much about conspiracy theories, except that I thought the phrase "conspiracy theories" sounded cool.

Also, despite my innocence (or perhaps because of it), I had the audacious idea that a compendium of conspiracy theories would make a good book. I began accumulating information as fast as I could. I can't recall the exact day the Skeleton Key arrived in the mail, sent by a friend in New York. But here's how I'd like to remember it: snowy, cold, dark, threatening — winter in Central New England where the Atlantic sea breeze can't reach. In Worcester, Mass., it's just plain snowy, cold and dark; ice on the front steps of century-old wooden three-deckers, dead cars rotting on the shoulder of every off-ramp, snow plows cutting through the night with their orange flashing lights. Like a lot of New Englanders, I'd get solipsistic on those days. The outside world is too hostile and people shut it out. For the *Gemstone File* to show up in the mail, it was a beautiful day.

There was a clandestine thrill on pulling the pages out of their manila envelope. They looked like a 20th-generation photocopy at least, typewritten, some passages too faint to read. What appeared to be the address of a real person (Stephanie Caruana) was typed at the top, but there was a date on it: 1975. The document was 13 years old, a slice of secret history.

Concealed in the file, I anticipated, was information so important that somewhere, after hours in a darkened office, some feverish soul — an anonymous drone during the day — was risking livelihood and reputation to run off multiple copies, forehead sweating in the rays of a photocopying bulb. The mysterious document yielded truth that gave the mad xeroxer a reason for coming to work every day, and a sudden sense of personal mission where before there had been little but confusion or a vague sense of despair.

I've since learned that the route by which the file came to me was not nearly so existential. (Strangely enough, I think my copy originated with the publisher of this book.) But when I read the file, I felt a connection to that imaginary person, a beam of transreality piercing the New England gloom. I got the conspiracy rush, a zap of adrenaline that hits when you apprehend a higher truth; the revelation sensation, I call it. Your mind expands, or so you believe. Everyone else now appears slower, plodding through life a little stupider than you thought they were before.

Of course, Socrates believed that the truly wise man knows but one thing; that he knows nothing. I remembered that later. The main point of my planned book was to prove Socrates right. Most of us, particularly those of us in the news media (where I earn my daily chips and dip) are insufferable know-it-alls, smug with the peculiarly American conceit that we've got it all figured out; whatever "it" may be. I set out to collect the craziest group of thinkers ("crazy" by societal definition) I could find, conspiracy crackpots. Then I'd show how they might, just maybe, be *right*. Perhaps not about everything (which would be tough because they often contradict each other), but right about enough to make so-called responsible citizens darn uncomfortable. In other words, by proving that conspiracy theorists knew something, I would prove that the rest of us intellectually self-satisfied bastards knew nothing.

Socrates' dictum, unfortunately for me, is incompatible with the conspiratorial state of mind, which is forged in a moment of gnosis, believing that you can grasp truth in your hands in the form of a fuzzy photocopy of somebody's typewritten notes. Or in the form of a skinny, yellowed paperback on a used-bookstore shelf. Or in the form of a Sunday night radio show on an obscure college station with a host who sounds like Edward R. Murrow on BZ. The conspiracy rush is addictive and eventually it develops into a conviction not that you know nothing and have everything to learn, but that you know everything and had better bring everyone else up to speed before it's too damn late. That was how I felt when I first read the Skeleton Key.

When I wrote my book, the prose style of the Skeleton Key, though not a model for my own, was an inspiration. Terse. Tense. Driven by certitude. I needed to give my readers shivers of sudden access to horrifying secrets, duplicating my first reaction to the *Gemstone File*. I was shooting for mental shock value, an experience that alters one's entire view of reality.

Was Aristotle Onassis global chieftain of the Syndicate? Did Johnny "Poselli" shoot President Kennedy in the head with a .38? Is apple pie America's leading health hazard? It doesn't matter much to me now (though I've no doubt there's more truth in the Skeleton Key than your average Joe Journalist cares to consider). I didn't write about the *Gemstone File* in my book. It fell off of my outline along with a lot else. But I regret the omission because the *Gemstone File* is a dangerous document.

Like all good conspiracy theories, Gemstone is dangerous not for what it says, as its adherents believe, but for how, twisting perceptions like a UFO abduction, it can change the way people think.

I wanted to be as dangerous as the *Gemstone File*, to subvert the way readers view American politics. But there is another danger: the danger that once revelation sensation sends the conspiracy rush shooting up the spine, Socrates' words of wisdom will be lost forever. Many of the conspiracy theorists I interviewed are caught in a trap. Conspiracy theories are used best as a way of digging to the truth with dynamite, blasting out crusty old paradigms. Too many conspiracy theorists, I fear, have let their own thoughts become encrusted in dogma.

I don't blame them. In our society, where good information is difficult to come by and the "official" versions of reality tend to ring false, it's easy to get stuck in a dichotomous view of things: if the *New York Times* is a pack of lies, the *Gemstone File* **must** be true. If not, what is? End of argument.

Something like that must have happened to Bruce Roberts. He probably wouldn't be pleased to see his "file" amended, altered and parodied as it's been for close to 20 years now. Conspiracy theorists, whose credibility is zilch in the straight world, are nonetheless preoccupied with credibility. Information in their view is not public, but personal property. Even when there is a sizable quantity of truth in what they offer — frighteningly often — their rigid attitude renders them useless.

As I was in Worcester, we're all in the dark, out in the cold and denying our hostile surroundings when it comes to interpreting what's going on in this ever-more deranged nation. Like the best conspiracy theories, the *Gemstone File* slashed through the darkness like white light. We're not certain what we're looking at, but it sure is dazzling. As if we'd just been given a private showing of the Holy Grail, viewing the everyday world in a "rational" way after peering through a gemstone prism becomes rather difficult. It teaches us what we don't know more than what we do. Understand the *Gemstone File* in that way. Conspiracy theories are too important to be left to the conspiracy theorists.

Is it True?

Jim Keith

Till tree from tree, tree among trees, tree over tree
become stone to stone, stone between stones, stone
under stone for ever.
  O Loud, hear the wee beseech of thees of each of
these thy unlitten ones! Grant sleep in hour's time, O
Loud!
  That they take no chill. They they do ming no mer-
der. They they shall not gomeet madhowiatrees
  Loud, heap miseries upon us yet entwine our arts
with laughters low!
  Ha he hi ho hu.
  Mummum.

Finnegans Wake
James Joyce

The *Gemstone File* is a mystery whose origins are partly
obscured by time, and so will probably remain, at least in
part, a mystery. There are Gemstone "facets," however, which
provide believability and importance to the document, and
apparently do so for other readers, considering its ongoing
hand-to-hand life.

In "A Skeleton Key to the *Gemstone File*," Stephanie Caruana indicates that the number of original Gemstone letters:
"...is well over a thousand, of which I have read about four
hundred." Mae Brussell set the figure at three hundred and
fifty.

The work involved in Bruce Roberts writing at such

length argues against Gemstone being a complete hoax. He may or may not have been correct in his beliefs about the forces that secretly control the planet, but the extent of Roberts' labors suggests he believed what he was saying.

Supporting my belief that Roberts was not attempting a hoax, Stephanie Caruana has stated she doesn't believe the original letters were ever intended for public distribution: "They were almost invariably addressed, and sent to, a specific person. Xerox copies went into the 'File,' and were only given, or sold, to people like myself or Mae Brussell, who had a special interest in them. As far as I know they were never publicly distributed."

Describing her editing of Roberts' letters, Caruana's description paints a surprisingly different picture from what I had imagined they might be like (namely, something on the order of the bare bones of the Skeleton Key): "Roberts was not only a mental giant and a powerful writer, but also a sort of poet. Reading his letters was like reading a history written by James Joyce in his *Finnegans Wake* period. All of historic time (that is, the threads Roberts was interested in) tended to be jumbled together in paragraph-long sentences. Some of my 'chronologizing' consisted of picking bits and phrases out of these sentences, and putting them under appropriate dates—sometimes, years apart. I stuck to Roberts' own words as much as I could, since I felt that any interpretation I might make of what might be a 'poetic' expression on his part, might well be wrong."

This might explain the patchwork construction of the Skeleton Key. It was apparently intended as a rambling, even poetic personal commentary and it seems to have been Stephanie Caruana who turned the letters into a focused expose and call to arms.

My first impression of Bruce Roberts from the Skeleton Key was that he was probably an outsider from mainstream life, a man painting himself into the partially fictionalized events in his conspiracy documents but most likely obtaining most of his information from books and the tabloid press.

In a note criticizing my interpretation Stephanie Caruana says, "He, as far as I knew, was brave, tough, real, a player and not a sideline sitter; sometimes scared, very angry, and not in the least way the silly wimp you describe! He wasn't 'trying to enter the world of James Bond' — he was James Bond, or his own version of it. Only, he wasn't 'On Her Majesty's Service.' He was a free-lancer. A street fighter, a Scotsman, a heavy drinker. I know it's difficult for most people who are not embroiled in the center of a universe such as his to imagine what it's like to be there, but your picture is just wrong."

Interestingly, Mae Brussell's assessment of Roberts seems to have been similar to my initial guess. Quoting Caruana again, "After reading the portion of the file that Mae had (possibly 200 pages, dating from around 1970 to 1972), I had been very curious about the author. I asked Mae what he was like, and she said he was 'Caspar Milquetoast!' ... She told me that she went to visit Roberts in S.F., and that he lived with his mother, a nice little old Scotch/Irish lady who served tea and wore white gloves..." Supporting this estimation, Robert Eringer in *Critique* magazine says that the portion of the File in Brussell's possession consisted of "300 pages of manic letters Roberts had written to his mother."

Caruana continues: "Roberts had mentioned that his phone was tapped, and I didn't want to call him, so I just drove to the address that he had put on the file, an apartment house in S.F., and rang the bell. I fully expected him to invite me in for tea with his mother. When I finally did meet him, it was clear to me that he wasn't Caspar Milquetoast at all. More like Clint Eastwood/John Wayne, if you want to go to Hollywood for images."

These conflicting views may contain a clue to Roberts' character and to the purpose and credibility of his letters. In addition, if they really were addressed to his mother, Roberts may have never anticipated any critical scrutiny being applied to his allegations.

The Skeleton Key tells us that Roberts "...was married to the daughter of the former French consul in Indochina. In that area Onassis's involvements in the Golden Triangle dope trade was no secret." This reference is one instance where Roberts, for a change, credits his sources. A former French consul could have been in the position to know about drug trade in the Golden Triangle, and since Roberts the person did exist (as some have doubted), the detail of his marriage to the consul's daughter is probably true. In addition, the File was distributed at least in part to people who knew Roberts (for instance, his mother), and who knew varying degrees of, or who could investigate his past. If he didn't want to be caught in lies, it is unlikely that he would have fabricated major details of his own past.

Another source Roberts credited was Admiral Noel Gaylor [sic], Naval Intelligence. Gayler is real, a resident of San Francisco, and was at one time commander of the Pacific fleet. This is another instance of Roberts' account bolstering his credibility: highly delusory characters do not usually name their sources (even if they misspell their names), preferring to take credit themselves for all insider knowledge.

Mae Brussell, who had spent time with Roberts, maintained that the source for his information was a local bar, reportedly a between-jobs province of CIA spooks. A descriptive bit of the Skeleton Key explains: "The Watergate team showed up at the S.F. Drift Inn [sic], a CIA-FBI safe-house hangout bar, where Roberts conducted a nightly Gemstone rap, for the benefit of any CIA or FBI or anyone who wandered in for a beer. James McCord, Martinez, Bernard Baker, Garcia, and Frank Sturgis showed up—along with a San Francisco dentist named Fuller."

While the idea of Roberts conducting a "nightly Gemstone rap," with full awareness of conspirators and witnesses to the Kennedy assassination dropping like flies, is astounding, it is possible that Roberts again points to sources. If the Drift In (which did, in fact, exist, and was owned by Al Strom, who Roberts names) was a gathering place for CIA and FBI (not to mention Mafia, Arabs, Russians and Chinese), then it is possible that Roberts might have picked up some amazing stories there, either true or false, even the type of stories that would impel him to go public.

"Next evening Brading and Frattiano [sic] showed up in the Black Magic Bar—Brading wearing his X-marked hat from Dallas—to see whether Roberts recognized it, how much he knew, etc. A S.F. MP from the Presidio piped up from the end of the bar: "I heard they let everyone with an X-marked hat through the police lines in Dallas."

From this and the preceding account I had already surmised that Roberts spent a good deal of time in bars; he was there "nightly," in fact, and Caruana calls him a "heavy drinker."

Roberts having the military policeman in the bar implicating Brading is another detail to his credit; if he had invented the story from whole cloth it seems likely that he would have done the whistleblowing as the insider in the scenario.

Conversely, Brading and Fratianno seeking Roberts out to find out how much he knew of the conspiracy particularly smacks of a self-aggrandizement that is not solitary in the Skeleton Key. We know of many instances of witnesses to the Kennedy assassination — both first and second-hand — being murdered. If these Mafiosi had any suspicion of him revealing their complicity in the assassination, why not search him out to to kill him, rather than question him? Caruana and Brussell have, at different times, suggested this is precisely what happened, although it is difficult to know for certain. In the world of the conspiratologist, all deaths are suspicious.

Another portion of the Skeleton Key contains both believable and unbelievable elements: "Roberts had made an agreement with a friend, Harp, of Kish Realty, over a bugged phone. Harp was to buy a Gemstone—with history—for $500, the price of a trip to Canada for Roberts to check into the 'Hughes' Mormon Mafia Canadian stock market swindle, and other matters. But Harp was sodium-morphate poisoned before the deal could go through—on this date."

X. Sharks DeSpot has determined that Gail "Larry" Harp of Kish Realty did exist. But would the Mafia have poisoned Harp, who, in fact, didn't have a copy of the File? Wouldn't they have killed Roberts and saved themselves a world of future trouble? And how would Roberts have known for certain whether Harp had been murdered, and by what method? The lingering smell of apple pie? His analysis of the event smacks of paranoia, another not-unfamiliar note in the Skeleton Key.

Roberts' Gemstone is obviously far from flawless. Numerous times events are related that Roberts could not possibly have been privy to, although he — via Caruana — is willing to admit that some aspects of the File are speculative. Much of the earlier chronology must have been second or third or fifteenth hand: Roberts was simply not in a position to be hobnobbing with Onassis, Roosevelt and others at the beginning of the century.

Some events he relates have a false ring to them: "Onassis had invited Jackie for a cruise on the Cristina, where she was when JFK got tipped off that big O planned to wipe him out." If JFK and RFK were doing everything in their power to thwart Onassis, as Roberts' account indicates, then there would have been no reason for JFK to need warning of a reprisal from his arch-rival. Especially with the factual penchant of the Mafia for knocking off their competitors by the busload, it seems unlikely that JFK would have let Jackie party with Onassis to begin with — unless Monroe's presence in the Lawford bathtub understandably caused the whole matter to slip his mind.

Matt Love's speculations may give a rationale for Kennedy's behavior (at least as Roberts describes it). "Question: Roberts implies that the Kennedies knew it was Onassis they were opposing. Why would Kennedy allow Jackie to go yachting with Onassis? Possible answer: he sent her as a courier, to make a deal with Onassis. Judith Exner has said that Kennedy used other public figures as couriers, too, and that may have included Jackie. That is why the Roosevelts went along; their old man was perhaps a bridge between Kennedy Sr. and Onassis. Kennedy had known that Exner was Giancana's mistress and she had been a courier of money and documents between them. So Kennedy figured he'd run the same operation with Onassis."

Roberts' whole tale of "hit and run" on the streets of San Francisco smacks of megalomania and paranoia, and I would dismiss it entirely except for the fact that it is curiously similar to Mae Brussell's tale of incidents surrounding her meeting with Roberts.

"Hit and run accident on Roberts' car, parked in front of the Russian consulate in S.F.—who routinely take pictures of everything that goes on in front of the consulate. Their photos showed the license plate of the hit-and-run car: UKT-264, on a blue Cadillac belonging to Mia Angela Alioto, Joe's daughter, being driven by Tom Alioto, Joe's son—whose driving license had been revoked. His license, and the car's license, were both fraudulent. To cover up the hit-and-run circumstances, S.F. MP's from the Presidio quickly staged a few more hit-and-runs on the same corner—all duly filmed by the Russians. Kathryn Hollister, the Alioto family nurse, was 'persuaded' to take the rap for the hit-and-run. Roberts threatened to spill the whole story—in court—with photos." And... "Roberts threatened to blow the hit-run story, plus its Mafia ramifications open if Humphrey came to S.F. Humphrey didn't come; Humphrey lost San Francisco, California, and the election."

Even though the sequence is imaginative, is it likely that the Mafia would have taken out their vengeance on Roberts' car, rather than him? Is it also likely that Tom Alioto, the Mayor's son, would have been the one tapped to do the job, even if they had resorted to such pettiness? And how about the Russian consulate taking pictures of the event? How would Roberts have obtained the shots from them, unless by bartering a handful of artificial rubies and sapphires? And were the Arabs, the Chinese and the Russians lurking on the sidelines, stealing hubcaps?

Throughout the tale, Roberts describes the event as "hit-and-run" which technically it is, but the term is more usually employed to describe leaving the scene after striking a pedestrian. This suggests that Roberts might be consciously — if crudely — weighting his words to make the incident sound more sinister than it was. It might even have been a verbal mechanism which he used to convince himself of the dark motives for the accident.

If Bruce Roberts was going to "blow the hit-run story," what would he have said to the press? That he had pictures of the mayor's son running into his car while driving with a revoked license, and that proved the Mafia link to the JFK assassination? All in all, it sounds like Roberts' car was struck by another vehicle and he got paranoid about it, imaginatively parlaying the event into a story about how he personally derailed Humphrey's candidacy. And what would have been the purpose of destroying Humphrey's chances, anyway, considering the alternative?

The story about Mary Jo Kopechne sounds fishy, with no pun intended. Roberts describes a curious combination of accident and Mafia hit taking place. Logically, if it had been a hit, then Teddy Kennedy certainly wouldn't have been the one to stage it, and not in the manner it happened, which would have required acrobatic — not to mention deadly — skill. A murder would have been better planned, furnishing Kennedy an alibi after its accomplishment. As a highly influential and loyal Mafia asset (according to Roberts' description), Kennedy would have been the last person the Mafia would have wanted compromised or discredited. If anyone in the Mafia had wanted Kopechne killed, Kennedy for instance, then she would have simply been detained and would have disappeared. Roberts even goes so far as to say: "It took her 2 hours and 37 minutes to suffocate," which puts in dramatic relief the unlikelihood of him being there with a stopwatch and bears the melodramatic flavor that the document is tinged with.

After the murder, "Cardinal Cushing's priests... appeared before the Kopechne's 'direct from God,' with personal instructions from Him that Mary Jo was not to be disturbed." How could Roberts have known this claptrap for certain? It sounds like he might have had a pronounced streak of anti-Roman Catholicism, and Roberts' other religious speculations in the Skeleton Key seem to bear this out.

Another illogic: "Eugenie Livanos Niarchos, in bed with her husband, overheard the conversation. Stavros was forced to beat her to death." It seems unlikely that Stavros would have been discussing matters so sensitive with a possible informant in bed next to him. It also seems unlikely that Roberts could have known the bedside details of the event, except through hearsay or (more likely) a newspaper account. As in the Kopechne sequence, one is tempted to think that this story might be a particularly transparent revelation of Roberts' working methods. The details of the alleged killing could only have been obtained through the workings of his imagination, embroidering upon details that were already common knowledge.

Roberts' account of the deleted Nixon tapes has Nixon raving about Canada, 'asshole Trudeau,' 'asshole Roberts,' Onassis, Hughes and Francis L. Dale. Again, how could Roberts have known the contents of the tapes? But it would have been rather flattering to Roberts to imagine that Nixon thought of him as an equal a danger as Onassis, if indeed Nixon thought Onassis was a danger to him.

Thanks to the research of Matt Love, we know where

Roberts obtained a good portion of his information about the John F. Kennedy hit: *Coup d'Etat in America* by Canfield and Weberman. The portions of the *Gemstone File* attributable to *Coup d'Etat* are numerous and include the naming of the overall assassination personnel (although not all of the actions Roberts attributes to them) and other details copied almost word-for-word including:

a) The story of the missing Kennedy brain.

b) Eugene Hale Brading's stay at the "Cabana Hotel" [sic], and his becoming "a charter member of the La Costa Country Club."

c) The Pepsi Cola factory in Laos that never "produced a single bottle of Pepsi," this a quote from *Coup d'Etat*.

Here is an essential dishonesty in Roberts' presentation that puts the File into doubt as the revelations of a man in the know. He takes the story for his. This is not an unusual tack in the world of underground "super-patriots," as Caruana terms them. In the heat of revelation about the evildoing of the Mafia or the Illuminati, sources are often neglected.

In the Skeleton Key Roberts has Fratianno shooting from the second story in the Dal-Tex building, with Roselli behind a fence in the grassy knoll area, Brading shooting from the pergola (which he mistakenly identifies as a 'pagoda'... Roberts apparently never examined Dealey Plaza in person) across the street from the knoll, and Oswald firing from the Texas School Book Depository.

A number of witnesses, including Fratianno, confirmed the Mafia's role in planning and carrying out the assassination, however it is curious that Roberts does not mention the abundant CIA and FBI (and Permindex, and Right-wing, and Nazi, and NASA, for that matter) connections to the event. Nor does he mention the intricate convolutions of the Garrison case or of the *Torbitt Document*.

Roberts correctly identifies Eugene Brading as being a member of the Denver Mafia Smaldones "family" and Jack Ruby as being Mafia.

Scheim in *Contract on America* confirms that Maheu was the go-between for the Mafia and the CIA. The idea that Onassis was ultimately calling the shots is plausible, since Maheu had worked for him in an important capacity prior to (and, following the Gemstone scenario, perhaps during) his employment with Hughes, as can be confirmed by any biography of Onassis. Here we have an intersection of detail which is about as close as we come to confirming Roberts' Gothic tale of Onassis as Godfather.

As far as the events of the shooting, Brading was arrested in the Dal-Tex Building shortly afterwards, making his described presence at the pergola possible, even though the Dallas County sheriff's office reported he was in the building at the time of the shooting. Ballistics reports and witnesses confirm that shooting took place from the locale of the Dal-Tex building. Another man was arrested at the Dal-Tex building and later released. This could have been Fratiano, if the Gemstone account is correct.

Another possibly true detail in the Skeleton Key: "Roselli and his timer went down a manhole behind the fence and followed the sewer line away from Dealey Plaza." In the *Spotlight* newspaper of August 29, 1988 investigators Kenneth and James Collier verify the existence of a storm sewer in the grassy knoll, leading to the sewer system.

Quoting the Skeleton Key: "After JFK's death, Onassis quickly established control over Lyndon Johnson through fear. On the trip back to Washington, Johnson was warned by radio, relayed from an air force base: 'There was no conspiracy. Oswald was a lone nut assassin. Get it, Lyndon? Otherwise, Air Force 1 might have an unfortunate accident on flight back to Washington.'"

As unlikely as the Air Force 1 message might seem, it is not impossible that it happened. Johnson had been the recipient of considerable mob funds during his career, including at least $500,000 while in the Senate and $100,000 from Jimmy Hoffa in 1964. The Mob presumably does not give away its funds without expecting something in return.

In the matter of Thane Cesar's possible role in the RFK shooting, Roberts is knowledgeable and, in light of recent research, perhaps correct. Roberts might have picked this information up from the source listed in the Skeleton Key, the movie, although the date on the movie's release suggests that this reference may have been added by Stephanie Caruana. In correspondence she tells of having met Ted Charach, the movie's director, at a party given by *Playgirl* magazine.

Surprisingly, the artificial gemstones which Roberts distributed with the Gemstone letters, were real. Caruana reports: "Yes, I did see a few of Roberts' gemstones. He invited me to meet him one day in front of 'Mrs. Giannini's Bank of America' in downtown S.F." Note Caruana's repetition of the Roberts' phrase, not the only time she has betrayed her absorption in his worldview, even 17 years after the fact. "He had a safe deposit box there, and he went in and got a few artificial diamonds, and I think, a sapphire, and showed them to me. They were to be sent out in connection with a letter or letters that he was sending to someone. At the time, I believe he was no longer making gemstones. He told me that he had done so in the past in a garage, which blew up one day due to some mistake, and singed off his eyebrows, etc. I think he may have run out of gemstones at some time, and of course could use anything he wanted as a symbolic 'Gemstone.' Sometimes a coin. Or even a pebble from a certain place. In this case, it was the 'history' that accompanied the object that would give it its value." Caruana mentions that the single Gemstone letter that she bought from Roberts was accompanied by a Kennedy dime, supposedly minted on the day of the assassination.

The Gemstone depiction of Howard Hughes is, interestingly, perhaps more believable than the accepted story of Hughes retiring from public life and holing up in assorted penthouses to watch television and the prolonged growth of his hair and fingernails, although Roberts was not alone in his belief about what had happened.

Howard Hughes did inexplicably vanish, supposedly going into seclusion at a bungalow at the Beverly Hills Hotel in 1957. Hughes refused to appear in court, even when control over his company TWA was at stake. At various times he also refused to submit his photo or fingerprints, even when applying for licensing of his casinos. During this licensing procedure, Governor Laxalt of Nevada was reported by the FBI as concerned "...that a grave hoax could be being perpetrated..."

An IRS agent at the time echoed Roberts' story by stating, "It is my belief that Howard Hughes died... and that key officials running his empire concealed this fact in order to prevent a catastrophic dissolution of his holdings."

Robert Maheu insisted that Hughes had been abducted. Carl Oglesby in *The Yankee and Cowboy War* gives some of his reasons for believing this, including: "Hughes's health was too poor for so sudden and hurried a trip. *Newsweek* magazine reported on these events in its issue of December 21, 1970. This story scornfully informed its readers that "Maheu's group spread another story that Hughes had been visited by a heart specialist (or in one version, three heart specialists) in November, that he was too ill to be moved anywhere but to a hospital, and that he had been kidnapped... Eikes gave him immediate blood transfusions and said later that he was still on transfusions at the time of his sudden departure for the Bahamas, a departure carried out so hastily, however long it may have been considered, that he actually left behind his till-then precious or even indispensable life-support equipment."

Also, Maheu argued that it was certainly peculiar for a man like Hughes, engaged as he was at that exact moment in a battle for control of the Las Vegas-Bahamas gambling axis, suddenly to abandon old friends and helpers in the game, people like Maheu himself and Hooper, and to leap headlong down the spiderhole of an organization like Resorts International, a company which operated a casino in the Bahamas... in direct competition with those in Nevada. This in spite of bad health and only on the counsel of formerly distrusted executives. On top of all, what would possibly lead him to employ as over-all manager of this trip a security organization, Intertel, 94 percent of which was owned by Resorts International?

Oglesby continues: "So even if Intertel was not the CIA of the Lansky Syndicate, it was still at least the CIA of Resorts International, and Resorts International, whether it was a syndicate front or not, was still Hughes's chief competition."

Other circumstances around Hughes's flight from Las Vegas to the Bahamas are questionable. "Hughes was met in the Bahamas on Thanksgiving Day by an Intertel official named James Golden, whose presence in the melodramatic episode is interesting because of his reputation as 'Nixon's man.' Secret Serviceman Golden was assigned to Vice-President Nixon in 1957. He accompanied Nixon to Russia and Central America. They got stoned together in Venezuala. They grew close. When Nixon left the White House in 1960, Golden left the Secret Service to take a job as security chief for

Lockheed. In 1968 Lockheed gave him a leave of absence to join Nixon's campaign as director of security. After Nixon's election he became Resorts International's deputy director of security on Paradise Island. He was a founding officer of Intertel and one of its vice-presidents at the time of the events of November. He later joined the Hughes Las Vegas staff. As of summer 1975, he was at the Justice Department as chief of the Organized Crime Strike Force of the Law Enforcement Assistance Agency.

"Golden's presence in the *Coup* raises the question of a Nixon influence since 'Nixon's man' either means nothing or something. Could Nixon have been involved in the plot of Thanksgiving 1970 to overthrow Maheu, abduct and confuse Hughes, and radically change the nature of the crime-connected, FBI-connected, and CIA-connected Hughes empire?"

Oglesby also asks: "What about Hughes's solitude? Why could he not show his face to save $160 million? [referring to the TWA case]. Does this not go beyond eccentricity? Sometimes it seems Hughes must have died, as so many insist, long before April 1976. The only people who claim definitely to have seen and had daily transactions with Hughes are the so-called Mormon Mafia, or the Big Five, the mostly Mormon superstraights who were said to tend him as nurses and secretaries. They were all recruited by Bill Gay of the Toolco board, and they are of course loyal to Gay. Parties to the events they served, partisans, these five men alone assured us of Hughes's existence. That he did as they say he did, willed as they say he willed, we have no word but theirs."

Maheu went so far as to attempt to rescue Hughes from the Bahamas. He sent a team of men there, and they checked in a floor below Hughes's supposed penthouse in the Britannia Hotel. With a boat waiting to spirit Hughes back the states, Maheu's men obtained a search warrant to break into Hughes's quarters, but Intertel's James Golden stopped the rescue attempt by having the team deported for "working without a permit."

Roberts' source may have been as obvious as the utilization of suspicions about the death of Hughes that were prevalent at the time of his writing. The information I have suggests that *Midnight*, the Canadian tabloid, was the basis for at least a portion of the story. Not exactly the most credible of sources (even though credited by Caruana and Brussell in their own research), although it is easy to imagine how Roberts might have read the *Midnight* story and worked backward from it, finally coming to the conclusion that he had "cracked" the Howard Hughes case.

If any portion of the *Gemstone File* is eminently debatable, and definitely stranger than fiction, it is Bruce Roberts' allegation that Aristotle Onassis was the head of the Mafia, and that he was ultimately responsible for the Kennedy hit. Steve Beard's assessment in the magazine *j-d: The Visionary Issue* is almost a typical reaction to the allegation: "Take the *Gemstone File*. ...Its solution to the riddle of the Kennedy assassination is astonishing. Aristotle Onassis dunnit. That's why he got to marry Kennedy's widow (it's a Mafia thing). But that's not all the wily old Greek tycoon did. He also kidnapped American billionaire Howard Hughes, put his double in his place and pumped him full of drugs so nobody would notice the swap, took control of the Mafia's rackets, ran the American elections and generally came on like the master of the universe. Perhaps he was the chief alien from Alpha Centauri. No matter. What's interesting about the *Gemstone File* is that buried in the dross is a lot of hard fact. It has become a polymorphous disinformation vector, continually remodified, reprinted and redistributed."

I admit that my own initial reaction was approximately the same. Onassis as Godfather was incredible and remained incredible because of a lack of substantiation on the part of Roberts (or perhaps Caruana). Researching Gemstone, though, I have been able to link Onassis to a variety of evils (if not proving that he was guilty of them), and have discovered that it is widely believed among conspiracy researchers (Dick Gregory, for instance) that Onassis made his money through drug smuggling. What had initially seemed completely wild claims on Roberts' part suddenly became more credible. There is even the sense that the Danny Casolaro "Octopus" might have revealed a draping tentacle.

The Skeleton Key states that Onassis, "a Greek drug pusher and ship owner" made a deal with Joseph Kennedy, Eugene Meyer, and Meyer Lansky to ship bootleg liquor. "Also involved was a heroin deal with Franklin and Elliot Roosevelt."

Joseph Kennedy's bootlegging activities are, of course, legendary. But according to Matt Love, "Roosevelt's grandfather (on the Delano side) made his fortune from opium trade in China at the time of the Opium Wars. Maybe the stories of Joseph Kennedy (with Roosevelt's help) bootlegging is only a cover story for a far more scandalous story. People laugh at bootlegging, but heroin is different story."

We do know that Franklin Roosevelt did aid the Mafia in a number of instances, the most important being "Operation Underworld," involving the trade of Lucky Luciano's freedom for the security of the Eastern seaboard docks during World War II. Since the Mafia controlled the Eastern seaboard, Meyer Lansky was able to make this offer to Roosevelt, presumably via J. Edgar Hoover.

Echoing Bruce Roberts, Oglesby speculates in *The Yankee and Cowboy War* that: "The offer Lansky made in particular was simply for Roosevelt to intervene in the Luciano matter, although from the prosperity enjoyed by organized crime during World War II, it may appear to imply that the deal went much further and actually entailed federal protection for certain areas of Syndicate wartime activity, e.g., smuggling."

Although I have not heard any speculation on it, it would not exceed known facts to suggest that Roosevelt was Mafia-allied, and J. Edgar Hoover has been shown to have been the recipient of Mafia funds and favors, while maintaining until his death that the organization did not exist. Oglesby provides the perspective, while not specifically making the connection: "With Operation Underworld, Roosevelt made the Mafiosi all but official masters of the U.S. East Coast docks and gave implicit protection to their activities everywhere. With his instructions to Patton in 1943, he restored the Mafia to power in Sicily. When he sent [Meyer] Lansky to Batista in 1944, he paved the way for the spread of Syndicate influence throughout the Caribbean and Central America. When he directed the CIA to use Syndicate thugs at Marseilles in 1945, he licensed the heroin factories that would be feeding the American habit into a contagion virtually unchecked over the years of the Cold War."

Since it has been established that the Syndicate controlled the Eastern seaboard during this period, and since this was also a period of huge profits for Onassis shipping through these same ports, how would it be possible that Onassis would not have at least been Mafia-connected?

Conspiratologist and Mae Brussell associate John Judge concurs with Roberts on Onassis drug trade involvement. In his recorded talk, The Secret Government, he says: "In 1949... The international heroin routes are re-established in force. The shipping done by Aristotle Onassis. Much of it runs from Marseilles where the OSS had had a hand in throwing out the Socialist and Communist governments and putting in Sicilian or Corsican Mafia... Lucky Luciano had been moved by that point into Italy and was able to set up the labs there necessary to break the opium down into heroin and the other derivatives, and Bishop Montini was hard at work in Southeast Asia with the French-Vatican ruling class, making sure that the opium came out of Vietnam and the other areas, in Laos where it was being grown. He eventually became Pope Paul VI."

Judge points out another sinister Montini connection that will become more significant as other Onassis associations are brought forth. "Monsignor Montini... used Caritas Internationalis, a welfare organization, to provide refugee travel documents to such Nazis as euthanasia killer Hans Hefelman, and Hitler's secretary Martin Bormann, aiding in their escape to Argentina."

What of the Roberts' statement that both candidates in the Kennedy/Nixon race were controlled by the Mob? A news story, written by Anthony Summer and published in the *Washington Times* in 1991, is worth quoting at length:

"What then of Miss [Judith] Exner's claim that, during the election campaign, Kennedy met with mobster Giancana and sent him bags full of cash designed to buy votes? Is it conceivable that Kennedy would thus compromise himself with the Mafia? Again the answer must be yes.

The mob connection ran in the family, more so than has ever been understood. Prominent underworld sources have said it began during Prohibition, when — like the mobsters — Joseph Kennedy made a fortune in the whiskey business. He was said to have played golf in the '30s with Giancana's associate Johnny Roselli [also implicated in the Kennedy hit by Roberts]. Years later, during John Kennedy's election campaign, an FBI report noted that Joseph Kennedy was "visited by many mobsters" while staying at the Cal-Neva Lodge in California. The hotel was partially owned by Giancana.

"A connection between Kennedy, the privileged Easterner, and Giancana, the Mafia graduate of a Chicago street gang, is not as improbable as it might seem. They shared a number of mutual friends, including Frank Sinatra, [and] Kennedy's brother-in-law Peter Lawford...

"In February 1960, when Sinatra introduced Kennedy to Miss Exner in Las Vegas, the presidential campaign was going into high gear. Sammy Davis, Jr., who was in Sinatra's show at the Sands Hotel, later recalled an odd incident. Mr. Lawford took him aside and whispered, 'If you want to see what a million dollars in cash looks like, go into the next room. There's a brown leather satchel in the closet. Open it. It's a gift from the hotel owners for Jack's campaign.'

"One of the criminal hotel owners in Las Vegas was Sam Giancana. The next month, just two weeks after Kennedy began his affair with Judith Exner, an informant told the FBI that Joe Fischetti and 'other unidentified hoodlums' were 'financially supporting and actively trying to secure Kennedy's election at the behest of the senator's friend Frank Sinatra.' Fischetti, whom Miss Exner also met that month, was one of Giancana's close associates.

"...Kennedy won the election as a result — Miss Exner's new testimony suggests — of a collaborative effort: mob muscle and money, and a liberal injection of greenbacks provided by Kennedy to Giancana for distribution by his henchmen.

"Heavily censored FBI documents show that Giancana was indeed in the Northeast in August 1960 when — according to Miss Exner — he again met the candidate and picked up a bag of money in New York. In November, when a razor-thin majority gave Kennedy victory over Richard Nixon in the state of Illinois, there were serious charges of vote fraud in the area of Chicago where Giancana ruled the roost.

"...Kennedy may have paid the ultimate price for his dalliance with Giancana. The Mafia, which does nothing for nothing, takes vicious revenge when it considers a pact has been broken. According to Skinny d'Amato, the price for a Kennedy victory was the return of deported Mafia boss Joe Adonis.

"If there was such a deal, it fell through, reportedly because Attorney General Robert Kennedy would have none of it. It was his crusade against organized crime that infuriated the mob most of all.

"Giancana, one of its prime targets, made threatening noises as early as July 1961, when — according to Miss Exner — he was still linked with Kennedy on the Castro operation [to assassinate him]. 'I know all about the Kennedy's,' he shouted at an FBI agent, 'and one of these days we are going to tell all.'

"By early 1962, ever more harried by Kennedy law enforcement, the mob felt cheated. 'He'll get what he wants out of you,' an FBI bug overheard Giancana say of the president, 'but you won't get anything out of him.'

"Around that time, Miss Exner says, the flow of envelopes between Kennedy and Giancana ceased. By the fall of the year, when her affair with the president had dwindled and died, she sought solace in a brief affair with Giancana. She recalls him speaking of Robert Kennedy 'with hatred,' of the president, 'without respect.'

"Also that fall, Florida Mafia boss Santos Trafficante, an accomplice of Giancana in the Castro murder plots — and a man with close links to the exiled Joe Adonis — made an ominous comment. The Kennedy's were 'not honest,' he told an associate. 'They took graft and they did not keep a bargain,' he said. 'Mark my words, this man Kennedy is in trouble, and he will get what is coming to him... He is going to be hit.

"... The House Elect Committee on Assassinations concluded in 1978 that President Kennedy was 'probably' assassinated as the result of a conspiracy. The staff was divided over whether the murderers were mobsters or U.S. intelligence operatives, or elements of both. In a book soon to be published, Sam Giancana's nephew and godson — also named Sam — will say the committee was right about the conspiracy, and that his uncle was involved. The book will also corroborate Miss Exner's claim that she acted as courier between Kennedy and Giancana, and will say that two others — public figures — were used the same way."

Nixon was financed by the Mafia, as well as by Hughes and, it turns out, Onassis. Davenport and Lawson, in *The Empire of Howard Hughes* relate a deal between John Mitchell and Onassis: "One... reads that Martha Mitchell, though highly discredited for her eccentricities and weird ways, had some knowledge of her husband's and Nixon's relations with the Onassis shipping industry and Hughes. ...Says Beale in her Washington column:

"She (Martha Mitchell) said Aristotle Onassis came to see John Mitchell immediately after she and John had moved in their New York apartment three years ago. She rushed to get to John's side of the apartment finished in time for the visit. Onassis, she said, came to discuss an over $900 million deal that he and John were supposedly involved in, but she did not know just what John's involvement was."

Documented contributions to Nixon from the Mob include $5,000 from Mickey Cohen for Nixon's first campaign for Congress, an additional $75,000 from Cohen during the 1950 Senate campaign, Carlos Marcello's $500,000 delivered to Nixon in 1960, and $1,000,000 given to him in 1977 by Frank Fitzsimmons and Tony Provenzano.

In an interview with reporter Dick Russell, printed in *Argosy* magazine in 1976, Charles Colson said he had heard the theory that Hughes's empire was actually, "...a headquarters of the Mafia's operation; that they owned Bebe Rebozo, they got their hooks into Nixon early, and, of course, that ties into the overlap of the CIA and the mob... Don't say that's my theory, but I've heard it expounded as a possibility and, of course, it is."

Although you'll hear nothing of it in any of the many Onassis biographies, it turns out that his links to Nazis, Mafia and the JFK assassination were legion. Although this naturally does not prove that Onassis was Nazi, Mafia, or involved in the assassination of Kennedy, it does open the door for speculation in those areas, and also lends more credibility to Bruce Roberts' claims.

In *The Secret Government*, John Judge says that the fictional Corsican Mafia ("Union Corse") figure Ernst Stavro Blofeld, in the Ian Fleming James Bond books, was based on Onassis. Not as unlikely as it might seem at first glance, since Ian Fleming had been an intelligence operative and, by his own admission, based some of his characters on real individuals.

William Taub was a middleman for Onassis, and had

other clients that included Nixon, Howard Hughes, and Jimmy Hoffa. According to Mae Brussell in her article "The Nazi Connection to the John F. Kennedy Assassination," printed in *The Rebel* in 1983, "Taub was especially close to Cardinal Alfredo Ottaviania of the Holy See, who arranged Mussolini's 1929 'donation' of $89,000,000 to the Vatican to ensure its neutrality with Mussolini and Hitler. The money went into a special fund in the Vatican Bank, and after the war part of it was entrusted to 'God's Banker' Michele Sindona [kingpin of the infamous Freemasonic P2/Vatican/Mafia connection, who began his career as a lawyer for the Sicilian Mafia] for investment. Sindona channelled a good chunk of it to the Nixon campaign." Sindona was also a guest at Nixon's inaugural ball, although this probably did not entirely discharge Nixon's debt to him.

Also implicated in the Vatican Bank scandal was Johnny Roselli, a prominent player in Gemstone, who, along with other Mafiosi, printed one billion dollars worth of counterfeit stock, which promptly vanished into the Vatican Bank and Banco Ambrosiano.

In *The Illuminoids*, Neal Wilgus says in 1968 "Agnew [was] allegedly chosen for Nixon's vice president to obtain CIA and Greek oil and shipping firms' contributions."

Aside from his Mafia associations, Nixon also had Nazi ties that overlap with those of Onassis. Again, according to Brussell: "In 1952 Nicola Malaxa moved from Whittier, California to Argentina. Malaxa had belonged to Otto von Bolshchwing's Gestapo network, as did his associate Viorel Trifia, who was living in Detroit. They were members of the Nazi Iron Guard in Romania and had fled prosecution. They had one other thing in common: they were friends with Richard Nixon.

"Trifia had been brought to the United States by von Bolschwing. Malaxa had escaped from Europe with over $200,000,000 in U.S. dollars. Upon arrival in New York he picked up another $200,000,000 from Chase Manhattan Bank. The legal path for his entry was smoothed by the Sullivan & Cromwell law offices, the Dulles brother's firm [which also represented a large number of Nazi interests]. Undersecretary of State Adolph Berle, who helped Nixon and star witness Whittaker Chambers convict Alger Hiss, personally testified on Malaxa's behalf before a Congressional subcommittee on immigration. In 1951 Senator Nixon introduced a private bill to allow Malaxa permanent residence. Arrangements for his relocation in Whittier were made by Nixon's law office.

"When Malaxa went to Argentina in 1952, he linked up with Juan Peron and Otto Skorzeny. Questions were raised at the time about J. Edgar Hoover, the Iron Guard, Malaxa and Vice President Nixon."

One of Onassis's documented Nazi associations was Hjalmar Schact, the president of Hitler's Reichsbank, who was released by John J. McCloy (later on the Warren Commission) from imprisonment for war crimes in Germany and later employed by the Greek shipping magnate. Schact was the son-in-law of Otto Skorzeny, the creator of the "International Fascista," buddies with John Foster Dulles in the banking schemes that put Hitler into power, and later employed by the CIA and the Reinhard Gehlen BND. Schact was also a close friend of Clay Shaw, charged by New Orleans District Attorney Jim Garrison with involvement in the assassination of John F. Kennedy. Brussell says that "Schacht guided Onassis's shipyards in rebuilding the German and Japanese war fleets." I see no reason to imagine, nor evidence to suggest that Onassis's Nazi connections were terminated after World War II.

Onassis was sexually involved with Eva Peron. Of Peron, John Judge says in the article "Good Americans": "Evita got her funds from the Nazi treasures stolen by Martin Bormann at the end of the war, and put hundreds of millions in the 'Evita Peron Foundation' and Swiss bank accounts. This money aided men like Josef Mengele, Heinrich Dorge, Hjalmar Schacht (who had worked under Herman Abs at the Reichsbank, Rudolf Freude, Dr. Fritz Thyssen, Dr. Gustav Krupp, Otto Skorzeny, and others." As Judge is apt to say, the same names keep cropping up.

Lebedev's *Treason for my Daily Bread* and Flammonde's *The Kennedy Conspiracy* implicate Bormann in the assassination of JFK. According to Edwards and Dunne in *A Study of a Master Spy*, "Official Washington knew Martin Bormann, Deputy Fuhrer of Hitler's Germany, master minded the international 'Die Spinne' (Spider) underground organization which is planning to revive Nazism as soon as West Germany is adequately rearmed by the United States. Official Washington seems disinterested."

Other correlations are provided by Mae Brussell: "The Howard Hughes organization... has long retained Carl Byour Associates [referred to as Byoir in the Skeleton Key] as its public relations arm. Throughout the war Byour represented Nazi bankers and industrialists and the I.G. Farben interests. One of its clients was Ernest Schmitz, member of I.G. Farben and the German American Board of Trade. A lucrative Byour client was the Frederick Flick Group. Flick, a Nuremberg defendant released by McCloy, was the single greatest power behind the Nazi military muscle."

Was Aristotle Onassis the monster that Bruce Roberts portrayed him as? All we can say with certainty is that he ran with the breed.

Roberts' story finally contains portions believable and unbelievable. I am left wondering whether Bruce Roberts really was privy to the inside track or making educated guesses based upon his research... or even making connections with stories in the tabloid press, as lurid then as it is now.

Prior to corresponding with Caruana I assumed that Roberts' contact with Mae Brussell was probably the key to much of his knowledge. I reasoned that if he was familiar enough with Brussell to give the *Gemstone File* to her, then he was probably no more nor less than an amateur conspiratologist, aware of the content of her encyclopedic conspiracy programs and conspiratorial worldview, as well as other cloak and dagger literature of the day. It is interesting that the Skeleton Key pointedly does not mention Brussell's researches (or precious little of anyone else's, for that matter, although other researchers were consulted in the preparation of Gemstone). Caruana, however, downplays Roberts' association with Brussell, who she knew as well.

"Roberts was far from an amateur conspiratologist. Between Mae Brussell, and Bruce Roberts, it was Mae who was the amateur. She was a 'filer,' as anyone who knew her would tell you. I don't think she ever had any direct connection with the events she described. (Except for her contact with Roberts, which she misunderstood at the time.)...

"Bruce Roberts, on the other hand, got a lot of his information direct from the source, and from his own experiences.

He also 'traded' his Gemstone letters to sources around the world, who in turn supplied him with information that was unobtainable elsewhere. It was a worldwide information network on the highest level."

Maybe.

Finally, was Bruce Roberts' purpose to paint himself as the consummate insider, hobnobber with kingmakers and kingslayers, or did he really have a true conception of the forces behind world events? The flawed nature of the Gemstone, its lack of sources and verifiable facts, make it difficult and perhaps ultimately impossible to tell.

Correspondence with Stephanie Caruana has filled in (at least in my mind) many key points that make Bruce Roberts a real person, "a player, not a sideline sitter," as she says. My own feeling is that he was sincere and, with his letters, attempting a work that is still continuing, primarily through the circulation of the Skeleton Key synopsis. I don't believe that he was the James Bond that Caruana maintains he was, but I don't believe he was Caspar Milquetoast, either. My guess is that he was something closer to human: a combination of both.

For making the attempt that Gemstone represents (and taking the chance, if only in his own mind, of dying for it), I respect Bruce Roberts, even though the product of his efforts (admittedly judged by the Skeleton Key and not his original letters) is in many respects uneven, derivative, and perhaps wrong.

The Skeleton Key exudes a subjectivity and paranoia that cripples much of its believability, that puts into question Roberts' discoveries and opinions. These are shortcomings that have kept Gemstone confined to the tight orbits of conspiracy aficionados and the reason I consider it unlikely that the Mafia ever considered the document a threat to their dominion. Still, I am convinced that Roberts did have contacts high and low, and pursued his quest in an attempt to fathom an evil that must have seemed to swirl about him. The *Gemstone File* was an honest attempt to expose international corruption, using whatever sources Roberts could find, and there is a possibility that it contains a clear reflection of the sinister shapes that continue to move in the darkness.

The Godfather, Part IV

Robert Anton Wilson

How much of the *Gemstone File* is true? Not much, I'd say; but I do feel sure that the basic thesis — America's conquest by gangsters and thugs — is substantially accurate, even though most "good citizens" would rather die, even in prolonged torture, than to face the facts.

Since thinking about conspiracies is neither illegal, nor immoral, nor fattening, I have often wondered why people have such a powerful tabu against examining who owns and runs this nation.

Why is it that, with a literary tradition in which conspiracy stories are among our "classics" — e.g. Shakespeare's *Julius Caesar, Henry IV, Parts I, II, III* and *Richard III*, Conan Doyle's *The Red Headed League*, most of Raymond Chandler, Dickens' *Oliver Twist*, all of John le Carre, Pynchon's *Gravity's Rainbow*, to name only a few — we still fear to think about such clandestine and murderous struggles in the "real" world?

Why is it that, in that "real" world, our legal system recognizes conspiracy as a criminal offense, but we still have a conditioned reflex that makes us regard any conspiracy researchers as a "nut case?"

And why is it that we all know the word "paranoid," but hardly anybody can think of words for *rational suspicion* or *rational fear* — even though both of these would appear necessary for survival in a world where every major government has a secret police agency and every corporation and political party has a "dirty tricks" department?

Thunder and Tabu

After decades of mulling this mystery — why are most people so terrified of tabu ideas about their rulers — I think I finally found the answer in the 18th Century Neapolitan sociologist Giambastica Vico, best known today as the inventor of what we call transpersonal linguistics (the study of how language influences perception and social "reality"). Vico had lots of other ideas, however, but wrote them in a rather opaque style — sensibly, since in Naples, at that time, the Holy Inquisition still occasionally barbecued people who had original notions.

Vico seems to imply, in his indirect Neapolitan way, that the first god was the thunder, and morality derives from traumatic experiences with thunder (i.e. "negative imprints"). Vico was the first to study the cave peoples, and to suggest that Bigfoot was a survivor of that age; and from cave art, Vico imaginatively deduced that anything that happened just before thunder roared in the sky was construed by our ancestors as arousing the anger of some giant being up there — i.e. "god."

Thus, imagine some caveman about to crack his brother on the head with an ax, when the thunder crashed. Obviously, the Thunder God disapproved of killing your relatives. For the next 30,000 years we have kept the tabu, "Never kill members of your own tribe." War goes on, perhaps, because in those early days the thunder never struck when somebody was getting ready to hit a "foreigner" (non-tribe member) with an ax.

Can you think of a better explanation of why most people, although they seem sane, look with natural horror upon murder (killing tribe members) but have no such horror or loathing or even mild discomfort about mass murder (war)? Or why they think those who do object to mass murder (war) are somehow "queer" or bizarre or (most amazingly) "indecent?"

Or consider the idiocies of our "decent" sexual codes. If I understand Vico's hints, some delightful sexual dalliances got put under Big Tabu because just when somebody was trying them, the sky roared again.

"Well, we can't do it that way after all. Damn!"

And another tabu lasted 30,000 years or longer...

In some cases, nobody could figure out what had pro-
voked the anger of the sky-god — why the thunder roared at
a certain moment. The early shamans must have given this a
lot of thought. They finally decided that since nothing had
happened, the god must have gotten royally pissed off at
something somebody said. And so, bit by bit, or byte by byte,
more and more ideas and images were denied verbal expression, because the Thunder God might get into a frightful snit
if he heard them being uttered.

Then the idea dawned that He Who Thundereth From on
High might get royally pissed over things we were merely
thinking...

Thus, we still have long lists of unspeakable words and
unthinkable ideas, because the old brain, where primitive imprints are stored, still fears that primordial Thunder God
(who appears, incidentally on the soundtrack of almost every
horror movie, when the director wants to activate our deepest
collective anxieties).

Even people who think they have outgrown the Thunder
God and the tabus of the Old Stone Age will find certain
atavistic fears creeping up on them, in some modern works
of art which deliberately violate tabu and conventional ways
of thinking. Sen. Jesse Helms — who is financed by people
who make their living by literally poisoning us — can always
make headlines by finding a new work of art which triggers
the dread of the Thunder God.

The same is true of the present book, so I warn you that,
if you think certain ideas and images can be dangerous to us
— can literally bring down "curses from heaven" (the roars of
the Tyrant in the Sky) — this book can be extremely hazardous to your health. If you are in the Political Correctness
business, perhaps the safest course is not to read the book
at all, and just issue a general condemnation of it based on
your ideas about what might be found in here if you dared to
read the eldritch and unhallowed pages that follow. Of
course, condemning books you haven't read always sounds
goofy to the uninitiate and ungodly; but then condemning
what you know nothing about represents a long and honor-
able tradition among censors, who have never worried about

the fact that they very often sound goofy, batty, buggy or just plain whacko to the rest of us.

After all, censorship consists chiefly of reading books that are suspected of causing degeneracy and depravity among their readers. The censor is therefore, by definition, a person constantly risking self-destruction and moral decay. What Dorian Grey—like loathesomeness must result after three or four years of hard work as a censor staggers the imagination — the mind conjures images from *Tales from the Crypt*. But some persist in this risky profession for five years, for ten, sometimes for twenty. The total corruption that must result involves thoughts of the lowest and most excremental pits of Dante's Inferno.

One can admire the courage of those who undertake such perilous quests, but one also wonders a bit about their fool-hardiness or downright masochism.

Consider: Charles Keating, who first came to the public notice as leader of the National Organization for Decent Literature, spent years scrutinizing the centerfolds of *Playboy*, which he suspected of being hazardous. After intensely studying 12 of these American beauties every year, Keating was indeed corrupted. He currently stands convicted of massive junk bond swindles and embezzlements, and is accused of bribing five U.S. Senators — who already proceeded to "the hard stuff" — *Penthouse* or *Hustler*.

Far more terrifying than erotica, certain ideas have been banned, repressed, outlawed, punished violently and generally forbidden to consciousness throughout history. Not surprisingly, the most damned of all damned ideas is the notion that the local rulers are not the benevolent Santa Claus types they always pretend to be but are quite the reverse of that.

Tabu on Thinking About Evil in High Places

Why was even a raving mad Hitler obeyed up until the last day in the bunker? Why did the Russian peoples try desperately to believe in Stalin until that bloody lunatic was dead and buried? For the same reason that the majority of Americans do not want to hear about the involvement of

George Bush and the CIA in the international drug business and its associated corruption of law enforcement and its trail of murder and neo-Nazi conspiracy. It is dangerous to talk about such things, and with the Thunder God still a living presence in the collective unconscious, it feels dangerous to even think about them.

Let us consider the "psychology" — or better yet, the physiology of the Power Elite, i.e. the men Buckminster Fuller called the "Great Pirates."

All of us, men and women and those who aren't sure, have some testosterone (the principle "male" hormone) and some estrogen (the principle "female" hormone) from conception onward, but before we even get out of the womb our chemistry starts to change. Males are born with more testosterone, females with more estrogen — and after puberty, the amount of testosterone in men and estrogen in women increases steeply, determining most of our adult behavior for the next 30 or 40 years, and only decreases again in old age. Let me quote some data from Michael Hutchison's *The Anatomy of Sex and Power.*

Men "see" more sexuality than women do. Psychologist Frank Sal, showing a film of a man and woman talking, found male students perceived more sexual flirtation in the film, while women saw only friendliness. We "see" what the chemicals in our brain program us to see.

There also seems to be a circular-causal or "feedback" loop in testosterone level. Testosterone makes men act "dominant," but acting dominant also increases the production of testosterone.

Thus, one study of male tennis players found higher testosterone levels among the winners than among the losers, one hour after competition. (Ct. Henry Kissinger's famous and quite accurate remark, "Power is the ultimate aphrodisiac.")

Wrestlers at Harvard also showed higher testosterone among the winners than the losers, and on a more intellectual level of competition, medical students showed higher testosterone one day after graduation. Conversely, the humiliating and terrifying experience of arriving at Army boot camp lowers testosterone.

The testesterone/estrogen ratio also relates directly to the fact that most men are more violent than women. Researcher June Reinisch of Rutgers University found that both boys and girls given certain precursors of the testosterone — chemicals that increase testosterone production in the body — immediately become more aggressive. In fact, Reinisch's subjects, both boys and girls became twice as aggressive as a control group not given the hormones. The aggressivity indexes were:

Boys given the hormone: 9.75; other boys 4.88.

Girls given the hormone: 4.0; other girls 2.6.

Note that testosterone boosters approximately doubled aggression in both sexes, and that boys already have so much more testosterone than girls that, even without boosters, they are still nearly twice as aggressive. This result was so totally contrary to previous scientific doctrine that Reinish was unwilling to publish her findings at first. As she later said, "The results were so shocking that I actually sat on them for a year. I was afraid to publish them."

Similarly, in a joint study by the Clarke Institute of Psychiatry and Mount Sinai Hospital, both in Toronto, the hormone levels of 20 rapists were compared with those of 20 nonrapists. The rapists consistently had higher precursors of testosterone.

In another study males with a history of low sex drive showed an increase in sexual fantasy and desire when given testosterone. Physiologist Julian Davidson, who did this research, says that "testosterone is the biological substrate of desire, at least in men."

These patterns took on new meaning when Frank Farley, a University of Wisconsin psychologist, found that male sensation-seekers or novelty-seekers have "rather high testosterone levels." Farley named these types Big T's and called the other extreme, those who want stability, little t's.

Farley found that the biggest Big T's are male and young (made up of the highest testosterone group in any society.) Big T adolescents tend to be very creative or prone to delinquency, or sometimes show both tendencies (like the charming and terrifying sociopath in Clockwork Orange.) Farley also found the Big T's, whether creative or criminal, are more inclined than average males to self-destructive behaviors like drug abuse, smoking and alcoholism, and have twice as many auto accidents as little t's. In short, they have the attitudes Nietzsche called "Herrenmoral" — the ethics of pirates, conquistadores and gunslingers.

Little t's, Farley says, "cling to certainty and predictability, avoiding risks and the unfamiliar — neither creative nor criminal — they're grey." They also like to fantasize that the Big T's are "protecting" them — a fantasy the mass media is paid to encourage — and never, never want to know about the "Herrenmoral" that actually guides Big T thinking. The little t's are governed by what Nietzsche called "Sklavmoral" — the morality of slaves and serfs, or paleolithic fear of the Thunder God, of the "domesticated primate."

Obviously, little t's are the wimps in any crowd, most people are middle t's, and the violent Big T's rise to the top in every society. If the *Gemstone File* reminds you of Seutonius' *Lives of the Caesars*, it is because the same types rule all empires, in ancient Rome or modern America. Bruce Roberts has merely given us the front names and hind names and home addresses of some of our current versions of Nero, Caligula, Tiberius and Company.

The Mafiazation of America

When my father was young, back around the turn of this century, the America Mafia was a small bunch of hoodlums in New York known only for extorting money from other Italian immigrants. Today, it is almost impossible to discover an area of American life and finance that the Mob hasn't penetrated and perverted. Businesses that do not at least occasionally deal with the Mafia are as rare as kangaroos in the Royal Ballet.

Mafiosi own major hotels; they're as ubiquitous as roaches in the restaurant business; they have funded their own banks and own shares in others; they own large hunks of movie studios (e.g. Paramount); they've taken over whole labor unions (e.g the Teamsters); they even have a weird (but well documented) symbiosis with the C.I.A. In a sense our whole national identity has been reshaped in the Mafia mold.

Nobody aware of the facts can deny that this much of the *Gemstone File* is true.

And the paranoia that infests any person or group that has to deal with the Mob has become pervasive in every aspect of American life. While naive professors write silly books about the "greening" of America or the "closing of the American mind," the major fact of our century goes unrecorded by Academia — the Mafiazation of the United States.

Bucky Fuller even claimed, in his last book, *Grunch of Giants*, that the Mafia is one of the four principle international powers in the modern world, along with the oil cartels, the Atomic Energy corporations and the international banks.

All this has been accomplished by our anti-drug laws, which allow the mob to sell for $200 (or more) a day's worth of heroin stupor or cocaine excitement that would sell for less than a dollar in a free market. Every year that these anti-drug laws continue, the Mafia gets richer and buys or bullies its way into more areas of previously "respectable" business.

Pulitzer Prize columnist Jack Anderson has charged, in his column and in a recent 2-hour TV documentary that the Mafia killed President John F. Kennedy, much as the *Gemstone File* claims. I happen to agree with Anderson and *Gemstone* on this issue, on the basis of the evidence; but in a sense it doesn't matter whether one agrees or not. The terrible fact is that the Mafia is known to be so powerful that most people are ready to believe they could kill a President and get away with it.

They kill politicians and investigating magistrates every week or two in Italy, don't they?

The major reason to end our "war against drugs," to me, is that the "war" is in practical terms a vast crusade to keep up the profits of the Mafia and to increase the power of organized crime in every nook and cranny of America. One has to be very naive to assume the Mob doesn't know this and isn't financing most of the "anti-drug" propaganda one sees on TV and reads in the press. The only people who have a sane and rational reason to keep recreational drugs illegal are the Mafia, George Bush and other Mobsters (in and out of the CIA) who profit from anti-drug laws and the black market these laws have created.

If drugs were legalized, the Mafia/CIA cabal would not go

away — it is too rich now, for that — but at least it would stop growing at its present alarmingly cancerous rate. It seems likely, reflecting on the Mafia's growth between 1907 (the anti-heroin law) and 1992 (laws against hundreds of drugs), that if these laws remain on the books another 20 years, the Mob will quite likely own just about the whole country. In that case, if you want to see America's future just sit through all three of *The Godfather* films twice and read the last two centuries of Sicilian history.

If drugs were legalized, every one of us would be safer in our homes and on the streets. Muggings, purse snatchings, burglaries etc. would decrease the first day addicts could get a fix for a dollar instead of having to steal $400 or more to feed the monkey on their backs. (Most male addicts have to boost that much in property to get $200 from an underworld fence, and $200 a day is about standard for a heavy heroin habit.)

If drugs were legalized, many female addicts would no longer be forced into lives of prostitution — and the Mob would lose another source of revenue, and become less powerful in our political and financial structure. "Politics" and "business" might not forever remain words that are largely synonymous with murder and robbery — as they are today.

If drugs were legalized, the abnormal and pathological crowding in our prisons would end. This overcrowding in our prisons is probably a major factor in the notorious inability of our penology to "reform" anybody — as illustrated by the fact that most ex-cons are imprisoned again within one year after release.

Any ecologist or ethologist will tell you that all animals, including humans, become perverse, violent and a bit crazy when overcrowded. Stuffing our jails until the walls bulge with largely harmless pot-smokers and acid heads is a formula guaranteed to increase our ever-accelerating high crime rate. Being in prison for 5 to 10 years is just like being on the New York subway during a "rush hour" that lasts that long: everybody comes out wired and mean.

If drugs were legalized, vast amounts of police time and energy would be freed up to deal with violent crimes, instead or being wasted on busting a few kids who like to smoke weed when they listen to their favorite Rock records — or using Machievellian techniques, elephantine patience and huge quantities of time and money to hunt down a few psychology majors who want to try LSD or MDMA to find out for themselves what altered consciousness is all about.

The cost of administering our anti-drug laws doubled under Nixon, doubled again between Nixon and Reagan, doubled one more time since 1980 when Nancy Reagan took office with Ronnie as her front, and is now doubling almost yearly — and there are more drugs everywhere, not less. Anybody who thinks this result was not planned with maximum profit in mind would believe in the chastity of Long Dong Silver.

As in all other cases where a government attempts to control the private habits of its citizens, the cost goes up and up, and up, and up, and the "problem" gets worse, not better. Have we completely forgotten the lessons of alcohol prohibition in which the same total failure to cure alcoholism resulted and nobody profited by the gangsters?

When she was president, Nancy Reagan once proposed that the government should attempt to arrest and imprison every drug user in the country. Nobody can guess how much it would cost to find and arrest everybody who uses an illegal chemical occasionally — and it would obviously require a completely totalitarian government to undertake such a task — but even if it were done, we would have a bill of $15,000,000,000 every year to keep all these people in jail, according to the calculations of congressman Pete Shark.

We are already the number one debtor nation in the world; can we afford to pay the taxes for $15,000,000,000 every year, to keep these galoots in jail, and for at least another $15,000,000,000 (or more likely $30,000,000,000) every year to maintain the totalitarian state necessary to ensnare them all?

At this point, does anybody still believe that the "war on drugs" can be successful at any cost less than that, and without utter totalitarianism — without a bug in every bedroom, a mail cover on every citizen?

If drugs were legalized, the court system might be unclogged to the extent that a civil suit brought in 1992 might actually get to judgement before 2002, or a teenage punk arrested for rape might stand trial before he gets his first social security check.

Considering that the profits from this racket run into hundreds of billions every year, does anybody still believe that the laws which create the racket remain on the books due to "prejudice" or "ignorance?" The laws remain because they are making huge profits for the Great Pirates — the Big T's. As J.R. "Bob" Dobbs, our greatest 20th century philosopher says, "The major errors by which most people are deceived are (1) the belief that our rulers are dumb, and (2) the belief that they mean well. They are not dumb and they don't mean well."

Tales from the Vatican Crypt

G.J. Krupey

Part 1

Gemstone Files entry for February, 1972:
"The day before [Bruce Roberts' father was allegedly murdered by Watergate 'Plumbers' Dale, Martinez, Gonzalez, and Barker in a San Francisco hospital], Tisseront [sic], head of the College of Cardinals at the Vatican, was pushed out of a Vatican window. Tisseront had followed the career of the present Pope, Montini (whose mother was Jewish). Montini sodium-morphate murdered Pope Pius XI; was banished from Rome for it by Pius XII; became Pope in 1963. Tisseront wrote it all down; called the Pope "The Deputy of Christ at Auschwitz," and the fulfillment of the Fatima 3 Prophecy: that "the anti-Christ shall rise to become head of the Church." Tisseront also wrote about all the suppressed secrets of the Roman Catholic Church: ie, that Jesus Christ was an Arab, born April 16, 6 BC at the rare conjunction of Saturn and Jupiter. Arab (Persian) astronomers (the Magi) came to Bethlehem to look for their king, an Arab baby and found him in a stable, because the Jews wouldn't let Arabs Mary and Joseph into their nice clean inns, even then. When Jesus overturned the tables of the money lenders at the Temple, the Jews had the Romans nail him to a Cross. He died

on the cross when the Roman soldiers stuck a spear in his side, pulled out his liver, and ate it. Tacitus, the Roman historian, described it all in a chunk of history deleted by the Church. Nero burned Rome but that didn't stop the spreading of Moses' teachings by the early Christians (Arabs). So the Romans decided to adopt the religion, clean it up, make Christ a Jew and Mary a virgin, and work out a Church State deal to fool the people in the name of God and country that had been operating ever since. Around 311 AD at the council of Nicasa [sic], the Christian Orthodoxy was established: a dissenting bishop had his hands chopped off; another bishop was assigned to round up all the old copies of the *Bible* and destroy them in favor of the "revised" de-Arabized version. Cleaned up Matthew, Mark, Luke, and John were declared "it," the other Gospels were declared apocryphal, and heretical. Roman Emperor Constantine became the first Christian emperor.

Later, during the holy crusades, the *Bible* was again rewritten to include Jesus's warning against the 'yellow race.'

And that is the Gospel according to Bruce Roberts, or whoever provided him with that bizarre revision of two thousand years of Christianity. Jesus an Arab? Suppression by the early Church of dissident gospels? The *Bible*, the sacred word of God, rewritten, revised, and altered to accomodate the changing political climate and the ambitions of Church and State? A half-Jewish Pope who collaborated with the Nazis and murdered his way to the Triple Crown? Absurd? Impossible? Unthinkable? Blasphemous?

Who else but a paranoid lunatic, one who thought that the Kennedy assassination was the result of a turf-war to control organized crime in America between Howard Hughes and Aristotle Onassis, who else but someone like that, like Bruce Roberts, would even entertain such ideas, let alone believe them? But is there any validity to what he claimed? To dissect his claims one by one:

According to his obituary in the *New York Times* (1) Eugene Cardinal Tisserant, age 87, died of a heart attack on 2/21/72 at the Regina Apostalorum Clinic in Albano, Italy, a "hill village twenty-six miles southeast of Rome." He had checked into the clinic in July of 1971 to be treated "for a form of prostatic hypertrophy," that is, enlargement of the

prostate gland, a common and potentially fatal ailment in el-
derly men.

Tisserant had a long and distinguished career in the
Church. An Oriental languages scholar (he spoke eleven different tongues), he did field research in Jerusalem and other
areas of the Middle East, he was curator of Oriental manu-
scripts in the Vatican library, and as administrator of it, he
reorganized and modernized it. If there was a suppressed secret at the heart of the Christian religion, and it was documented, Tisserant would be the man who would have known.

Tisserant was Dean of the College of Cardinals during the
elections of Popes John XXIII and Paul VI, two Popes who
initiated the reforms that proceeded from the Second Vatican
Council. As a conservative, Tisserant felt "uneasy about the
tides of change swelling the Church," yet it was also claimed
that he "had little interest in Church politics."

A workaholic despite his advanced age, Tisserant retired
only because of "papal pressure"—from Paul VI, the Pope that
Bruce Roberts claimed poisoned Pius XI, and which Tisserant
documented in his diary. The fact that Tisserant was being
pressured by the Pope to retire [Paul VI had apparently insti-
tuted mandatory retirement for Vatican clerics, another inno-
vation], and that Tisserant was visited on the morning he
died by Vatican Secretary of State Jean Cardinal Villot, who
was as liberal as Tisserant was conservative, and who "con-
veyed the blessings of Pope Paul VI" may have led Roberts to
believe that Tisserant was murdered. It was sometime between February 1972 and January 1973 that Roberts received—or claimed to receive—a copy of Tisserant's diary:

"January, 1973: Tisseront [sic] was dead—but as the
Church rushed to destroy every copy of his papers, Roberts
received one—and wrote a few of his own, released over New
Years':

1. "The Cover-Up of the Murder of Christ";.....

4. "Vietnam—Fatima 3—Holy Crusade."

[Numbers 2 and 3 are not relevant to this discussion.]

It is not impossible that Roberts received a document—
from what source he doesn't even hint—that purported to be
a copy of Tisserant's secret diary. It was apparently common
knowledge—or at least a common presumption—among
Vaticanologists that Tisserant was keeping diaries for the

purpose of eventual publication. Roberts could have been the victim of a hoaxer, if we charitably disregard the possibility of Roberts himself being that hoaxer. Or Roberts may have been merely guessing at solutions to fragmentary information that he may have been receiving from a variety of contradictory sources, and claiming to have the elusive documentation from high places in order to confer the aura of authority upon his own pet theories.

Whatever the reason, Bruce Roberts did not make up the claim that Pope Pius XI was murdered by poisoning, he merely added his own twist to it by accusing Giovanni Battista Montini, the then current Pope Paul VI, of being the guilty party. Other fingers have pointed at one Dr. Francesco Petacci, a Vatican physician and father of an actress, Clara Petacci, who just happened to be the mistress of Italian dictator Benito Mussolini (the pair would be executed together, and their corpses exposed to the abuses of a crowd of disillusioned former admirers).

Pius XI had been an early supporter of Mussolini's, having once declared him (December 20, 1926) "the man sent by Providence." (2) In 1929, Pius and Il Duce signed the Lateran Treaty, which in essence recognized Roman Catholicism as the sole official religion of the Italian state even as the Vatican itself was recognized as a sovereign state and the Pope as inviolable. Mussolini, for his part, received the tacit approval, if not blessings, of the papacy, which at this time feared the imminent eruption of godless Bolshevik revolutions. But Mussolini didn't uphold his end of the bargain on all counts, and in 1931 Pius gave the dictator a tongue-lashing in an official encyclical. Pius didn't seem to learn his lesson, because in 1933 he forged a similar concordat with yet another champion of Christian civilization, Adolf Hitler. The Nazis also reneged and Pius denounced Nazism in yet another encyclical in 1937. By this time even Pius had wised up, and regretting his former accomodationism with the two fascist regimes (not, it must be emphasized, because of their flagrant abuses of human rights, per se, but because of their flouting of the agreed-upon privileges and perogatives of the Catholic Church), he resolved to correct his error by condemning fascism-nazism in no uncertain terms. In February 1939, with the wholesale attacks on Jews and the rapid escalation towards another world war, Pius fell ill while working on his speech, and begged his doctors to keep him alive long enough to deliver it.

It was only twenty-four hours before he was to deliver the speech, on the tenth anniversary of the concordat with Mussolini, ironically enough, that he suddenly died. The text of the speech disappeared. Allegedly, Petacci, in his role as a Vatican physician, killed Pius by injecting him with a poison (probably not Roberts' ubiquitous sodium morphate), and embalming the body before an autopsy could be conducted. (3)

According to John Cornwall, this revelation originated in "a scurrilous book entitled *The Vatican Papers* by one Nino LoBello" whose source "was the private diary of the powerful French cardinal of that period, Eugene Tisserant." (4) Anthony Rhodes, in his book on the relations between the Popes and the fascist dictators, states:

"Since this was written [the passages dealing with the death of Pius XI], allegations have appeared in the French and Italian press (1972) that Pius XI in his last illness was assassinated at the order of Mussolini, who had learned of the contents of the Pope's coming speech. They are based on the revelations said to be contained in the memoirs of the late Cardinal Tisserant...Arguments for and against this thesis continue to be bandied about, and will doubtless be repeated when Cardinal Tisserant's memoirs are published." (5)

Rhodes discounts the assassination theory, noting that Pius, aged 82 years when he died on February 10, 1939, had nearly died in 1937 of a combination of "cardiac weakness, arteriosclerosis, and asthma", and he suffered another heart attack in November, 1938, (6) implying that it wouldn't have taken much to kill an old and ailing man like Pius. Rhodes also notes that the British Ambassador to the Vatican, D'Arcy Osborne, did not refer to any rumors or suspicions of assassination in his diplomatic cables to London at that time, and he would have had ample reason for publicizing any accusations of fascist murder of the Pope.

Another writer who recounts the tale of Mussolini's poisoning of Pius is Avro Manhattan (7). He also attributes Tisserant's unpublished diaries as the verification of this claim. Unlike Bruce Roberts, he does not claim to have seen a copy of Tisserant's actual papers, but claims for his source a mutual friend of both himself and the deceased Pope, Dom Luigi Sturzo, priest and founder of the Italian Catholic Action Party in the 1920's. Manhattan claims that Tisserant's diaries were removed from the Cardinal's home in France (he doesn't say by whom) upon his death, and taken to the safety of a Swiss bank vault. Supposedly, Tisserant himself had given strict instructions (again, Manhattan does not reveal to whom) that under no circumstances were the diaries to fall into the hands of the Vatican. No doubt, as one well advanced in the Vatican hierarchy, Tisserant (8) knew only too well the Church's penchant for rewriting history to its convenience.

Contrary to the Roberts-Gemstone version, none of these sources implicate Monsignor Montini, later Pope Paul VI, in the murder of Pope Pius XI. It is significant that Rhodes indicates 1972, the year of the deaths of both Tisserant and Roberts' father, as the year when the French and Italian press began to publicize the rumors that Pius XI was murdered on orders from Mussolini. Roberts could have gleaned this from readings of the foreign press, and as speculated before, twisted the theory to suit his own purposes. Roberts could not have gotten his information from either Manhattan or Cornwell since their respective books were published after the *Gemstone Files* were initially released, and after Bruce Roberts died in 1976 (1982 for Manhattan's, 1989 for Cornwell's). However, Manhattan wrote many books on the Vatican, and could well have recounted the Pius XI murder story in an earlier volume than the one cited here, and which Roberts could have conceivably read.

The other allegations made against Montini/Pope Paul VI in the *Gemstone Files* also do not seem to bear any resemblance to reality. There is little reason to believe that Montini's mother was Jewish. This just seems to be a gratuitous dose of anti-Semitism, as Roberts seems to be implying that Montini's alleged Jewish maternity (which would officially make him a Jew, no matter what his religion, by Orthodox Jewish law) made him a fraud, unfit to be Pope. Whatever Montini's mother's ethnicity, she was an apparent devout Catholic who had married into an upper-class Lombard family which had produced clerics over the past five centuries. Montini's "banishment" from Rome by Pius XII (Eugenio Pacelli) came in 1954—fifteen years after Pius XII's coronation and fifteen years during which Montini served Pius as an advisor and unofficial Secretary of State—and came a year after he had fallen afoul of arch-conservative Pro-Secretary of State for Extraordinary Affairs, Cardinal Tardini, over the issue of Montini's advocacy of the French "worker-priest" movement, a precursor of the current Liberation Theology. His banishment consisted of being named Archbishop of Milan, barely a hardship considering that the position was practically assured, traditionally, election to the office of cardinal; an office Tardini rejected in 1953, according to rumor, merely to prevent the (as he saw it) pro-Socialist Montini from accepting the Red Hat when the Pope offered it to them both. (9)

As for Montini/Paul VI being "the Deputy of Christ at Auschwitz," the closest Montini got to the site of the infamous Nazi concentration camp was in 1923 when he served as secretary to the papal nuncio in Warsaw, when Auschwitz was still an obscure village in the south of Poland, near Cracow, called Oswiecim. Montini's health failed him in Poland, and after six months he was sent back to Rome, not to step foot out of Italy again (at least according to available records) until his papacy. (10)

The allegation that Montini was the fulfillment of the third Fatima prophecy—that "the anti-Christ shall rise to become head of the Church"—is more hearsay. It not only requires a belief in the veracity of the Fatima incident, but in the reality of the anti-Christ and its converse, in other words, in a belief in Catholic theology. Without that belief, terms like "anti-Christ" are meaningless, even as metaphor. No doubt many outraged traditionalist Catholics, and Cardinal Tisserant may or may not have been one of them, viewed Paul VI as the very devil in view of the Vatican II reforms for which he was primarily responsible, but Christians have been in the habit of playing pin-the-tail-on-the-anti-Christ since the Book of Revelations was written, and one man's anti-Christ has often been another's saint. As for the "Fatima 3 Prophecy," it refers to what was supposed to have been told to three shepherd children near Fatima, Portugal in 1917 by none other than the Virgin Mary herself. She prophesied to them, so the story goes, that the world would witness a "horrible, horrible war" (the world was already in the middle of a horrible war), that Russia must be converted (to Catholicism) or else this horrible, horrible war was guaranteed, and a third, allegedly even grimmer prophecy that the Church refused to make public. (11)

Over the years, rumors have circulated as to the contents of that third prophecy. Every possible assertion has been delivered, with varying degrees of conviction, including the one favored by Bruce Roberts. It has been claimed that Montini's patron, Pope Pius XII, a man given to seeing "apparitions," nearly fainted upon being told what the third prophecy was. This legend may have given rise to the speculation on the part of Roberts and others, that the revelation was the near-future succession to the papal throne of the anti-Christ.

In the January, 1973 Gemstone entry, Roberts cryptically links "Fatima 3" with "Vietnam" and "Holy Crusade." It was actually no secret that the Vatican considered—and used—the Fatima "prophecies" as one of its most effective weapons in its Holy Crusade against godless communism, a Crusade engineered by none other than Pius XII, the firm believer in the Fatima "visitation," himself.

Ironically enough, Roberts may have confused Montini with Pius XII when he accused the former of being the "Deputy of Christ at Auschwitz." The controversy still rages over the extent of the Vatican's complicity with the fascist states. Pius XI championed and engineered concordats with both Mussolini and Hitler before the scales fell from his eyes. His successor, Pius XII, has been the focus of even more bewilderment and invective over his official silence in condemning the *Nazi Endlosung*—Final Solution—of the Jews and fascist war crimes in general. As papal nuncio to Germany in the 1930's, Pius XII (then Cardinal Pacelli), according to Avro Manhattan, helped pave the way to power for Hitler by ordering the Catholic Center Party to dissolve, thus making it easier for the Nazis to win the 1933 election. By his lack of forceful condemnation of Third Reich policies, Manhattan and similar critics charge, Pius XII tacitly encouraged Hitler's intransigence and helped bring the onslaught of World War II and its accompanying horrors. Other critics have been even more severe, accusing Pius XII of having been pro-German (he spent many years in Germany as nuncio, and often expressed his affection for the German people, which as one of his defenders correctly states, is not the same thing as being pro-Nazi) and anti-Semitic. Whatever the consequences of Pius XII's policies, his major intention seems to have been securing the Church from persecution in the fascist states, a policy that was not always successful. A common explanation by Catholic apologists for the Vatican's reluctance to condemn the fascists in blunt, unmitigated terms was the fear that by such harangues the Pope would endanger not only Catholics under fascist sway, but also provoke the Nazis into committing even more brutal atrocities against Jews and other minorities. (12)

The current Pope, John Paul II (Karol Wojtyla) has also been accused of being a Nazi collaborator, even before he entered the Church. According to some Jewish authors, fundamentalist Protestant preachers, and certain disciples of conspiriologist Mae Brussell, John Paul II worked in Nazi-occupied Poland for either Solvay Drugs of the I.G. Farben cartel in a factory at Auschwitz, or as a salesman for Farben's chemical division, selling Zyklon B, the deadly cyanide gas, directly to the Nazi camp at Auschwitz. Supposedly, John Paul, an actor by inclination, entered the priesthood in 1946 in order to escape arrest and trial as a Nazi war criminal. (13) While fundamentalists of certain sects cannot be regarded as objective or reliable in matters concerning the Catholic Church, Avro Manhattan (14) reports that not even Wojtyla's closest friend and confidante, Bishop Andre Deskur, would reveal what John Paul did during the war years. Manhattan calls this "Wojtyla's twilight period, not to be found in any public record." (15) It is possible, but extremely unlikely, that Roberts may have heard something about the alleged Nazi connection of this then obscure Polish cardinal, and either deliberately or unwittingly confused him with Pope Paul VI. But it is most likely—barring the even more unlikely possibility that Roberts did have a copy of Tisserant's papers and faithfully paraphrased them in the *Gemstone Files*—that Roberts merely let his paranoid imagination run wild with certain persistent rumors that appealed to his anti-Catholic prejudices, and mixed them together to villify the Pope at that time, Paul VI.

But if Bruce Roberts was really the insider that he liked to portray himself as, why did he not mention in the *Gemstone Files* the allegations that Paul VI was a CIA asset?

Despite his upper-class background and the patronage of the reactionary Pius XII, Paul VI developed left-wing sympathies and continued, as Pope, the "dialogue" between the Church and the Kremlin begun by his predecessor John XXIII. When John XXIII died in 1963, CIA analysts predicted Montini's election to the papacy, an event that did not please them, Montini being too "liberal" for the company's liking. Yet Montini had ties to the CIA going back to World War II when, in his capacity as officer of the Papal Secretariat, he had passed on information to the OSS, the CIA's wartime parent agency. As Montini was one of four heads of Vatican Intelligence and the keeper of the key to the Vatican's secret code, it was a role he was well suited for. (17) After the war, as archbishop of Milan, "he turned over to the CIA comprehensive dossiers on politically active priests. These were to be used to influence the Italian elections of 1960." (18) To express their gratitude, the CIA made generous donations to various Milanese charities under Montini's benefaction. Despite his services to them, the CIA was leery of Montini and was determined to do what they could to prevent him from becoming Pope, which in hindsight, must not have been very much. (19)

It would seem difficult to understand what sort of game Montini/Paul VI was playing until one reflects on the simple, constant fact of Catholic foreign policy: no matter what the relationship between the Vatican and any state or ideology, or the personal political implications of individual Popes, the Vatican's chief concern is the preservation and extension of its own power and influence. the Vatican accomodates itself with whatever secular ideology happens to be currently dominant, and looks to the future to ascertain the likelihood of that dominance continuing. In the 1960's, many in the Vatican hierarchy, including two Popes (John XXIII and Paul VI) were convinced that capitalism was waning and the future was assured for communism. It was an opinion that millions of people believed—or wanted to believe—and there seemed a great deal of evidence to support it. The Church was preparing itself for existence in a potential communist world, at the same time as it continued to placate the power of the still dominant capitalist West, namely the United States. The Church was never in favor of either system, because neither system placed the Church at the center of its ideology. So the Church, being the repository of truth for all mankind, knew how to play the two off against each other by appropriating selected rhetoric from both sides for its own propaganda purposes, to appear the lone voice of sanity and humane philosophy in a world menaced by the militance of the two contending nuclear super powers. (20)

It was this inability to see the big picture, to reduce everything to the Machiavellian machinations of diabolical individual conspirators, that I think discredits the *Gemstone Files* — at least in this particular instance — as being a reliable source on covert politics. If anything went out a window anywhere on February 21, 1972, it was Bruce Roberts' credibility.

Part 2

It is the second part of the February, 1972 Gemstone entry that makes the most mind-blowing claims, those dealing with the true identity of Jesus and "The Cover-Up of the Murder of Christ" (as he puts it later in the January, 1973 entry). While there is never any shortage of those willing to believe the worst — no matter how bizarre — accusations against the Catholic Church, it never seems to occur to many of these non-Catholic Christians, who hold that "true" Christianity was perverted by Rome until rescued by Protestantism, that there may be something wrong with their religion in essence, and not merely in the Roman version of it.

These are the same sorts who would lap up everything Roberts claimed about the Vatican and its "anti-Christ" Pope, and then go into a state of hypertension upon reading Roberts' "revelations" concerning Jesus from Tisserant's alleged secret diary. Whether Roberts really believed these things or whether he was just gleefully indulging in a little subversion of cherished certitudes is neither verifiable or relevant. He had to have made it up, because he got too many minor details wrong for it to have come from the papers of a

Middle Eastern scholar like Tisserant. Roberts claims that the Magi who came to Bethlehem were "Arab (Persian) astronomers." The original Magi—the Three Wise Men—were "the three stars in the belt of Orion, pointing to Osiris' star Sothis (Sirius), which 'rose in the east' to announce the coming of the Savior at the season of the Nile flood. These three belt stars were still called Magi in the Middle Ages." (21) By Roman times, when Jesus was said to have been born, Magi meant Persian astronomer-astrologers who were associated with the cult of Mithra, a Persian deity whose mythology and rituals were appropriated nearly wholesale by the later Christian cult as it sought to Romanize itself. In fact, the very story of the Magi searching out the newborn Messiah came directly from Mithraism. Roberts correctly surmised the astrological allegory of the nativity story, but muddled the Magi's ethnicity by claiming Persians (Iranians) are Arabs. They are a distinctly different ethnic group, and the only reason many people today confuse them with Arabs is because they are now Muslims, and most Americans think all Muslims are Arabs. It is unlikely that the exact date of Jesus's birth could have been known. Traditionally, December 25 has been regarded as the date of birth because it was the birth date of Mithra and a host of other pagan sun gods who were born during the winter solstice, the Dies Natalis Solis Invictus, birthday of the Invincible Sun. December 25 was not even officially adopted by the Christian Church, in Rome, until the fourth century CE, nearly four hundred years after Jesus's alleged birth. The Eastern Christian Churches never have accepted the date. The early Christian Church didn't even find the Savior's birthdate relevant. (22)

Roberts uses his claim of Jesus's concealed Arab identity to dish out some more anti-Semitism, making a crack about the Jews being unwilling "to let Arabs Mary and Joseph into their nice clean inns, even then." An ironic joke on Israel's ongoing expulsion of Palestinians from their land in order to provide more *Lebensraum* for Jewish immigrants (for those who think the analogy strained, consider that many Israeli critics of their government's policies, such as Israel Shahak, have described Israel as an apartheid state comparable to its ally South Africa), it is the only example of real humor in the

Skeleton Key, causing one to wonder if one of Gemstone's
many samizdat compilers didn't insert it.

Roberts sticks to the conventional outline of Jesus's life
when discussing the Crucifixion, until he claims that "the
Roman soldiers stuck a spear in his side, pulled out his liver,
and ate it." Obviously these legionnaires were the first and
ultimate communicants of the Eucharist!

Roberts' Christ does not rise from the dead, nor does he
indicate why a religion would rise—or be engineered—around
a crucified prophet who failed to come back to life. He next
claims that Tacitus, the Roman historian (c.55-117 CE) recorded the true story of the Crucifixion, but the Church "deleted" it. Not all of Tacitus's works have survived, and the
Church certainly did alter, rewrite, expunge, and destroy
works which ran counter to its self-image, so this is not an
impossibility. But as the Church was usually very thorough
in its destruction, it would be impossible to know that Tacitus had written such a thing unless it had either been referred to by some other contemporary writer (usually a Christian writer eager to refute it), or the Church had kept a copy
secretly. Since this information supposedly came to Roberts
from the secret papers of Tisserant, it would do to remember
that Tisserant was an expert on ancient documents and one
time head of the Vatican Library. Roberts then asserts that
Nero burned Rome (64 CE), a popular rumor at the time
which Tacitus believed and reported in his Annals. Nero
blamed the fire on the then-insignificant sect of Christians,
and began the first persecution of them, burning many of
them alive in his gardens.

However, there are scholars who doubt both the story of
Nero setting Rome on fire (he certainly didn't fiddle while it
happened, as there were no violins then) and the persecution
of the Christians, and point out that the Annals of Tacitus
are incomplete and most likely tampered with. The passage
which details the persecution of the Christians by Nero was
unknown, never referred to by any other writer, pro- or anti-
Christian in antiquity. It first surfaced in an edition printed
in Venice in 1468. (23) Despite this fact, it continues to be
cited as a genuine passage proving the existence, thirty-some
years after the crucifixion, of a large colony of Christians in

Rome and their unjust persecution by an emperor regarded as one of the wickedest and most depraved. (24)

Then, according to Roberts, to counteract the growing popularity of the Christian cult (who are here Arabs engaged in the "spreading of Moses' teachings"—if these Arabs accepted Moses' teachings, then wouldn't they be Jews?), "the Romans decided to adopt the religion, clean it up, make Christ a Jew and Mary a Virgin, and work out a Church State deal to fool the people in the name of God and country that has been operating ever since." This all sounds perfectly logical (except to those who persist in believing in the supernatural origin of Christianity), except for one thing: why would Romans, who were engaged for many years in a bitter war with Israel, make their new Savior/Son of God one of the despised Jews?

One theory holds that Christianity was in fact the product of the Roman ruling class who, in their efforts to subvert the Jewish rebellion against Roman rule in Palestine, devised the cult of the other-worldly, pacifist Messiah to castrate and contain the Jewish rebellion, as well as counter its growing influence within the Empire, especially among the slaves and other downtrodden, who were harkening to its apocalyptic egalitarianism. The primary exponent of this theory (if not the inventor of it) was Abelard Reuchlin, a Jewish apologist who claimed that the aristocratic Roman Piso clan actually wrote the *New Testament* and even cynically encoded the proof into the text itself. (25)

An obverse theory to the above suggests that the Jews devised Christianity as a Trojan Horse to subvert and overthrow the Empire of their conquerors, playing upon the seething discontent of the oppressed masses to overthrow the Empire. This theory is popular among certain anti-Semitic and white supremacist groups (those not enamored with the Christian Identity/Aryan Israel thing), and was supposedly verified by a Jewish writer, one Marcus Eli Ravage, in the 1920s. (26)

Both theories have their problems. While certain passages in the *New Testament* do indeed counsel a pacifist, quietist ethic that would ideally benefit an authoritarian power structure seeking to stifle all dissent and rebellion to funnel it into a scheme of post-mortem deferred reward (better known as pie in the sky by and by; see especially the Epistles of Paul), there are those troublesome passages such as Matthew 10:34-37 and Luke 22:36, which show so much ominous fascination with swords. A warning to the Jews and other malcontents, perhaps? If Christianity were a Jewish Trojan Horse, its success would have been a bittersweet, Pyrrhic victory, as well as a belated one: nearly three hundred years after the introduction of Christianity, after the Roman-Jewish war, after the destruction of the Jewish nation, the Roman Empire, still standing, became Christian and the Jews were scattered to the winds.

Fusing the two theories together results in a hybrid not too dissimilar to the Gemstone one: in brief, the Jewish resistance movement developed Christianity to subvert the Roman Empire, the Romans either caught onto it and rewrote it to their designs before the destruction of Jerusalem or after when they realized its value as a unifying cult for a restless, multi-ethnic population and a weapon against potential revolts. They rewrote the Gospels to put the blame for the death of Jesus on the Jews, thereby creating the "blood-libel" that fueled anti-Semitism down to the present. The main divergence from Roberts' version is the historical existence of Jesus and his secret Arab identity.

The preceding theories have all been offered as only speculation, any suspicions being currently unverifiable, but certainly not irrelevant. But none of these conspiracy theories regarding the possible origins of Christianity can discredit the fact that the quest for the historical Jesus has led scholars of integrity, both believers and unbelievers alike, into a dead end (just as the unreliability of the *Gemstone Files* does not discredit the conspiracy theory of the Kennedy assassination because it hinges upon it). The lack of non-Biblical evidence has led many investigators to ask not only "Who was Jesus?" but, even more importantly, "Was Jesus?"

Among those who assert the historical reality of Jesus while disbelieving the *New Testament* claims for his divinity and resurrection are Hyam Maccoby (27) and Hugh J. Schonfield (28), both Jewish apologists eager to reclaim Jesus as an exemplary Jew with no intention of starting a new religion and no pretensions to divinity. Michael Baigent, Richard Leigh, and Henry Lincoln (29) contend in their controversial books that not only did Jesus not die on the cross, but he fathered a son with Mary Magdalene and that the descendents of that union are today at the head of a secret society, the Priory of Sion, plotting to place someone of Jesus's lineage on the throne of a united Europe. What all these authors agree upon is that Jesus was a rebel against Rome and a claimant, whether legitimate or not, to the throne of David.

Morton Smith (30) also maintains Jesus's historicity, but contends that he was a magician, executed as much for sorcery and blasphemy as subversion. These comprise the most extreme and imaginative speculations on Jesus's possible real identity. A currently less popular theory (although it ruled in free thought circles a century ago) is that of the completely mythical nature of Jesus Christ. This claim was first put forth by the German Bruno Bauer who argued that Jesus was invented by the author of the *Gospel of Mark*. The French Count Volney argued in his *Ruins of Empires* (1872) that Jesus was the personification of a solar god originating with Krishna of India. J.M. Robertson, a Scotsman, was the most dedicated proponent of the idea (31), and currently the torch is being carried by G.A. Wells (32), who has written several books on the subject.

In outline, Robertson's theory postulates an ancient cult of Joshua (Jesus is merely the Greek for the Hebrew Joshua, or Yeschua) among the ancient Jews, which practiced human sacrifice and cannibalism, a common practice in the primitive religion of all cultures. This bloody practice is dimly hinted at in the Gospel accounts of the Crucifixion and Last Supper-Eucharist. Joshua may have been a Hebrew-Canaanite sun god supplanted by Yahweh, and relegated to the status of a legendary warrior-hero secondary to Moses, the champion of Yahweh. The Joshua cult may have had to go underground during the reign of the Yahwehistic-Mosid party, only to surface once again in the chaos of the Jewish rebellion against Rome.

"The oldest documents and tradition show that the cult of Jesus the Christ was being pushed in rivalry to pure Judaism among the Jews of the Dispersion before the destruction of the Temple. Such competition was the more easy because the life of the synagogues was largely independent of the central temple and craved for rites and teaching which should make up for the sacrificial usages at Jerusalem... The Jews of the Hellenistic period regarded him [Jesus/Joshua] as the actual founder of the rite of circumcision. According to tradition he began his work of deliverance on the day fixed for the choosing of the paschal lamb and concluded it at the Passover. The hypothesis that Joshua is the original Jesus—the origin of the myths which blended in a composite pattern mistaken for real history—solves many problems." (33)

However, Robertson doesn't discount the possibility that a real person may have served as the focus for the Joshua cult's savior. Saint Paul's Jesus, as opposed to the Jesus of the Gospels, does not seem to have lived in any time recent to the writer of the Epistles (which are generally regarded by most scholars as pre-dating the Gospels). Paul does not give any of the biographical details that the four evangelists do, and he never mentions Pontius Pilate. His Jesus is obviously not the same character as that of Mark, Matthew, Luke, and John.

"The Jesus of the Pauline doctrine was either a mythical construction or a remote figure thought to have been crucified but no longer traceable in history. A Jesus ben Pandira is said to have been stoned and hung on a tree under the Hasmonean king, Alexander Jannaeus, nearly a hundred years before the Christian era. It is conceivable that Paul's Jesus is merely a nominal memory of the slain Jesus ben Pandira." (34)

This Jesus ben Pandira, although an obscure figure, managed to cause the early Christians some problems and some embarrassment. Strangely enough, they did not try to discredit him by denying his existence or any connection to Jesus Christ. In fact, Church fathers like Eusebius and Epiphanius felt obligated to find ben Pandira a place in Jesus's family tree, explaining that he was Jesus's paternal grandfather, that is, Joseph's father. But if the virgin birth of Jesus was true, then there was no genetic relationship between Jesus and Joseph, and Jesus ben Pandira. And according to Matthew, Joseph's father was Jacob, but according to Luke his name was Heli. So who was Jesus ben Pandira (also Pantera, or Panthera), and what, if any, connection did he have to Jesus called the Christ (Anointed One, or Messiah)?

The pagan philosopher Celsus, arch-enemy of the early Christians, claimed Jesus was "a Jewish sorceror from Egypt" who was also the illegitimate son of "a soldier named Panthera." (35) This charge was repeated in the Talmud, from which Celsus may have gotten it.

Celsus's works were destroyed by the Christians once they came to power, but most of his anti-Christian polemic, *True Words*, is known almost word-for-word because the Christian apologist Origen quoted it extensively in his rebuttal to it, *Contra Celsus*. The charges that Celsus made must have been taken seriously enough to warrant such a detailed response, and not merely shrugged off as the jibes of an anti-Christian bigot. Celsus "was a man who relied not on rumors and hearsay evidence but on personal observation and careful study. Because he had read both the Old and the *New Testaments* and was familiar with Jewish and Christian literature... his book is on the whole free of mistakes and misconceptions... It contains none of the popular pagan antagonism against Christians and makes no unsubstantiated charges." (36) If a man like that accused your savior of being a sorceror and a bastard, it's no wonder you would feel obligated to answer the charges.

Regarding the father of Jesus ben Pandira, Morton Smith says: "It was not a very common name, but we do know of a Sidonian archer, Tiberius Julius Abdes Pantera, who was serving in Palestine about the time of Jesus's birth and later saw duty on the Rhine. It is possible, though not likely, that this tombstone from Bingerbrucke is our only genuine relic of the Holy Family. (37)

(Sidon was—and still is—a city on the coast of Phoenicia, now called Lebanon. Perhaps Bruce Roberts wasn't that far off the mark after all.)

Other Jewish sources claim that Jesus was the son of a ben Stada, also a magician, and that he—Jesus—"brought magic marks from Egypt in the scratches of his flesh," that is, tattoos, most likely of magical sigils. (In Galatians 6:17, Paul claimed to "bear in my body the marks of the Lord Jesus." Was Paul claiming to be a stigmata, bearing—metaphorically—the same wounds as Jesus, or was he claiming to have the same magical tattoos as Jesus on his flesh?) A third century rabbi Hisdu claimed that ben Stada was the husband of Jesus's mother Miriam (Mary), a hairdresser, and Pandira was her lover. The implication being, of course, that Jesus was a bastard born out of adultery. Yet another rabbi said that Pappos ben Judah was the father of Jesus and Stada referred to his unfaithful wife, *s'tal'da* meaning one who has fallen away from her husband. (38)

These were the sort of contradictory rumors and legends that early Christians were assailed with. Tertullian, a Church Father, summarized the standard Jewish allegations against his God circa 200 CE:

"Son of a carpenter or a prostitute, profaner of the Sabbath, a Samaritan who had a demon... whom his disciples spirited away [from the tomb] so they could say he was risen, or whom the gardener hauled off, lest his lettuces be damaged by the crowd of sightseers." (39)

Some clarification is needed to explain how Jesus's father, Joseph or whatever his name was, could possibly be both a carpenter and a magician. The Hebrew word for carpenter, najjar, also meant Nazorite or Nazorean, a mystic brotherhood of wood-workers, the same sect that the Old Testament Samson belonged to. This could account for the (mistaken) reference to Jesus as being "of Nazareth," a town which is not known to have existed during that time. (40)

As for the mother of Jesus, Miriam of Magdala may not have been a prostitute in the modern sense of the term, but a "sacred whore" or *hierodule,* a Virgin Bride of God, dedicated from an early age to the temple and to be the future bride of a sacred king. This according to the *Protoevangelium,* or *Revelation of James,* a second century CE gospel eventually eliminated from the official canon at the Council of Nicea, "declared apocryphal and heretical" as Roberts (for once) correctly pointed out. That Miriam (or Mary) Magdala (or Magdalene) was a title rather than a personal name (as both Joseph and Jesus Christ/Joshua Christos probably were). As well as being the son of a sacred virgin/whore, Jesus may have been raised to be the husband of one as well. It would certainly explain the confusing plethora of Mary's and Joseph's within the gospels (including the suppressed ones), the obliquely sexual relationship of Jesus and

Mary Magdalene, and how a virgin can give birth to a son yet still remain a virgin, in a manner of speaking. (41)

That these names were the titles of players in a ritualistic drama, perhaps one acted out for real with a knowing and willing sacred-king/scapegoat, perhaps one trained from birth for the role, lends credence to J.M. Robertson's theory of an underground Joshua cult running throughout Jewish history, surfacing during times of crisis when the Mosaic Yahweh cult was flagging, or impotent in the face of a major threat (such as Roman oppression). It has been said that Jesus ben Pandira was executed by his own wish. (42)

The Talmudic version, dating from no earlier than the early second century CE (43), goes like this: Yeschu (Jesus) was found guilty (by the Sanhedrin) of being a sorceror and a false prophet, and condemned to death. Forty days prior to his death, a herald was sent out to urge anyone with anything good to say about Yeschu to come forward (and presumably stay his execution). No one did, and on Passover Eve, Yeschu was stoned (to death presumably) and then (therefore his corpse) hung from a tree (not a cross). (44)

Anyone familiar with the *New Testament* will see obvious parallels here.

Finally, in the light of the ponderous evidence given above, what can be said of Bruce Roberts' revision of Catholic dogma? That, while justified in its skepticism, once again he missed wide of the mark. Unless the improbable be true, and Roberts actually received a copy of Cardinal Tisserant's secret diary, and that diary made the bizarre claims published in the *Gemstone Files* (which I won't believe until I am personally given verifiable evidence to the contrary), the only conclusion that can be reached is that Roberts, letting his prejudices once again get in his way, guessed at what might be the truth behind the inconsistencies and impossibilities of the Jesus story. Without doing any research into the subject, or knowing that he was far from the first to realize that two plus two does not equal five, he jumped to conclusions that—somehow—validated his (to be charitable) eccentric worldview. Surely, to his mind, it was no coincidence that his father died the day before Tisserant died, was murdered, as Roberts would have it. It was the same evil conspiracy at work in both deaths, the same conspiracy that killed Kennedy. Jesus an Arab or a Jewish sorceror-heretic crucified, or stoned or hung for blasphemy, or subversion, or treason or jaywalking: does it really matter, is it less shocking than the possibility that Jesus never existed at all? There have been plenty of people who freed themselves from the thrall of religion before Bruce Roberts, more will do so without ever reading the *Gemstone File* or suspecting some dark secret hidden away deep in the Vatican Crypt, other than that truth does not abide there.

But there is still one question remaining that the *Gemstone File* leaves unanswered: what was it really on the end of that sponge offered to Jesus at the crucifixion, vinegar or sodium-morphate wine?

Notes:1) *New York Times*, February 22, 1972, p. 40.2) Blanshard, Paul, *American Freedom and Catholic Power*, 1949, Beacon Press, p. 245.3) Manhattan, Avro, *The Vatican-Moscow-Washington Alliance*, 1982, Chick Publications, pp. 27-8.4) Cornwell, John, *A Thief in the Night: The Mysterious Death of Pope John Paul I*, 1989, Simon & Schuster, pp. 47-8.5) Rhodes, Anthony, *The Vatican in the Age of the Dictators* (1922-1945), 1973, Holt, Rinehart, & Winston, pp. 216-17.6) Ibid, p. 2157) Manhattan, pp. 91-99.8) Manhattan, p. 27.9) Anonymous, "Paul VI, Pope" in Current Biography: 1963, H.H. Wilson Co., pp. 316-19.10) Ibid.11) Blanshard, pp. 226-27,11a) Manhattan, pp. 143-4. The Fatima cult was suppressed by Pius XII's successor, John XXIII, who "being the matter-of-fact man that he was, and fully realizing the political implications of the Fatima revelations, ordered the Portuguese hierarchy to drop at once 'La pulcinellada,' a word which, in Venetian slang meant leg-pulling or burlesque." John XXIII was known in some circles as "the Red Pope" for his apparent pro-communist leanings. 12) Rhodes, pp. 337-49.13) Anonymous (Tony Alamo?), *Fugitive Pope: John Paul II, A Catholic Nazi World War II Criminal*, no date, tract published by Tony Alamo Ministries, 14) Manhattan, pp. 40-5.15) Ibid, p.41.16) Lee, Martin A., "Their Will Be Done," July 1983, *Mother Jones* magazine, pp. 25-6.17) Baigent, Michael, Richard Leigh and Henry Lincoln, *The Messianic Legacy*, 1986, Henry Holt & Company, pp. 304-06.18) Ibid, p. 306.19) However, according to Manhattan, they never stopped trying to sabotage Paul VI's papacy, and may have ultimately succeeded. See pp. 23-5.20) "The Vatican is accustomed to think in terms not of any particular country, but of whole continents as single political units. Hence the necessity of carrying out such policies on a continental scale as part of a later strategy integrated with plans it is implementing in other parts of the world." Manhattan, p. 298. See also Manhattan's *Catholic Power Today*, 1967, Lyle Stuart, dated in some incidentals but generally still applicable. 21) Walker, Barbara G., *The Woman's Encyclopedia of Myths and Secrets*, 1983, Harper & Row, pp. 565-66; Doane, T.W., *Bible Myths and their Parallel in Other Religions*, 1882, *Health Research* 1985 reprint, pp. 151-53; Graves, Kersey, *The World's Sixteen Crucified Saviors, or Christianity Before Christ*, 1875, Health Research reprint, no date, pp. 63-7; Graham, Lloyd M., *Deceptions and Myths of the Bible*, 1979, Bell Pub. Co., pp. 307-08.22) Walker, pp. 166-67; Doane, pp. 473-74; Graves, pp. 68-71.23) McKinsey, Dennis, in Biblical Errancy (periodical) #33, September, 1985, p. 3.24) "Therefore to scotch the rumor [that he had set the fire], Nero substituted as culprits, and punished with the utmost refinements of cruelty, a class of men, loathed for their vices, whom the crowd styled Christians. Christus [sic], the founder of the name, had undergone the death penalty in the reign of Tiberius, by sentence of the procurator Pontius Pilatus, and the pernicious superstition was checked for the moment, only to break out once more, not merely in Judaea, the home of the disease, but in the capital itself, where all things horrible and shameful in the world collect and find a vogue. First, then, the confessed members of the sect were arrested; next, on their disclosures, vast numbers were convicted, not so much on the count of arson as for hatred of the human race. And derision accompanied their end: they were covered with wild beast's skins and torn to death by dogs; or they were fastened on crosses, and, when daylight failed were burned to serve as lamps by night. Nero had offered his gardens for the spectacle, and gave an exhibition in his circus, mixing with the crowd in the habit of a charioteer, or mounted on his car. Hence, in spite of a guilt which had earned the most exemplary punishment, there arose a sentiment of pity, due to the impression that they were being sacrificed not for the welfare of the state but to the ferocity of a single man." Tacitus in the *Annals*, as quoted by Benko, Stephan, *Pagan Rome and the Early Christians*, 1984, Indiana University Press, p. 15. McKinsey, op. cit., dissects this passage, putting its veracity in doubt. 25) Reuchlin, Abelard, *The True Authorship of the New Testament*, Abelard Reuchlin Foundation. Reuchlin's work has been carried on by John Duran whose unpublished manuscript *The Origin of Christianity* takes the theory into more detail. 26) Ravage, Marcus Eli, "A Real Case Against the Jews: One of Their Own Points Out the Full Depth of Their Guilt," *Century* magazine, January, 1928, as quoted in Graham, pp. 276-77. The name sounds too coincidental to be real, but apparently Ravage really existed and probably wrote this article. The possibility of tongue in cheek satire cannot be dismissed, but why any Jew would want to fool with such volatile material is puzzling. 27) Maccoby, Hyam, *Revolution in Judea: Jesus and the Jewish Resistance*, 1981, Taplinger. 28) Schonfield, Hugh J., *The Passover Plot*, 1966, Bernard Geis. 29) Baigent, Michael, Richard Leigh, and Henry Lincoln, *Holy Blood, Holy Grail*, 1982, Delacorte Press; Baigent, et al., *The Messianic Legacy*, (see note # 17). 30) Smith, Morton, *Jesus the Magician*, 1978, Harper & Row. 31) Robertson, J.M., *Pagan Christs*, 1987, Dorset Press, reprint of 1903 original. 32) Wells, G.A., *Did Jesus Exist?* 1986, Pemberton. 33) Robertson, p. 21. 34) Ibid, pp. 67-8.35) Wells, p. 15; Benko, pp. 147-51. 36) Benko, p. 148. 37) Smith, p. 61. 38) Ibid. 39) Smith, p. 61. 40) Walker, "Jesus ben Pandira," p. 463.41) Walker, "Mary" pp. 604-05; "Mary Magdalene," pp. 614-15.42) Walker, p. 463.43) Wells, p. 12.44) Wells, p. 16.45) The author regrets being unable to find reference to any Arian bishop having his hands chopped off (though it is plausible, this was, after all, the Age of Faith), or to any warning by Jesus against the "yellow race" in the Bible. He trusts that those who do find them will be sure to let him know.

Is Gemstone a Hoax?

Kerry W. Thornley

Whenever I read an expose holding the Queen of England responsible for Communism, Nazism, Zionism, Cosa Nostra and AIDS, I assume it is Irish Republican Army propaganda. That is not to assume it is Irish Republican Army propaganda. That is not to say I think Queen Elizabeth and her German relatives are entirely innocent. Nor is it to say I am unsympathetic with Irish Republican aspirations.

But once upon a time I was a believer in the notion that lone nuts and lonely potentates — Aristotle Onassis was a little of each — are great makers of history. Not any more. Now I blush to recall that I once thought Lee Harvey Oswald, acting alone, killed the President — when in fact I was probably more involved in that assassination than he was.

In the *Illuminatus* trilogy we encounter an English spy named Fission Chips who becomes obsessed with an organization called B.U.G.G.E.R. which he always concludes is behind any case to which he is assigned. Such obsessions are common enough, whether they target outfits or misfits.

Having read at least two slightly different versions of "A Skeleton Key to the Gemstone File" more than once, I'm inclined to suspect such an obsession on someone's part about Aristotle Onassis.

A central concern of Gemstone is the John Kennedy assassination. Without effort on my part, I have met an unusual number of accused John Kennedy assassins.

In 1958, I attended the University of Southern California at the same time as Garrison probe suspect Gordon Novel.

That seemed like no big deal when Garrison first mentioned it, because so did 73,000 other students that year. But it so happens that one of my pledge brothers in the Delta Sigma Phi fraternity there was named Gordy — and upon much pondering, I think he said his last name was Novel and that it was Hungarian.

In 1959, I was in the Marines with Lee Harvey Oswald. When I read of his Moscow defection attempt, I wrote a novel about a Marine who winds up going to Russia.

In 1961 in the New Orleans French Quarter I was introduced to a man named Guy Banister who said he was very interested in literature and who asked me a great number of questions about my book inspired by Oswald. Hardly an assassination theory exists which does not include Banister — who did not tell me he was a former FBI man coordinating anti-Castro activities in New Orleans.

That year or the next I attended a party on Louisiana Parkway in the home of a homosexual airplane pilot named David Ferrie. We met and shook hands that night, but did not engage in conversation. My invitation had originated with the faculty advisor of the Tulane University Conservative Club, who then took me to another party at the residence of Suki Waguespack — whose family is rumored to be involved deeply in conspiracy politics. Ferrie is of course star of theories about the Kennedy assassination ranging in scope from blaming Carlos Marcello to the Joint Chiefs of Staff.

Then in late October or early November of 1963, I breakfasted with a man named Dave Chandler — a stringer for *Life* magazine of whom Jim Garrison and his own boss, Richard Billings, both expressed suspicion in 1968. What did Chandler and I discuss? Assassinating John F. Kennedy — although we never got beyond agreeing that he should be assassinated, except for Chandler's suggestion that there might be some way to crash his plane.

In November of 1963, shortly before the assassination, I met Clay Shaw — who happened to be my landlord's best friend. My landlord said his mother was a writer who wanted to read my manuscript about the Marine who went to Russia. He borrowed it on a Friday and returned it Sunday afternoon, upon which occasion he also introduced me to Shaw who seemed quite interested in the book himself.

After the Kennedy murder I crossed paths with Jim Garrison, who has been accused by the likes of Robert Sam Anson of covering up the assassination — upon which occasion I stood in the same waiting room with Marina Oswald, who figures in many conspiracy theories and is suspected of ordering the famous Italian rifle. One day later in 1968 in New Orleans I hopped into a taxi cab driven by Perry Raymond Russo, Garrison's infamous "drugged witness" against Shaw and Ferrie.

In 1966 I was working as a night PBX operator in a highrise apartment building called Glen Towers near Los Angeles, California. An especially colorful resident of that building was a Mafia don known as Johnny Roselli — accused by Gemstone of firing the shot from the Grassy Knoll that blew John Fitzgerald Kennedy's brains out. From time to time we would catch two men in suits searching Roselli's car in the basement garage. One evening when I came on duty I was told such an event had occurred that afternoon. As always, the two men produced FBI identification but admitted to having no search warrant. As usual, they were asked to leave and complied.

So when Roselli came in that night I told him, "We caught the Feds searching your car again today."

"They don't scare me," he said with a rather forced, tight toothy grin. "They're so stupid. But, you know, who is really stupid is the CIA. They killed their own President, trying to get some bookie."

Our conversation continued for some minutes and he wound up loaning me a copy of a book called *The Invisible Government* and specifically instructing me to read the chapter about a raid on an ammunition dump in Hammond, Louisiana, in which Gordon Novel was involved.

My friends ask me how I do it. My enemies think they already know. I would be the last to insist on coincidence. Obviously, I am somehow in the thick of the Dallas plot. My hunch is that a weird Nazi in New Orleans with whom I also used to discuss killing the President was E. Howard Hunt in disguise. While that would explain much, it still leaves my prior associations with Oswald and (probably) Novel unaccounted for.

My point here is that whatever forces have been at work

to dump into my lap so much information about the Kennedy assassination have never once brought me in contact with anyone who claims to have seen the original, unabridged *Gemstone Files*. Nor, to my knowledge, have I ever met Bruce Roberts or anyone who has known him.

That is one good reason among many why I suspect a hoax. As one who has been accused wrongly of a hoax or two about the assassination myself, I think I have an eye for what a hoax is not.

First to accuse me of such disinformation was District Attorney Jim Garrison. A charismatic culture hero, Garrison commands the unwavering faith of a small cult. These people believe that I testified to the Warren Commission that I thought Oswald was serious about Communism, because Jim Garrison says that is what I said. My Warren Commission testimony, which is a matter of public record, does not say that. These Goosestepping Garrisonites, as I call them, also think I decided to write a book about Oswald when he was just a common Marine — forgetting, because Garrison never reminds them, that common Marines don't walk into the U.S. Embassy in Moscow and plop down their passports.

More recently, Jonathan Vankin in *Conspiracies, Cover-Ups and Crimes* has expressed the suspicion that my explanations of my involvement in the Kennedy assassination constitutes "a philosophical prank." What in hell's name a philosophical prank is never becomes clear, but evidently my Discordian Society activities make me suspect. Putting aside that only a monster would engage in jokes involving Nazi genocide plans, no one — as I tried to point out in a letter to Vankin — complains bitterly for a decade and a half about being persecuted just to lay the groundwork for a prank, philosophical or otherwise.

That brings me to the second reason why I am skeptical about Bruce Roberts. Like a comic book hero, this guy is nearly always on top of his shit. When you poke your nose into political assassinations — or when you help those who do — you are poisoned, beaten up, threatened with death, spied upon and tormented psychologically without respite — when they don't just kill you.

A couple of months ago I met a woman who said she could get me on the tabloid television show, *A Current Affair.*

I told her I was being persecuted. I don't think she believed me; I didn't quite believe her. But she came through and, what is more, now she believes me. For the past few weeks she has been in hiding. Weird things, you see, started happening to her.

Back in 1975 and 1976, when I first became aware of my involvement in the assassination — largely because of Watergate — the first two people who tried to help me were hit by cars. Neither man was killed, but both Reber Boult and Ward Silver were hopping about Atlanta on crutches for awhile.

But Bruce Roberts is not hit. Instead, he hits them. Do they retaliate? Perhaps not — if only because they are somehow unaware of him. So what does he do? He pushes his luck. He keeps extensive files and leaks them — spreading it about that, among other things, he has hit Alexander Onassis.

While I am party to no hoaxes involving the Kennedy assassination, I readily admit to a few pranks about other things in my time. Once, with the help of a few friends, I convinced the officers of Marine Air Group 11 that a private with an I.Q. of 157 who spoke 17 languages and drove a truck in motor transport was A.W.O.L. That no such man even existed did not keep him from being the object of an extensive manhunt. So, as one thief recognizes another, I think I can often spot another joker in the deck. And if Bruce Roberts was not himself a put-on, then he was putting us on or someone was putting him on.

Certainly the first likely suspect that comes to mind is G. Gordon Liddy. Not only does Gemstone sometimes read like an advertisement for Liddy's services as a hit man, Liddy is also enough of a screwball to go to the trouble involved. Moreover, G. Gordon Liddy's intelligence connections suffice to lend the necessary ring of truth to many of the charges. I find it hard to believe that Johnny Roselli was not involved in the assassination, for example. And the section about the Communists blackmailing Nixon over the murder of Howard Hughes is almost too funny not to be true.

Stan Jamison, one of my informants who, like Liddy, was reputedly a Royal Arch Mason, said once that to make a lie stick it must at least approach the truth.

If Liddy is too young to have been in Dallas on 22 November 1963, many of his Watergate co-conspirators were not. But would Liddy have been so hard on Nixon? And wouldn't he have picked on Larry O'Brian or Senator Howard Baker, or even Jimmy Carter, before singling out Onassis?

A hotter suspect than Liddy is to be found.

Aristotle Onassis had a brother-in-law who was also his arch enemy. Stavros Niarchos was even suspected in the death of Alexander Onassis, as well as those of two of his own wives. Certainly his rivalry with Aristotle was not a one-sided affair. Ari stabbed Stavros in the back at least as often as Stavros ripped him off.

A typical tale of their relationship is told in *The Fabulous Onassis* by Christian Cafarakis:

"One day, for instance, Stavros Niarchos came to see him on the ship, the *Penepoli*, which was for sale at a very good price in Marseilles. Onassis was also aware of this deal but until that point had been in no hurry, since he thought he was the only one interested in the ship. On hearing this, however, he asked to be excused for a moment and left Niarchos sipping whiskey, while he radioed ashore that he wanted to buy the *Penepoli* immediately.

When he returned, Niarchos picked up the conversation and asked him what he thought about the deal. Onassis admitted that he thought it excellent, but that unfortunately the boat was already sold.

"And to whom?" Niarchos asked, very surprised.

"Why, to me, of course," he said with a smile.

In *Onassis: Aristotle and Christina*, L.J. Davis says of Ari:

"His money and his rivalry with Niarchos were important elements in his struggle to define himself..." Among the tactics Ari used against Stavros was, according to Davis, disinformation: "Misinformation was deliberately planted, usually by the transparent expedient of discussing it in an unnaturally loud voice in the presence of the hired help." Onassis even created "a private intelligence apparatus" to spy on his brother-in-law. (p. 77)

There is every indication Stavros Niarchos responded in kind, but — if anything — with considerably more vindictiveness. Peter Evans in *Ari: The Life and Times of Aristotle Onassis* goes so far as to call the rivalry between these two "a fatal contest." (p. 88) Onassis once accused Niarchos of sending a hostile report on him to the FBI. (p. 94) Evans accuses Niarchos of never "missing an opportunity to irritate Ari." (p.130)

Says Nigel Dempster in *Heiress: The Story of Christina Onassis*: "It was not simply that when Ari built a tanker, Niarchos built a bigger one. Niarchos also troubled him in ways that transcended business competitiveness." And "the mutual animosity went much deeper than a conflict of styles." (pp. 21-2)

William Wright in *All the Pain that Money Can Buy*, a biography of Christina Onassis, refers to Niarchos as her "despised uncle." (p. 235) He also describes in detail Aristotle's frantic efforts to convict Stavros Niarchos for the murder of Christina's aunt Eugenie — Stavros' wife. (p.120-3) Ari suspected both Niarchos and the CIA in the plane-crash death of his son, Alexander. (p. 175)

Camden Benares once brought to my attention the great bullshit controversy in American literature. Hemingway spelled it as two words. Faulkner and Kerouac spelled it as one. Someone else hyphenated. But no matter how it is written, it always smells the same. So do both versions, for the most part, of "A Skeleton Key to the Gemstone File."

Outlaws and Inslaw

Ben G. Price

Background

The National Security State and the C.I.A. were born under the same sign; they share identical natal characteristics. And they serve the same master. Ensconced above the portal to the C.I.A. building is the prophetic phrase, "Ye shall know the truth and the truth shall make you free." The truth that is known is that the price of liberty is eternal vigilance. But knowing the truth and sharing it are antithetical to the notion of national security, as it has evolved in the shadowy realm of secrecy.

"Freedom Shrines" are liberally erected across land, where liberty and justice are laminated under thick layers of transparent hypocrisy. The truth, like liberty itself, has been preserved as a paleo-ontological specimen and enshrined in tyranny's branch offices, including the National Security Agency ("The Puzzle Palace"), the Justice [sic] Department, the FBI, CIA, DEA, NSA, DIA, IRS, and other repositories of a bygone democracy. Freedom itself is thus secured, protected from the clawing mass of huddled and betrayed, who press their noses where, according to freedom's new curators, they don't belong.

The fetish of National Security was stroked into its current enormity over five decades of governmental self-indulgence. World War II saw the birth of the great international spy networks. Industrial spying is mistakenly thought to be a recent outgrowth of the cult of secret vices, but the reality is that spying has never had any more signature quality than its allegiance to industry and its captains. I.G. Farben and Krupp armaments earned both loyalty and untouchability during the international conflagration of the forties, not because of aloof indifference or neutrality, but because they owned controlling interest in the outcome of the contest, and whatever transpired on the battlefield, and arms monopoly in time of war is an amoral thing of beauty, which is to say an obscenity.

The transformation of the industrial revolution into its geo-political convolutions was immediate, but not until industrialization had gone to seed throughout the "Western World" did mechanized war ascend to central stage as history's Golem. The theatre of war had been, until this century, a flood of morality plays recounted in glowing self-congratulatory memoirs by colonizing zealots, who with only marginally superior technology managed to subdue aboriginal populations in far-flung corners of a globe. The globe shrank geometrically as the engines of industry grew linearly. But always the force of superior arms lead the way, and the technological knowledge to manufacture and distribute weapons became a commodity more precious and guarded than any in history.

Our current world is in disarray as industry's overreaching feelers, sent forth in opposite directions to span the globe, at last touch and lock their grip. In the path of industry's explosion lie mass graves, denuded cultures, and more graves. Dwight Eisenhower saw firsthand the industrialization of death. As one of its orchestrators, he dared question the motives of the captains he served only at the end of his political career when he warned the citizens of an expired democracy about the dangers of the entrenched and expanding "military industrial complex."

Behind the national security dam that keeps the flow of information from irrigating the withering patches of democracy and freedom that remain, a potential deluge of outrage has been harnessed and scientifically managed. Its trickle-down privileged information becomes ever more distilled and bland as it filters through the "need to know" aquifers of bedrock bureacracy. The watershed event in 20th century America has been the erection of National Security as the organ of State perpetuity, with general ignorance powering the turbines of capitalized politics.

Industry discovered in its infancy that a domestic population can be colonized as lucratively as a foreign one. Urbanization served the crude necessities of industry, while destroying long-established social structures as basic as the family. Transforming the nation into a protector of corporate rights over and above citizen's rights has made-over the national character as an extension of industrial domestic colonization. The promise of a "new world order" arising from the dust in the dried-up sea of promises has been signed with the inky deception of a fleeing, multi-legged cephalopod. Freedom lovers intrepid enough to challenge the veil of secrecy for a glimpse of the truth as it writhes in the clutches of an American shadow government in the employ of organized corporate criminals often as not die premature and mysterious deaths. Enter and as quickly exit Joseph Daniel Casolaro.

Tentacles

"The Octopus" is the term Casolaro used to describe the nefarious Mafia-like network of national and international conspirators that had infiltrated the American system so successfully as to virtually control finance, industry, and government without the inconvenience of public accountability. Casolaro was investigating several leads that he saw as connected to one controlling entity. The tentacles included the theft from Inslaw Corporation of sophisticated computer software by Ed Meese's Justice [sic] Department, the "October Surprise" [the Casey, Meese, Reagan, Bush scheme that guaranteed weapons to Iran in exchange for holding American hostages until after the November 1980 presidential elections], and the involvement of U.S. intelligence agencies in the drug, arms, and graft money laundering services of B.C.C.I.

Casolaro never got the chance to deliver the finished manuscript of his book, *Behold a Pale Horse*. He was found dead in a Martinsburg, WV motel room on August 10, 1991, where he was to meet one of his sources who, he had told friends, would bust the entrails of the octopus wide open. His papers and the manuscript of his book were not to be found when he was discovered in a motel tub with a half-empty bottle of wine, a broken beer bottle, and his wrists slashed. The October Surprise and the B.C.C.I. scam were just hitting the front page.

Casolaro's faked suicide shared the limelight briefly. He was embalmed immediately on the authority of no one willing to take responsibility, and before his family was notified of his death. The verdict of psychologists, the local coroner, Eliot Richardson (Inslaw attorney), Jack Anderson (sydicated columnist) and others is that a wide open inquiry into this death is needed. To date, it's all been hush-hush.

On September 27, 1991, one of the "sources" named by the *Washington Post* as involved in Casolaro's investigations, William Richard Turner of High View, WV, was arrested on suspicion 90 minutes after the Gore branch of Dominion Bank was robbed. Turner is a former employee of Hughes Aircraft in Herndon, VA. He claims he gave Casolaro documents pertaining to corruption in the military defense industry. The Martinsburg, WV police chief Perry Smith, head of the only law agency officially involved in investigating Casolaro's mysterious death, said of the equally mysterious arrest of Turner for bank robbery charges, "That's a separate incident." Asked if he saw any possible connection between Casolaro's death and Turner's incarceration, he said, "I don't see how you could."

"The Octopus" also has been used to refer to an international business network linked circumstantially to prior knowledge of John Kennedy's assassination in November, 1963. According to Mae Brussell (*The Rebel*, Nov. 1983), Allied Crude Vegetable Oil Refining Corporation, controlled by the U.S. American Bunge Corporation, may have helped set the stage for a half-billion dollar windfall as the stock market crashed with news of Kennedy's death. American Bunge was financially controlled by "Bunge and Born, LDA," a group of expatriate German shareholders in Argentina. Brussell quotes Helmet Streiker, Nazi trained CIA recruit: "John Kennedy's murder was a two-part conspiracy murder by the intelligence apparatus that controls the way the world operates. It had to happen. The man was too independent for his own good."

Again according to Brussell, Martin Bormann, Deputy Fuhrer under Hitler was reported by European news agencies to be behind the Kennedy assassination. And in 1961 a member of British Parliament published documentary evidence that Allen Dulles of the CIA was aware, after consulting with Hitler's SS Security Office in February and March, 1943, of a secret international organization, "Die Spinne" (The Spider), which planned to revive Nazism once Germany became rearmed by the U.S.

Whether it's The Octopus or The Spider, the industrialization of politics (and the politicization of industry) respects no national borders, nor is it amenable to community standards of "decency," as Linda Hunt reports in her 1991 book *Secret Agenda: The United States Government, Nazi Scientists, and Project Paperclip, 1945 to 1990*. According to Hunt (former executive producer of CNN's investigative unit), with the fall of Nazi Germany a cadre of American military and intelligence operatives actively recruited German scientists and engineers and brought them secretly to America in direct contravention of U.S. law and specific orders from the president barring Nazis from entering the country. Once here they were distributed among private military contractors and universities. Bogus organizations were concocted to smuggle them in; records were altered and destroyed, investigations were obstructed, critics were harrassed, and officials lied and perjured themselves in order to secure the benefits of advanced German technology for the American military industrial complex. Eisenhower's warning was too little, too late. And it seems clear that he never shared what he knew with Kennedy, his presidential successor, who, if he had known, might have acted differently in affairs affecting international arms issues (e.g. the missile crisis) and domestic campaigns against organized corporate crime.

The National Security State (NSS) is not merely a quasi-political arm of government. Increasingly, every facet of public and private life is becoming incorporated into the crystallizing matrix of the NSS. The "new world order" is user-friendly, but the users are not you and me. We are the used. If just government derives its power from the consent of the governed, then governmentally deceived citizens are right to charge their leaders with treason. The NSS hasn't allowed the governed to know that there's been a coup d'etat. The degree of secretiveness in the political arena is inversely proportional to the degree of liberty available to the citizen. The more secrecy, the less liberty. It isn't surprising that liberty seems such a smothered and mysterious concept in this land that hypocritically dedicates itself in song and legend to the very ideals with which its government is constantly at-odds.

Multinational corporations invest fortunes in surveillance, psychological profiles, disinformation, and behavioral conditioning. The target of these activities is not "foreign" competition, but their own employees and market consumers. Every organ of public "service" and community access is used; education, media, legislation, employment, jurisprudence and electoral herding. Lobbying (bribery) is only the most benign manipulation, and it is openly perpetrated with obvious contempt for desensitized citizens. Other more hideous practices are becoming increasingly common. Cases such as Karen Silkwood's industrial homocide are repeated but go uncounted, like so many Iraqis buried in the desert.

Dan Casolaro died trying to uncover the truth about why the U.S. Justice [sic] Department had stolen software useful in tracking dissidents. Why, you might ask, should he bother when the whole thrust of government is now so obviously against individual aims and in service of corporate, cartel, and Mafia-like agendas? Why risk going against such a strong current?

Alyeska Pipeline Service Company, a consortium of seven oil firms, spied on Congressman George Miller, who was investigating the violation of environmental law by that multi-tentacled organization. At the same time (September 1991), Rochester Institute of Technology president, M. Richard Rose, resigned after it was learned he was a CIA operative overseeing the institution's work on advanced imaging technology, which is used for spy satellite surveillance. Coupled with the Inslaw dissident-tracking software, post "cold war" spy satellites might have a whole new agenda to support. And they say George Bush doesn't have a domestic policy!

The confirmation of Robert Gates to head the CIA became problematical only when the facts of agency involvement in the Iran-Contra affair (drugs for money for arms) kept being exhumed from the grave of secrecy dug by national security, and when hints of agency involvement in the breaking B.C.C.I. scandal leaked, and Noriega's trial started falling apart, so that it looked like the Bush invasion of Panama was just another gripping-post for The Octopus. Gates' boss, Casey, was also posthumously implicated in the treasonous "October Surprise." In the face of such an onslaught of substantive challenges, what was the CIA-trained president to do?

Just then, another round of confirmation hearings was under way. A perfect chance to set up a media circus and distract attention from the larger issue at hand. Appointing a conservative black judge to the Supreme Court, which was in the process of dismantling the *Bill of Rights* even without the help of another right wing associate justice, was clearly secondary to putting the right man in charge of state security and intelligence. Suddenly, thanks to a "leaked" FBI interview with another conservative, Anita Hill, the offensive and intimidating sexual bantering of Clarence Thomas was put on pages one through twenty, thus relegating B.C.C.I., Gates, Casolaro, Noriega, Casey, Meese, Thornburgh, Bush, and the whole interconnected, writhing can of worms to the limbo of non-news.

Eyes Only

Smoking guns and direct lineage are certainly preferable to baroque reality if what you want to do is construct a neat, clean, concise conspiracy theory. The *Gemstone File* supplies a sharp outline, but for all its linearity and attempt at offering cause and effect analysis of nefarious political events, not beginning with the JFK assassination but certainly climaxing with it, the *Gemstone File*, even if correct in most details, fails to answer the more fundamental questions. If a Greek Mafia under Onassis took control of American politics, what relationship did Onassis forge with the American technocrats with whom any political arrangement would have had to be negotiated?

Arms manufacturers and arms dealers, like drug manufacturers and drug dealers, are powerful to the degree they can command interest in their wares and to the degree they can artifically perpetuate a shortage of their products among interested (habituated) and potential customers.   Saddam Hussein's "secret" arms build-up was closed-down by the U.S/NATO arms cartel through the auspices of the newly co-opted U.N. This was accomplished only after the global net-work of arms dealers was finished extracting from Iraq the mega-dollars it spent to buy those weapons. The Lord giveth and the Lord taketh away.

There are reports leaking out of the congressional com-mittee investigating B.C.C.I. criminal activities (chaired by Senator Kerry) that huge private business deals between George Bush and Saddam Hussein, and between George Bush and Manuel Noriega were handled through B.C.C.I. and its affiliated laundering operation, Banca Nazionale Del Lav-oro, according to journalist Sherman Skolnick. The exchange of funds was reportedly enormous between Bush and Saddam, but BNL records have not been forthcoming through Justice Department subpoenas. Something apparently went sour between these secret global business partners. Guns and drugs were likely at the heart of such gigantic transac-tions. But in the afterglow of the honeymoon between the CIA, Noriega, and Hussein, Panama and Iraq faced full scale military invasions. Meanwhile, bewildered Americans tried to sort out the facts from the hype that was offered alongside orchestrated news black-outs and battlefield censorship in both campaigns.

The "new world order," we are to understand by these global Pax Americana manipulations, each a manipulation of the Octopus's tentacles, touches all of us as if God were touching our lives. The "new world order" is a kind of god, born of the self adoration of industrial zealots. The "new world order" is an insidious side-effect of industrial warfare. It is a social result of industrial toxicity, a cultural mutation. The will to power, coupled with technology, yields exponential growth in the realm of tyranny. Industrialized tyranny has grown tentacles with which it grasps and probes into every corner of individual life. Tribal totems are deformed into na-tional symbols; taboos are magnified to advance genocide; and the secrecy of intelligence professionals supercedes the quiet but once shared wisdom of silenced and ridiculed elders.

At first, tyrants grasped blindly. It seemed a simple matter of justified greed back in the old days of political "machines" and bosses, and turf run by Alpha Male inheritors of fear-surrendered liberty. Industrial bosses realized exactly how powerful they were in contrast to an indigenous, uninitiated populace. Tyrants co-opt existing hierarchies and symbols, like those of organized religion, in order to manipulate large populations. Nixon, for instance, flattered Billy Graham and made him his personal symbol of solidarity in faith with the common man. He also drafted Spiro Agnew as his running mate, a Greek American, perhaps with equal deference to Onassis and the criminal elements in American government who were really in charge. But it was Reagan and his handlers who turned politics into a religion. They had Jeeeeeesuuuuus announce from every pulpit that He would register as a Republican, then Reagan's persona drafted HEEEM who would prophesy the "new world order" on his ticket and nailed-down the election with a few well-timed arms deals with the Iranians. Christianity as a state religion hasn't done so well since the last days of a decaying Rome.

Bush, in the hoofsteps of Reagan, has derided drug addicts as public enemy number one. Not savings and loan embezzlers. Not banking fraud perpetrators. Not arms traders willing to barter hostages for arms. Not lieutenant colonels coordinating illegal covert wars. Not generals willing to plow-under surrendering conscripts. Not Haitian generals overthrowing democratically elected presidents. He does not side with independence-seeking Soviet nations, nor with America's own unemployed.

Who does he side with? Arms manufacturers, no matter who they sell to, no matter what money they launder or what populace the weapons terrorize. Drug suppliers, who can afford to buy arms and trade for them. The shadow government is on its own side of the street, and if we as citizens try to cross that street to see just what it really is that casts such a large shadow, a shadow that darkens all our horizons, we risk being crushed under the wheels of the caissons being wheeled off to the next covert battlefield, under cover of darkness. The Mafioso-like black market, trading in death and slavery, has grown larger than anyone could have ever dreamed possible. It sets up its own banking systems, subverts elected governments by enlisting unscrupulous politicians into covert wars and illegal trade in arms and drugs. It assassinates those it can not co-opt. It manipulates elections in order to put into place the gangsters who will smile and make speeches, all the while selling-out the nations to the lumbering cephalopod lurking beneath the surface, plotting to engulf them in a sea of treason.

On this ocean of betrayal, what did Onassis ship?

Appendix:
Sodium Morphate

Yael Dragwyla and Gary Csillaghegyi

We cannot find a reference to "sodium morphate," anywhere. We assume that "morphate" is an ion of the compound morphine. If so, neither the Chemical Rubber Company Handbook nor any enclopedia we can find has anything
remotely related to such a thing listed, and the CRC Handbook is the authority on all possible organic compounds. The
CRC Handbook does list toxins, an enormous number of
them, some of them too insidious and/or cruel for Lucrezia
Borgia, so the CRC editors are not suppressing evidence
when it comes to poisons!

It is not listed under either "Poisons" or "Morphine" in the
1911 *Encyclopedia Britannica*, which surely would have included data on a sodiumized morphine compound if any
such existed (we assure you, neither then nor now has the
Mafia been in control of the editing & publication of the *Encyclopedia Britannica!*).

Morphine does not occur in nature, and it is extremely
unlikely that it could have been synthesized by a medieval
chemist. Once you had it, however, it would not be possible
to ionize it and replace the methyl group in the pyridene ring
with an oxygen — which then would be the morphate —
without the sort of temperature control that simply did not
exist prior to 1900 (which was about the time mustard gas
was first synthesized). In other words, the sort of technical

expertise and equipment necessary to produce any morphate, sodium or otherwise, did not exist before 1900. Therefore, the alleged compound, if it exists at all, certainly was not "used by the Mafia [or anyone else] for centuries." At most, it could only have been used by anyone since 1900, as it could not have existed prior to that.

Something that would qualify as "sodium morphate" — an ion of the morphine molecule with sodium plugged in as a carrier ion — could be synthesized now, but it could not have been so before 1900, at which time the sort of temperature-control necessary to synthesize it in a laboratory first became possible. Morphine is an extremely delicate compound; it falls apart rather easily into smaller compounds, which are the chemicals that do its real work, such as analgesia and anesthesia, and, of course, poisoning. The latter it achieves by binding up blood oxygen, after the fashion of carbon monoxide, so that the victim of morphine overdose dies essentially of anoxia. To tinker with this very fragile molecule without destroying it requires extremely elegant, fine-tuned temperature control. Since this did not exist until this century, surely "sodium morphate" could not have been artificially created before then.

If it did exist before that time, then it would have been a botanical alkaloid. Plants, like animals, achieve metabolic processes and syntheses of chemicals in their tissues which, in a laboratory, would require temperatures far too high to enable life to continue or processing too touchy for our technology, by means of enzymes. These chemical templates enable assembly of extremely complex, fragile molecules at very low temperatures and in very short time, relatively speaking. In other words, by means of enzymes, plants routinely synthesize within their tissues certain molecules, such as plant alkaloids, that could not otherwise be created, except under conditions that would destroy the plant, or else at a rate so slow as to be useless for the plant's needs. Morphine is an opiate derivative — and opium is, of course, made by the opium poppy as a matter of course. So, at least in theory, morphine or one of its derivatives, such as "sodium morphate," could be a botanical alkaloid. One that could have been discovered, extracted from the plant and put into use quite long enough to qualify for the supposed Mafia poison Roberts writes of in the *Gemstone File*.

Considerations such as whether indeed synthesis of an alkaloid contructed of ionized morphine bonded to sodium would be useful to any plant, or useful enough to justify expenditure of the energy and resources necessary to synthesize it aside, there is another problem. Such a compound would not, under the Geneva conventions of the naming of chemical compounds, be called "sodium morphate," at least not scientifically. It might be called "sodium morphate" in the same way that acetylsalicylic acid is called "aspirin," as somebody's shorthand or trade-name. But "sodium morphate" would not be its real chemical name.

One has to ask: Where did Roberts get the term and the information concerning use of the compound by the Mafia for a great length of time? If he isn't talking about a plant alkaloid, then you can be sure that it certainly could not have existed before 1900.

There is no way to know whether sodium morphate, if synthesized, would be a poison, without knowing how stable the ion is — the more stable, the less poisonous. Poisons fall into two groups: (a) simple, highly active compounds which replace nutrients, and therefore do their dirty work; and (b) complex compounds which fall apart into simpler compounds, one or more of which is the active toxin.

There are no common rat poison ingredients which Roberts might have mistakenly called sodium morphate. The commonest staple ingredient of rat poison is arsenic or strychnine. Another, warfarin, is a colorless, odorless, tasteless, crystalline anti-coagulant, causing fatal internal bleeding in rats. It is successful because it acts too slowly for the rats to catch on. Its formula is $C_{19}H_{16}O_4$ — not a relative of the opiates. It is neutralized with sodium hydroxide (NaOH, common lye, as is used to make soap). It is derived from coumarin, $C_9H_6O_2$, originally extracted from the tonka bean.

Strychnine is also a common ingredient in rat poison. None of the chemicals we have mentioned are opiates, or related chemically to opiates. All are simple compounds, working directly on the tissues of the body, rather than breaking down into simpler compounds which are the actual toxins, as is true of all opiates. All are cheap, readily available and eas-

ily synthesized, which makes them all eminently more desirable for the job than any alkaloid, which is expensive, usually controlled by law, and difficult to extract or synthesize.

As far as sodium morphate only being detectable in the
vomit, this is not likely at all — all opiate residues are readily
detectable in blood, brain and other tissues, as well as in
vomit.

Notes

X. Sharks DeSpot, Jim Keith,
G.J. Krupey and Matt Love

1) I received a copy of the Christic Institute's affadavit to the court, re: their lawsuit against what they call "The Secret Team," and noticed a lot of familiar names started turning up from Gemstone re: the Iran/Contra affair. So, I merged the two, with dramatic results. I started wondering if Roberts had access to secret info — or info that was secret when my version was drafted. I started doing serious research, and have so far concluded that everything in Gemstone that can be verified by other sources was known by the public from the Church Committee hearings on organized crime. I base this belief on the fact that Gemstone makes no mention of Kennedy's relationship with Judith Exner Campbell. Church, a Kennedy friend, suppressed that information. If Roberts had inside information, he certainly would have mentioned that. Some of the things that can't be verified, I believe, are outrageous fabrications, such as the kidnapping of Hughes by Onassis. But then, I thought that Jacqueline sailing with Ari just before Kennedy was killed fell into that category, and it turned out to be true... Even better, Franklin Roosevelt, Jr. and wife were also on board, strengthening the highly dubious (in my opinion) Onassis, Roosevelt, Kennedy and Lansky heroin connection. — ML

2) The names of the 'Seven Sisters' are Exxon (also known as Esso), Shell, BP (British Petroleum), Gulf, Texaco,

Mobil, and Chevron (also known as Socal). *The Seven Sisters: The Great Oil Companies and the World They Made* by Anthony Sampson, 1975 Viking Press, p. 5. — XSDS

(3) In July of 1928, five American companies led by Exxon signed the 'Red Line Agreement' by which none of these companies would independently seek to drill for oil in the territories of Turkey, Syria, Jordon, Iraq and Saudi Arabia, but only through a joint company, the Iraq Petroleum Company. Because of the reluctance of the IPC companies to drill and exploit quickly enough, Chevron (Socal), Texaco and American Mobil signed later. Sampson, p. 74. — XSDS

4) In early 1928 the heads of Exxon, Shell and BP (British Petroleum) met at a castle called Achnacarry to create the Achnacarry Agreement, nicknamed the 'As Is,' which allowed "...the oil barons [to] reach a basic agreement to divide the world into an international cartel." 15 other companies, including Gulf, Chevron (Socal), Texaco and American Mobil signed later. Sampson, pp. 73, 74. — XSDS

5) Aristotle (Socrates) Onassis (1922 — March 15, 1975) purchased his first oil tanker in 1938, and owned two more by World War II. Onassis experienced a 'golden age of profit', and in the mid-1950's he purchased 17 new tankers in one year. *Encyclopedia Britannica,* 15th edition, Vol. 8, p. 949. *Facts on File,* 1975 edition, p. 204. — XSDS

6) The loan to Nixon's brother took place and was reported in the press at the close of the 1960 election, at which time Roberts may have heard of it. Other known Hughes "loans" to Nixon included $50,000 to his campaign in 1968, $100,000 in 1969 and 1979 through Bebe Rebozo, and $150,000 to the Nixon campaign in 1972. Other money parcelled out to candidates by Howard Robard Hughes during his stay in Las Vegas include $50,000 to Senator Alan Bible, $70,000 to Senator Howard Cannon, $10,000 to Nevada Lieutenant Governor Harry Reid, $9,500 to State Attorney General Robert List, and $5,000 to District Attorney George Franklin. *Citizen Hughes* by Drosnin, Holt, Rinehart & Winston, 1985, p. 519. — JK, XSDS

7) Tax exempt status was granted to the Howard Hughes Medical Institute, not Foundation, in 1957. Drosnin, p. 312. — JK

8) Roberts is apparently pointing out another Mafia/Onassis connection here by mentioning Davis's Sicilian nationality. — JK

9) The timeline for Hughes's disappearance is correct, according to Drosnin, p. 52. — JK

10) "If you wanted to know what Hughes looked like after some years in captivity, brain injured, heroin-addicted, confined to a wheelchair, there was a photo of him printed in *Midnight*, a Canadian tabloid that Mae [Brussell] had. Of course, it wasn't labelled 'Howard Hughes,' but 'JFK is alive and an invalid on Skorpios (Onassis's private island).' The CIA/Mafia frequently leaks info, stories, photos, etc. in the mass-media tabloids. The purpose is multi-fold: to confuse and bamboozle the public, (the stories are always a bit screwed up, and they usually represent a 'fail-safe cover-up' of some important matter) and at the same time, to fish for any information anyone not in the club might have produced in responding to this bait. Anyone responding with too much information, of course, is turned into fishbait himself." — Stephanie Caruana in correspondence, 1991. — JK

11) Fratianno is misspelled 'Frattiano' throughout the *Gemstone File*. — ML

12) "In September 1963, even as he was taking the first perceptible steps toward a Vietnam pullback, Kennedy ordered the FBI to raid secret CIA guerrilla training camps and staging bases in Florida and Louisiana. Dave Ferrie, linked by New Orleans District Attorney James Garrison to Clay Shaw and the CIA, was involved in the operation of the Louisiana camps. The camps were situated on land owned by a gambling associate of Jack Ruby's, Bill McLaney. The McLaney brothers, cogs in the Lansky Syndicate, were among the big losers when the Cuban revolution ejected the Syndi-

cate and its casinos from the island. Frank Fiorini (aka Sturgis) of the Watergate burglary was also connected to the base Kennedy closed at No Name Key. Sturgis was visible at Dallas two months later and was actually questioned by the FBI in connection with the Assassination." — Carl Oglesby, *The Yankee and Cowboy War*, Berkeley Medallion, 1977, pp. 73-74. — JK

13) (Carey) Estes Kefauver suffers heart attack August 8, 1963, dies from burst aorta August 10, 1983. *Facts on File*, 1963, p. 287. — XSDS

14) It is well-documented that Jackie and friends went on this cruise. The official version has JFK asking Jackie to come back from the cruise because it was making all the papers and people were talking. It undermined the dignity of the office of the presidency, etc. My nod goes to the official version. If Kennedy knew Onassis was going to kill him, would he have been stupid enough to go to Dallas, riding in an open-topped car, after cancelling Chicago? — ML

15) Kennedy cancelled a scheduled appearance at a Chicago football game held on November 2, 1963 (not November 1, as in Gemstone) and spent the rest of the day, after two conferences, with his wife. She was not on board Onassis's yacht November 2, as Roberts claims, at least not according to the *Chicago Tribune*, November 3, 1963, "Presidents Trip to Chicago Cancelled." — XSDS

16) "A secret CIA memorandum says that E. Howard Hunt was in Dallas the day President John F. Kennedy was murdered and that top agency officials plotted to cover up Hunt's presence there.

"Some CIA sources speculate that Hunt thought he was assigned by higher-ups to arrange the murder of Lee Harvey Oswald.

"Sources say Hunt, convicted in the Watergate conspiracy in 1974, was acting chief of the CIA station in Mexico City in the weeks prior to the Kennedy assassination. Oswald was in Mexico City, and met with two Soviet KGB agents at the Russian EEmbassy there immediately before leaving for Dallas, according to the official Warren Commission Report.

"The 1966 memo, now in the hands of the House Assassination Committee, places Hunt in Dallas Nov. 22, 1963.

"Hunt's appearance on the scene in Dallas and in Mexico City at the time of the murder adds strength to a theory shared by some internal CIA investigators. They believe Oswald was working for U.S. intelligence, that he was ordered to infiltrate the KGB, and that this explains his life in Russia. They also believe Oswald proved to be so unstable that he was handled by the KGB into becoming a triple agent and assigned for the Dallas job.

"The same investigators theorize that Hunt was in Dallas that day on the orders of a high-level CIA official who in reality was a KGB mole. Hunt allegedly thought he was to arrange that Oswald be murdered because he had turned traitor. Actually he was to kill Oswald to prevent him from ever testifying and revealing the Russians had ordered him to kill Kennedy, the CIA sources speculate." *Sunday News Journal,* August 20, 1978, otherwise unidentified. — ML

17) One thing I find to be a glaring error in Gemstone is Roberts' insistence that Fratianno and Roselli were two of the hit men. They were capos in the Mob, and therefore would not have dirtied their hands (as well as incriminated themselves with hard evidence) in attempting to kill the President — what if they failed and were caught? — that being left to the torpedos and other expendable types. Mafia dons never carry guns, it being considered incriminating evidence. That's why the phalanx of bodyguards. The whole point is that the Mob does everything possible to minimize if not eliminate the role of their top dogs in crime, especially something like the magnitude of killing the President of the United States. So why would Roselli and The Weasel take such a risk? — GK

18) I think Roberts used *Coup d'Etat in America* by Canfield and Weberman as his main reference work. Page after page, the same cast of characters turn up that you find in Gemstone, the same CIA and Mafia personnel. Could it have been the other way around, that Canfield and Weberman used Roberts as their source? Well, *Coup d'Etat* seems to be

well footnoted, with pretty solid sources, whereas Roberts is almost without any sources listed. Most of Canfield and Weberman's sources were from 1973 on, and it seems like they speculate a lot, starting with Bay of Pigs at one end, Watergate at the other, and moving in. Suppose Roberts and *Coup d'Etat* had the same sources. They cite *Ramparts* from time to time. Could it have been a source for Roberts? — ML

19) Roselli also said that Jack Ruby was "one of our boys," and that Ruby was acting under orders to silence Oswald. Roselli was found dismembered in an oil drum shortly following his Senate testimony. Jack Ruby's testimony in the Warren Report on the matter is chilling and should be read in its entirety. Ruby says, in part, "...And I wish that our beloved President, Lyndon Johnson, would have delved deeper into the situation, hear me, not to accept just circumstantial facts about my guilt or innocence, and would have questioned to find out the truth about me before he relinquished certain powers to these certain people. ...Consequently, a whole new form of government is going to take over our country, and I know I won't live to see you [Justice Warren] another time." *Contract on America* by Scheim, Zebra, 1989, p. 156. — JK

20) Could the coverup have included Nixon's (and George Bush's) role in the Kennedy assassination? "On the Watergate tapes, June 23, 1972, referred to in the media as the 'smoking gun' conversation, Nixon and his Chief of Staff, H.R. Haldeman, were discussing how to stop the FBI investigation into the CIA Watergate burglary. They were worried that the investigation would expose their connection to 'the Bay of Pigs thing.' Haldeman, in his book *The Ends of Power*, reveals that Nixon always used code words when talking about the 1963 murder of JFK. Haldeman said Nixon would always refer to the assassination as 'the Bay of Pigs.'"

"On that transcript we find Nixon discussing the role of George Bush's partner, Robert Mosbacher, as one of the Texas fundraisers for Nixon. On the tapes Nixon keeps referring to the 'Cubans' and the 'Texans.' The 'Texans' were Bush, Mosbacher and Baker. This is ... [a] direct link between Bush and evidence linking Nixon and Bush to the Kennedy assassination.

"In the same discussion Nixon links the Cubans, the Texans, Helms, Hunt, Bernard Baker, Robert Mosbacher and the Bay of Pigs. Over and over on the Watergate tapes, these names come up around the discussion of the photos from Dallas, that Nixon was trying to obtain when he ordered the CIA to burglarize the Watergate." (Source: "Three Men and a Barge," Teresa Riordan, *Common Cause* magazine, March/April 1990, and *San Francisco Chronicle*, May 7, 1977, interview with Frank Sturgis in which he stated that "...the reason we burlarized the Watergate was because Nixon was interested in stopping news leaks relating to the photos of our role in the assassination of John F. Kennedy." Paul Kangas, "The Role of Richard Nixon and George Bush in the Assassination of President Kennedy," *The Realist*, No. 117, Summer 1991. − JK

21) Allegedly quoting Howard Hughes in *Citizen Hughes*, "I want to consider a development in Baja that would be similar to the all-inclusive arrangement Onassis had in Monte Carlo. I don't mean that I aspire to take over the Mexican government as he did Monaco..." Drosnin, pp. 386-387. −JK

22) Carl Oglesby's description of the event sounds like a Mafia operation. "...[Chester] Davis commanded his 'small army of special agents from Intertel,' flashing their mysterious credentials, to move with no more than necessary force into the sacrosanct cashier's cages in all the Hughes casinos. The Intertel men stuffed the cash into paper bags and boxes with no explanation other than their story about 'a new management' and no credentials other than their advantage in surprise and force. They could as easily have been robbers as cops." Oglesby, p. 218 − JK

23) Correct spelling: Byour. Also, note the Byour Agency's Nazi connections in "Is it True?" in this volume. − JK

24) There is evidence that, at some time, Onassis and Maheu had a parting of ways. "The Case of the Greedy Greek was a classic tragedy. At least for Aristotle Onassis. In his

hubris, the tycoon had made a secret deal with the dying king of Saudi Arabia that gave him a virtual monopoly on shipping oil from the Persian Gulf. It was Maheu's mission to scuttle that contract. Ostensibly he was working for Onassis's blood rival Stavros Niarchos. But the CIA was definitely in on it and so was then Vice-President Richard Nixon, and while not even the players seemed to be sure who was using whom on whose behalf, Big Oil was probably pulling the strings to make the world safe for Aramco. Still, it was Maheu's show. He bugged Onassis's offices in New York, Paris and London, got proof that the contract had been bought with a bribe, exposed the scandal in a Rome newspaper secretly owned by the CIA, and finally journeyed to Jidda, where he personally presented his evidence to the Saudi royal family and killed the whole deal." Drosnin, pp. 71-72. – JK

(25) Robert Kennedy actually shot on June 5, 1968. *Facts on File*, 1968, p. 226. – XSDS

26) Roberts was mistaken about Kennedy's book. It was published in 1960 by Harper & Row (with, obviously, nothing about his brother's assassination in it), and was reprinted by Greenwood Press in 1990. –ML, JK

27) If Bobby Kennedy didn't know who killed his brother, at least he had suspicions. Arthur Schlesinger, Jr. reports that RFK asked CIA Director John McCone, "Did the CIA kill my brother?" in *Robert Kennedy and His Times*, Arthur Schlesinger, Jr., Houghton Mifflin, 1978, pp. 615-616. – JK

28) *The Second Gun* was shown at Boston University in 1975. This may be one of Roberts' sources or a later addition by Caruana. – JK

29) Cyril Magnin, the father of Mae Brussell... – JK

(30) Roberts says that Kennedy bailed out of the car before it hit the water. The car was going 30-38 miles per hour at the time, and Kennedy could not have bailed out without injuring himself. The most likely source for this account is

Teddy Bare: The Last of the Kennedy Clan by Zad Rust, Western Islands, 1971, pp. 24-25. Western Islands is the publishing arm of the ultraconservative and conspiracy-oriented John Birch Society. *Chappaquiddick Revealed*, Kenneth Kappel, St. Martin's Paperbacks, 1989. Pp. 257-260. — XSDS

31) Robert Sam Anson suggests that JFK's brains are probably being withheld by members of the Kennedy family for reasons of discretion. *They've Killed the President*, Robert Sam Anson, Bantam, 1975, p. 340. — JK

32) Conspiracy researcher John Judge offers an alternative scenario to what happened at Chappaquiddick. He claims that Ted Kennedy wasn't even in the car when it went off the bridge, and points out that even Leo Demore, the author of the anti-Kennedy book *Senatorial Privilege*, "had to admit that Ted wasn't in the car. He (Demore) claims he (Kennedy) opened the door and jumped out at the last minute which is ridiculous because the windows are shut and the doors locked on that side. If he was in it, he wouldn't have bothered on the way out to lock it or even shut it." Judge goes on to claim that Mary Jo Kopechne, a former employee of George Smathers, "friend of Bebe Rebozo and the Nixon mob," was placed as an infiltrator in the Kennedy camp. "She thought she was taking him out to be killed, I believe. He was drugged at the party. He was ambushed, taken out of the car and back to the motel. He didn't have any wet clothes. He didn't swim anywhere that night, and he wasn't in the car. He was in a jovial mood the next morning. He didn't know anything had happened. They came to him and told him, 'She's dead in your car and we have blackmail letters signed by her. We can make it a murder rap or a manslaughter charge,' threatened his children and his life, and got him to lie about it."

Judge thinks Kopechne was already dead when she was put in the car and the car was pushed into the water. He says it was the same modus operandi in the murder-made-to-look-like-an-accident that killed TV journalist Jessica Savitch, who was investigating the Vatican-P2 Lodge scandal, and was beginning investigations into the U.S. government's recruitment and sheltering of Nazis after the end of the Second World War.

Judge claims that "there was a $10,000 payoff to Tony Vlaczewitz by Jack Caulfield mentioned during Watergate, for that summer called 'Operation Sand Wedge.' It was never explained or asked about. I think 'Sand Wedge' was 'wedge the Oldsmobile in the sand' in the little pond there and take care of Tony Vlaczewitz, who was up on the island. Local people in Martha's Vineyard I talked to said it was crawling with Nixon's men the day before. Lasowitz said that he got a phony press pass to ask embarrassing questions of Ted Kennedy at the press conference afterwards. But the date he said he went to get the press pass was before the accident happened. So what was he going to ask about? And he didn't show up at any of the press conferences. This was all nonsense. He was up there with the bag money, ready to take Teddy out."

Judge doesn't elaborate on how he knows this, and he doesn't mention how the locals in Martha's Vineyard that he talked to knew that the place "was crawling with Nixon's men." But if we can believe that John and Robert Kennedy were both murdered by conspiracy, then we must at least concede the possibility that Ted Kennedy could have been framed for the murder of Mary Jo Kopechne and let go via a cover-up in high places so as to keep him from ever being elected President, to tarnish forever his and the Kennedy name with the spectre of Chappaquiddick, and to keep him in line while in the Senate. After all, a third assassinated Kennedy might have been too much coincidence for even the mainstream media to swallow. "The Fourth Reich," John Judge, a talk given in *Judge For Yourself: A Treasury of Writing & Speeches* by John Judge, 1990, Prevailing Winds Research — GK

33) "The immediate postmortem examination of Eugenie's body... listed fourteen injuries on [her] body. They included a bruise on the left eye and swelling on the left temple; an elliotic hemorrhage on the right side of the neck; three parallel smaller bruises on the left side of the neck above the collarbone; injuries to the skin below and the fibers of the muscle; a hemorrhage to the left of the larynx; a two-inch bruise

on the abdomen with internal bleeding and bleeding behind
the diaphragm in the region of the fourth and fifth vertabrae;
bruises on the left arm; bruises on the left ankle and the left
shin; a bruise on the ring finger and a tear on the little finger
of the left hand. The doctors concluded that these injuries
were commensurate with 'old-fashioned attempts at resusci-
tation.' Death, in their view, was caused by an overdose of
sleeping pills." *Aristotle Onassis* by Fraser, Jacobsen,
Ottaway and Chester. JB Lippincott, 1977, pp. 290-291. —
JK

34) "Another of the many reasons to believe the real
Hughes is not in existence or hasn't been since 1971 has to
do with a January 28, 1971 *Los Angeles Times* article which
described a computer which had been programmed to write
the signature of Hughes. Although handwriting experts argued that the computer signature at that time was a possible
facsimile, it was noted that the 'digitizer-computer-plotter
system' could be used with greater sophistication to produce
handwriting good enough to fool a handwriting expert. Too, it
is important to note that Hughes aides were actually working
on special computerized devices to duplicate voice-prints and
were, back in 1968, hastily buying up every old newsreel
they could find with Hughes on it and had ordered a 'chronological synopsis of every news story or book which had ever
been published about Hughes.'" *The Empire of Howard
Hughes* by Davenport and Lawson, Peace and Pieces Foundation, 1975, p. 79. Although one is inclined to think that stories such as this prove Gemstone, note that the publication
date is within a time frame so that Roberts might have read
the story, too. —JK

35) As for Roberts' sources, often he gives them in the
Skeleton Key itself. If he was trading Gemstones with Mafia
and the CIA for information, why does he have to get information from supermarket tabloids? — ML

36) Through the witness informer called Tiger Eye as reported by researchers Mae Brussell and Stephanie Caruana
[in the article, "Is Howard Hughes Dead and Buried off a
Greek Island?" December, 1974, *Playgirl* magazine], Howard

Hughes probably died in Tenos, a Cycladic Greek island about 75 miles southeast of Athens, where he may have been buried at sea (the Aegean) possibly on April 17, 1971... A Greek national and registered nurse, Koula Markopolis who had, according to the Canadian newspaper, *Midnight* (dated October 18, 1971), revealed that Ms. Markopolis was the employee of Aristotle Onassis from November 1968 to January 1969. Her patient, called 'Mr. Smith,' weighed practically nothing, 'just skin and bones, no muscles,' and 'his body was wasted away.' The paralyzed and brain-damaged patient had apparently been badly injured, but was treated like a 'prince' by Mr. Onassis and staff. Could one billionaire after another's interests take on the benevolent role of a caretaker? Why not? But according to the same newspaper, an Army Major David Cordrey witnessed, in a somewhat conflicting report, the burial of a Hughes 'double' or possibly Hughes himself on April 18, 1971 in the Ionian Sea... Cordrey's statement in part said, "Later in the day people gathered on the rocky point. I was curious and watched through my binoculars. One was a priest. One was Jackie Onassis, and one was Ted Kennedy. They and the others went through a ceremony over a coffin, and then watched while it was lowered into the sea." Witness Tiger Eye believed the man thought to be Hughes, however did die on April 16, 1971 and was buried the next day at Tenos on April 17th. Whatever the case, Hughes, according to more than one report had been quite ill and helpless since 1957 and perhaps had given control of much of his empire to the CIA and the others in the late sixties. Davenport and Lawson, p. 77. Tiger Eye is no doubt a pseudonym for "Gemstone," suggesting that Bruce Roberts or his letters were the source for the article. *Midnight* was very likely the source for Bruce Robert's description of the burial, which is at least as damning a piece of information for Robert's veracity as any. — JK

37) John Judge: "I talked to someone in Washington, D.C. whose father had embalmed JFK. They wouldn't just let anybody embalm John F. Kennedy and see the wounds. I said, 'Did he embalm any other famous people?' and she said, 'Yeah, he embalmed Howard Hughes.' This guy's in Arlington, Virginia. They don't have any embalmers in Texas?"

John Judge, transcript of the talk, "The Secret Government," *Dharma Combat* magazine no. 10, 1991. — JK

38) Omar Garrison relates an interesting story of a journalist (who he chooses not to name; perhaps it is Garrison himself) who was contacted by Ralph Howard, a mysterious Texan, re: Hughes. A note sent to the journalist said, "Howard Hughes is dead. We have definite proof of it. We know where the remains are, and we have a signed affadavit from the doctor who pronounced him dead. We also have dental x-rays that have been positively identified as being those of Howard Hughes." Note the similarity to the Gemstone account. Garrison states that the Texan wanted to interfere with an Air West stock deal, but when he requested $1,000 for his evidence, the anonymous journalist terminated contact. *Howard Hughes in Las Vegas,* Omar Garrison, Lyle Stuart, 1970 — JK

39) The Golden Triangle is not Vietnam, Laos, and Cambodia, but the area where Laos, Burma, and Thailand meet. For someone who was allegedly married to the daughter of the former French consul in Indochina, this is a glaring error. It was a popular misconception at the time of the Vietnam War however, when some anti-war activists tried to explain the real American agenda in Southeast Asia with the perhaps too simplistic explanation of a drug war to seize control of the drug trade. Or was it too simplistic an explanation? The U.S. was waging a not-so-secret war in Laos even before sending any troops to Vietnam, where discovery of vast offshore oil tracts made it suddenly loom in importance. In any event, Roberts got the names of the countries that comprise the Golden Triangle wrong, and he also apparently neglected to mention his debt to Alfred McCoy's *The Politics of Heroin in Southeast Asia* (first printing 1972) for the story about the Pepsi-Cola plant in Laos that was used to produce heroin. — GK

40) In testimony before the Ervin Committee on May 20, 1973, James McCord gave a description of the contents of Greenspun's safe. "Liddy said that Attorney General John Mitchell had told him that Greenspun had in his possession

blackmail type information involving a democratic candidate for President, that Mitchell wanted that material, and Liddy said that this information was in some way racketeer-related, indicating that if this candidate became President, the racketeers or national crime syndicate could have a control or influence over him as President. My inclination at this point in time is to disbelieve the allegation against the democratic candidate referred to above and to believe that there was in reality some other motive for wanting to get into Greenspun's safe. To me this sounds like anti-democratic disinformation and an attempt to cover for Nixon. It is also a close rendering of the Roberts' thesis.

I find, after having written the above interpretation, that Carl Oglesby has reached the same conclusion in *The Yankee and Cowboy War*: "Decoded, his [Liddy's] original statement would then read: Liddy said that Mitchell told him that Greenspun had in his possession blackmail type information involving NIXON (not Muskie) and Mitchell wanted that material, and Liddy said that this information was in some way racketeer-related, indicating that if this candidate, NIXON (not Muskie) became President, the racketeers or national crime syndicate could have control or influence over him as President." — JK

41) Liddy's "Gemstone Plan" and *Gemstone Files*: I think this is central to the Roberts' Gemstone. I believe that Roberts read about these files and began to speculate about what was in them. He took the code name "Gemstone" and applied it literally, as meaning physical gemstones. I think for me it was a turning point from belief to disbelief, the mainstream reporting of *Gemstone Files* without mention of any of the rest of Roberts scenario. — ML

On the other hand, Roberts' telling of the story is more believable if you take into consideration that he did manufacture artificial gemstones, as witnessed by Caruana. It strains credulity to think that Liddy came up with the name "Gemstone" by accident, and that it happened to coincide with Roberts' line of work. — JK

42) Giovanni Battista Montini became Pope Paul VI June

21, 1963. *Columbia Encyclopedia,* article "Paul VI," p. 1613. — XSDS

43) Pope Pius XI held office from 1922-1939. Pius XII 1939-1958. John XXIII 1958-1963. Paul VI (Montini) 1963-1978. John Paul I, 1978, John Paul II 1978-. World Almanac, "Noted Personalities—Popes/Chronological List of Popes" 1983, Newspaper Enterprise Association, Inc., p. 409 — XSDS

44) The Arab world is usually thought to have begun in the 6th or 7th century, with the growth of Islam and the Prophet Mohammed (570?-632). However, the word Arab existed as early as the 9th century B.C. "In classical times the term was extended to the whole of the Arabian peninsula and to all the desert areas of the Middle East..." *Columbia Encyclopedia,* article "Arabs," p. 93 and "Mohammed," p. 1397. — XSDS

45) It was "only during the last century that historians have been able to fix satisfactorily Jesus's birth year..." as being at the conjunction of Saturn and Jupiter. Early Church scholars place Christ's birth six or seven years too early. *6000 Years of the Bible,* Gunther S. Wegener, Harper and Row, 1963, p. 103. — XSDS

46) In the *New Testament,* Luke 2:7 makes clear that Jesus was laid in a manger due to overcrowding in Bethlehem, caused by people arriving from all over the Roman Empire for a tax census. Matthew 2:11 says only that Christ and Mary were at a house together when found by the chief priests and scribes of the people, the Magi. — XSDS

47) Luke 19:45, Mark 11:15, Matthew 21:12. — XSDS

48) "But everything speaks for Jesus having been arrested as a troublemaker, informally interrogated and handed over to [Pontius] Pilate as the leader of a political revolt by the pro-Roman priestly Sadducean (traditional ruling class of priests rejecting doctrines not in the law such as resurrection, retribution in a future life and the existence of angels),

members of the Sanhedrin [supreme council of the Jews having religious, civil and criminal jurisdiction] who were dominant in Jerusalem society in those days. *Encyclopedia Britannica*, 15th edition, 1986, Volume 22, p. 360. — XSDS

49) In John 19:33 it says that Christ was already dead when the spear was stuck in his side. In John 19:34 the soldiers pierced Christ's side and blood and water came out of his body. There is no mention of the soldiers eating Christ's liver in either of these documents. — XSDS

50) Publius (or Gaius) Cornelius Tacitus (b. circa A.D. 56-D. circa A.D. 120) was an orator and held official office within the Roman empire. He wrote many works, the most important of which was his *Annals* (in Latin *Ab Excessu Divi Augusti*). The *Annals* covered the Roman empire from the start of the reign of Tiberius until the end of the reign of Nero. This was A.D. 14 until A.D. 66. The most important passage in the *Annals* is in Book 15, part 44, in which he mentions the crucifixion of 'Christus' during the reign of Tiberius (A.D. 14-March 16,37.). The *Annals* are fragmentary, and the years 29-31 A.D. are incomplete. Chapter 5 covers 29-31 and the crucifixion of Jesus took place in A.D. 30. Only one copy of Tacitus' work survived the Middle Ages. *The Complete Works of Tacitus*, Moses Hadas editor, Random House, 1942. *Encyclopedia Britannica*, Volume 11, p. 487. — XSDS

51) A possible source for this description of the life and crucifixion of Jesus Christ was a supposed official report to the Emperor Tiberius from Pontius Pilate. It is mentioned by two early Church scholars, Justin in his *Apology* around 150 A.D. and Tertullian in another work titled *Apology* in 197 A.D. It is now believed to have been a hoax, but, if authentic, may have been available to Tacitus for his *Annals*. *New Catholic Encyclopedia*, McGraw Hill Books, 1967, Volume 11, pp. 360-361. 'Pilate, Pontius' entry. Justin Martyr, vol. 8, pp. 94, 95. Tertullian, vol. 13, pgs. 1019, 1020, 1021, 1022. — XSDS

52) In the 15th century the *Apocrypha of Sulpicius Servus*

was added to Tacitus' *Annals*. It's possible that this was believed authentic by Bruce Roberts or by Cardinal Eugene
Tisserant, and that the Servus writings were actually true
writings of Tacitus supressed by the Church for political reasons. *Encyclopedia Britannica*, vol. 8, p. 606. — XSDS

53) Nero (his full name was Nero Claudius Caesar Augus-
tus Germanicus). B. A.D. 37- D. A.D. 68. He was the fifth
emperor of Rome. He ruled from A.D. 54-A.D. 68. In his biography *Nero*, author John Bishop argues that the fire was accidental, not deliberately set. After the fire, rumors spread in
Rome that Nero had sought to burn Rome to expand his own
residence and to rebuild Rome to his own design. According
to Tacitus in book 15, part 38, there were some who spread
the fire and prevented it from being extinguished, "and kept
shouting that there was one who gave them authority, either
seeing to plunder more freely, or obeying orders." John
Bishop argues that Nero tried to frame the Christians as
scapegoats, only to discover to his surprise that many freely
admitted to spreading the fire. Bishop argues that many of
the Christians intentionally spread the fire at Rome because
they believed the Apocalypse and Second Coming of Christ
were at hand. They confessed to it because they refused to
deny their actions in Christ's name. The conventional view of
history sees no reason to believe that Rome was burned to
stop Christianity, only that they made a convenient scape-
goat for Nero to blame the fire on. In fact, Poppaea his wife
may have actually been a Christian, and he held no personal
animosity against them. He did, however, brutally punish the
Christians accused of burning Rome, and it is understand-
able that these people became martyrs to the early Christians. But this was apparently not a religious persecution set
on destroying Christianity, as the *Gemstone File* implies, just
a brutal search for scapegoats. *Encyclopedia Brittanica*, vol.
8, pp. 605-607. *Nero: The Man and the Legend*, by John
Bishop. A.S. Barnes and Company, Inc. 1964. pp. 88, 192. —
XSDS

54) The first Council of Nicaea was held at what is now
Isnik, Turkey. It was called by Emperor Constantine I (The
Great) to solve the problem created in the Eastern Church by

the heresy of Arianism. The year was 325 A.D. and the problem was that Arianism declared that Jesus was not of the same substance as the Father, but was instead created as an agent for creating the world. Since Christ was lesser than God, the Holy Trinity of Father, Son and Holy Ghost would have been impossible. Its proponent, Arius of Alexandria, was exiled, and Arianism condemned. It continued to exist until 381, when the Nicaean view was affirmed by the Eastern Church at the Second Ecumenical Council of Constantinople. *Encyclopedia Brittanica,* vol. 8, p. 875. *Webster's New Collegiate Dictionary,* 1979. *Encyclopedia Americana,* 1990, vol. 2, p. 281.

The first attempt to create a list of proscribed Christian writings was done by a heretic named Marcion, who disbelieved in Christ being a fulfillment of the *Old Testament* prophecies. His volume was made up only of Luke and ten of Paul's epistles, both purged of any mention of Judaism. "Contemporary Christians were unanimous in stigmatising Marcion as an imposter, though they followed the main lines of the skeleton canon he had laid down, chiefly because nobody else had proposed one." He was excommunicated in 144 A.D. He started his own Church, which became widespread and powerful, the first heretical challenge to Catholic Christianity. He rejected Gnosticism, preferring salvation by faith. Later, Marcionism was absorbed into Manichaeism. Wegener, p. 142. *Columbia Encyclopedia,* p. 1307, "Marcion." – XSDS

55) There were a wide variety of early Christian writings, including heretical writings, hoaxes, Gnostic writings attributing Gnostic beliefs to Christ, stories of early Christian martyrs, honest letters by bishops, and clumsy translations of the writings of the Apostles. Literally hundreds of dogmas and sects produced their own writings. When the New Testament canon was formed, some writings were rejected as being supplemental, that is to say, acceptable but unecessary because Matthew, Mark, Luke and John had already done the job for such writings as the *Gospel of Peter* and the *Gospel of Nicodemus.* Peter and Nicodemus were not considered heretical, but merely redundant. Wegener, pp. 125-135. *The Lost Books of the Bible,* Bell Publishing Co., 1979, p. 9. – XSDS

56) Constantine I (the Great) had adopted the faith of Christianity by at least 313, twelve years before the Nicaean Council of 325. It was not an act of dishonesty embracing the Christian faith for power. Constantine's mixing of faith and politics was normal for the times. *Encyclopedia Brittanica*, "Constantine," Macropedia section, vol. 16, p. 730. — XSDS

57) "While Constantine was not... the good Christian that later tradition depicts, he consolidated, in the name of unity and uniformity, the status of Christian orthodoxy. In A.D. 325, for example, he convened the Council of Nicaea. At this council the dating of Easter was established. Rules were framed that defined the authority of bishops, thereby paving the way for a concentration of power in ecclesiastical hands. Most important of all, the Council of Nicaea decided, by vote, that Jesus was a god, not a mortal prophet. Again, however, it must be emphasized that Constantine's paramount consideration was not piety but unity and expediency. As a god, Jesus could be associated conveniently with Sol Invictus. As a mortal prophet he would have been more difficult to accomodate. In short, Christian orthodoxy lent itself to a politically desirable fusion with the official state religion; and insofar as it did so Constantine conferred his support upon Christian orthodoxy.

"Thus, a year after the Council of Nicaea he sanctioned the confiscation and destruction of all works that challenged orthodox teachings — works by pagan authors that referred to Jesus, as well as works by 'heretical' Christians. He also arranged for a fixed income to be allocated to the Church and installed the bishop of Rome in the Lateran Palace. Then, in A.D. 331, he commissioned and financed new copies of the *Bible*. This constituted one of the single most decisive factors in the entire history of Christianity and provided Christian orthodoxy — the 'adherents of the message' — with an unparalleled opportunity.

"In A.D. 303, a quarter of a century earlier, the pagan emperor Diocletian had undertaken to destroy all Christian writings that could be found. As a result Christian documents — especially in Rome — all but vanished. When Constantine commissioned new versions of these documents, it enabled the custodians of orthodoxy to revise, edit, and rewrite their material as they saw fit, in accordance with their tenets. It was at this point that most of the crucial alterations in the *New Testament* were probably made and Jesus assumed the unique status he has enjoyed ever since. The importance of Constantine's commission must not be underestimated. Of the five thousand extant early manuscript versions of the *New Testament*, not one predates the fourth century. The *New Testament* as it exists today is essentially a product of fourth-century editors and writers — custodians of orthodoxy, 'adherents of the message,' with vested interests to protect." *Holy Blood, Holy Grail*, Baigent, Leigh, and Lincoln, Dell Publishing Co., 1983. — JK

58) The Crusades were fought between 1095 A.D. and 1272, nine in all. *Columbia Encyclopedia*, article "Crusades," pp. 517-518 —XSDS

59) "In 1953 George Bush raised $500,000 through Brown Brothers Harriman and joined forces with Huge and Bill Liedtke to form Zapata Petroleum. They drilled in West Texas and by the late 1950s were millionaires. In 1959 the Bush family bought out the Liedtke's share of Zapata Offshore, a subsidiary of Zapata Petroleum. Hugh went on to become chairman of Pennzoil and Bill raised money for Nixon's 1968 and 1972 presidential campaigns. In 1972 Bill gathered $700,000 in anonymous contributions and had the cash, checks and securities delivered to the Committee to Re-elect the President (CREEP) one day before a new law prohibiting anonymous contributions took effect. Bill says his fundraising efforts were done as a favor for George Bush." *Bush League Trading Cards* by Paul Brancato and Salim Yaqub, 1989, Eclipse Enterprises, Forestville, CA., citing information from various news periodicals and The Christic Institute. — GK

60) "While the White House burglars plotted the break-in back in Washington, Hughes lay in a stupor watching *Diamonds Are Forever*, a James Bond movie about a reclusive billionaire held prisoner in his Las Vegas penthouse, his em-

pire run by an evil imposter." — Drosnin. Is it possible that Bruce Roberts might have seen this movie and based his Hughes/Onassis scenario on it? This anecdote at least shows that the Hughes abduction theory was common conspiratorial currency prior to the *Gemstone File,* while not proving whether it was true or not. — JK

61) This segment, from the reference to Nixon's alleged "asshole Roberts" remark to the bizarre gibberish about the "Yellow Race Dead-Fucks Mary Jo Kopechne," does more to discredit the *Gemstone Files* and portray Roberts as a mentally disturbed paranoid-obsessive than any other segment, with the possible exception of the "Hughes sea burial-casket stolen by Albanian frogmen" episode lifted from a Canadian tabloid. One possible explanation might be that the "Yellow Race Dead-Fucks Mary Jo Kopechne" is some sort of code phrase that only certain individuals might be privy to. — GK [Note Caruana's explanation in her interview in this volume]

62) Attempting to sort out what possible connection there could be between the Yellow Race and Mary Jo Kopechne, is it possible that Roberts was referring to the familiar conspiratorial theme of the Khazar Jews and their international controls (primarily via banking and high finance) when he speaks of the Yellow Race? In the far right wing *Affirmations,* Hillman Holcomb says, "The talmudic, mongoloids who now rule Christendom should be symbolized as khazar-askenazim... The only semites on earth are the Semitic Arabs of the Levant, Asia minor or the Near East. The only anti-semites on earth are the talmudic, mongoloid Kikes who call themselves Jews and Israelites. Their ongoing persecution and extermination of the Semitic Arabs demonstrate this truth." Roberts' previous slighting statement about the Jews not allowing Arabs into their 'nice, clean stables' may confirm this bent in Roberts' worldview, and also suggests the possibility that Caruana may have deleted that slant when editing Roberts' letters. *Affirmations,* Hillman Holcomb, Christian Technocracy, Las Vegas, 1990.

I am also reminded of a broadside that was distributed in Miami after JFK ordered that military activity against Castro be ceased. Bearing pictures of cowboys and the Alamo, the document reads: "Only through one development will you Cuban patriots ever live again in your homeland as free-men... [only] if an inspried [sic] act of God should place in the White House within weeks a Texan known to be a friend of all Latin Americans... though he must under present con-ditions bow to the Zionists who since 1905 came into control of the United States, and for whom Jack Kennedy and Nelson Rockefeller and other members of the Council of [sic] Foreign Relations and allied agencies are only stooges and pawns. Though Johnson must now bow to these crafty and cunning Communist-hatching Jews, yet, did an act of God suddenly elevate him into the top position [he] would revert to what his beloved father and grandfather were, and to their values and principles and loyalties. [Signed] A Texan who resents the Oriental influence that has come to control, to degrade, to pollute and enslave his own people." — JK

63) David Atlee Phillips said in his autobiography that he had been recruited by the CIA while publishing a small newspaper in Chile. Phillips was a good friend of Katherine Graham. Is it going too far to suggest, given all the known intelligence service connections between the *Washington Post* and the CIA, that it is a virtual CIA proprietary? The *Post* and the *New York Times* have been willing and often knowing channels of CIA disinformation... but could the *Post* connec-tion be even tighter? — ML

64) Hearings actually began May 17, 1973. *Facts on File* for 1973, p. 394, E1. — XSDS

65) Admiral Noel Gayler is a real person, however Roberts got the spelling of his name wrong. — XSDS

66) U.S. District Court Judge Bruce R. Thompson (not Thomson) dismissed indictment. Second indictment dis-missed by Thompson November 14, 1974. *Facts on File* 1974, p. 89, F3, F.o.F. p. 1036, C3. — XSDS

67) [See also Robert's entry on the "Zebra killings."] "The Los Angeles Police Department's 'Special Unit: Senator' was formed and run by Evelle Younger, current attorney general

of California. After it had completed its apparently successful cover-up of the RFK evidence, SUS was given permanent form as the Criminal Conspiracy Section, remaining under Younger's control. The CCS shortly had taken over the war against local reds and organized blacks. In support of its antisubversive purposes, it got involved deeply in the behavior-modification work going on in the California prison system, notably at Vacaville, a psychofactory turning out police zombies the likes of Donald 'Cinque' Defreeze and others involved in the formation of the Symbionese Liberation Army. Defreeze was explicitly a CCS creature. The thesis has thus formed that the SLA was always a play thing of the CCS and through it of the Southern California far right, and that the kidnapping of Patty Hearst was part of a larger project, possibly including also the Zebra killings of the same period and the murder of Oakland school superintendent Marcus Foster, the purpose of which was to generate a public demand for wider police repression. (Based on material developed by Donald Freed and the Citizens Research and Investigating Committee of Los Angeles. SLA leader Emily Harris has denounced Freed as a conspiracy patsy.)" Oglesby, pp. 349-350. — JK

68) On June 30th, 1974 Alberta Williams King, mother of Martin Luther King, was shot and killed by Marcus Wayne Chenault at Ebenezer Baptist Church in Atlanta, Georgia. This is four months later than in the *Gemstone File*. Facts on File 1974, p. 562, E2. — XSDS

69) Gail "Larry" Harp of Kish Realty did die on September 7, 1974. — XSDS

70) It is interesting that people involved with the Kennedy assassination have a high rate of heart attack, or what may have been heart attack. Tom Howard, Jack Ruby's first chief attorney until he was relieved, died of a heart attack at the age of 48 on March 27, 1965. Earlene Roberts, who was Oswald's landlady at the time of the shooting, testified that, after Oswald had returned from Dealey Plaza and was in his room, two uniformed policemen pulled up in front of the rooming house and honked twice. She died of a heart attack

on January 9, 1966. Lee Bowers, a key witness in the Warren Investigation and observer of activity on the Grassy Knoll
was driving on August 9, 1966 when his car veered into a
bridge abutment. A doctor who examined him afterward
stated that, "He was in some strange sort of shock. A different kind of shock than an accident victim experiences. I can't
explain it. I've never seen anything like it." He was cremated
without autopsy.   Harold Russell saw the Officer Tippet
shooting. He exhibited extreme signs of paranoia in July of
1965, stating that he would be killed. Police appeared and
one of them hit him over the head with his pistol. He was
taken to a hospital where he was pronounced dead by "heart
failure." Guy Bannister, a detective involved with the Garrison trial, died of (according to the official report) a heart attack, although witnesses say that a bullet wound may have
complicated the matter. Clay Shaw, the businessman implicated by Jim Garrison in the assassination, died under
mysterious circumstances and was embalmed before the
cause of death could be determined. Dorothy Kilgallen was
the only journalist allowed a private interview with Jack
Ruby (Judge Joe B. Brown later bragged about the price
paid). After Kilgallen stated that she was going to "break the
case wide open" she died, supposedly of alcohol and barbitu-
rate poisoning. Mrs. Earl T. Smith, a close friend of
Kilgallen's, died of undetermined causes two days later. Dr.
Nicholas J. Chetta, a key witness against Clay Shaw, died of
a heart attack before the case could be tried in Federal
Court. Source: *Disappearing Witnesses* by Penn Jones — JK

71) According to Stephanie Caruana, one of the Roberts
letters in her possession is addressed to Anwar Sadat. — JK

72) "Basically, [Kirlian] photography with high frequency
electrical fields involves a specially constructed high frequency spark generator or oscillator that generates 75,000 to
200,000 electrical oscillations per second. The generator can
be connected to various clamps, plates, optical instruments,
microscopes or electron microscopes. The object to be investi-
gated (finger, leaf, etc.) is inserted between the clamps along
with photographic paper. The generator is switched on and a
high frequency field is created between the clamps which ap-

parently causes the object to radiate some sort of bio-luminescence onto the photographic paper. A camera isn't necessary for the photographic process." *Psychic Discoveries Behind the Iron Curtain*, Ostrander and Schroeder, Prentice-Hall, Inc., 1970., p. 199. — JK

73) The story of the top secret mission of the Glomar Explorer is confirmed by Drosnin, p. 23. — JK

74) One recurring theme among people interested in the *Gemstone File* is the suggestion that it might be disinformation, a hoax document written to confuse researchers or throw them off the trail of real conspirators. Yael Dragwyla offers: "Is it possible that the *Gemstone File* is itself disinformation deliberately created and disseminated by the CIA, the KGB or some other agency to confuse and distract Americans from what's really going on? It's so easy to write down a bunch of clever, sensational rumors in a gosh-wow style and spread them around; but how accurate they are, and/or useful, is another matter. There is a fellow here in Seattle, 'She-Bop Steve,' who is totally convinced that Senator Alan Cranston of California is the Evil Genius Behind Everything, and he can prove it —by his lights. But emotionally satisfying verbal linkages don't constitute solid proof of anything; nor do blunt, sensationalistic allegations which, however tittilating they may be, are backed up by nothing whatsoever at all. It takes hard, nasty cutting research and tight analysis to get at the meat of anything — if, in fact, the meat is there at all. The *Gemstone File* looks like nothing more than a list of allegations, with nothing to back them up. Innuendo and rumor are cheap 'n' easy — but what real use are they, ultimately, save maybe to whip up mob violence... or sell more copies of *The National Enquirer?*"

Quoting X. Sharks DeSpot from his informal essay on the subject, titled "Could It Have Been a Hoax?": "The specific claims in the File sound crazy: Bruce Roberts' father, favorite bartender and good friend at Kisch Realty were all killed because he got too close to the truth. They didn't just shoot him outright in a dark alley, they killed three friends of his over four years, and let him live until 1977. He hired G. Gordon Liddy to kill LBJ and Aristotle Onassis's son by 'quoting the Chinese price in ears,' the price on LBJ's head. Later he tries to get $500 from Harp at Kisch Realty. The only thing that makes sense is that the People's Republic of China paid G. Gordon Liddy to kill four people, with Bruce Roberts as the middle man, because he obviously didn't have the money himself. And, of course, my favorite quote, in 1963: 'Get it, Lyndon, otherwise Air Force One might have an accident on the way back to Washington.' Aristotle Onassis was threatening to kill the President of the United States at a time when the country was on full alert status and in danger of starting World War III. To kill LBJ would have pushed the country over the edge into war, and Onassis is talking like a Grade-B movie gangster!

"From this, I think that Roberts was crazy and meant every word of it. But that may not be true. First, simple substitution could have taken place: Navy Intelligence could have sent around a man pretending to be Bruce Roberts to disrupt things and spread disinformation; or Roberts himself may have made up the whole thing as a joke to mess with [Mae] Brussell's head.

"A teacher of mine wonders if the *Gemstone File* could have been disinformation. Certainly the FBI during the 60's and 70's spread disinformation among the Ku Klux Klan and Black Panthers during the years of turmoil and protest. This was nothing new. During the 1920's Alexander Mitchell Palmer, United States Attorney General, would have his agents infiltrate Socialist political parties and have the agents write things into the party platforms. Then, having created a pretext for arrest, he would arrest the party members. The U.S. government has a long history of disinformation activities abroad: it's called the United States Information Agency.

"Since the *Gemstone File* focused mainly on Bruce Roberts and the Mafia, I don't know what the Navy (or FBI, CIA, etc.) would be trying to disrupt, unless it was an attack on Daniel Ellsberg or San Francisco Mayor Joseph Alioto.

"My argument against the *Gemstone File* being disinformation intentionally planted is the simplicity of creating an 'underground' newspaper: it's so easy. What do you need? A printer and some lies. That's all there is to it. The idea that Bruce Roberts was spreading disinformation to Mae Brussell is easier to believe. Any group which actively sticks its nose into CIA affairs like Mae Brussell's World Watchers did, should expect at least a passing interest from the agency's employees. And disrupting Brussell could not have been very difficult. In 1988 she came to the conclusion that a neutron bomb had been detonated by Israel and the U.S. in Africa. She had almost no evidence of anything of the sort, and jumped head-on into that conclusion. This does not mean she was wrong, it only means that she had very little information to back up her conclusions.

"It is worthy to note that the FBI supposedly went to columnist Jack Anderson and tried to convince him that a white dentist killed Martin Luther King because King was having an affair with his wife. If the FBI is that looneytunes, you can bet they'll say almost anything." — JK